The War after the War

A New History of Reconstruction

JOHN PATRICK DALY

D1564744

The University of Georgia Press *Athens*

© 2022 by the University of Georgia Press
Athens, Georgia 30602
www.ugapress.org
All rights reserved

Set in 9.75/13.5 Baskerville 10 Pro Regular
by Kaelin Chappell Broaddus

Most University of Georgia Press titles are
available from popular e-book vendors.

Printed digitally

Library of Congress Cataloging-in-Publication Data

Names: Daly, John Patrick, 1964– author.
Title: The war after the war : a new history of Reconstruction / John Patrick Daly.
Other titles: Uncivil wars.
Description: Athens : The University of Georgia Press, [2022] | Series: Uncivil wars |
Includes bibliographical references and index.
Identifiers: LCCN 2021050469 | ISBN 9780820361895 (hardback) | ISBN 9780820361901
(paperback) | ISBN 9780820361918 (ebook)
Subjects: LCSH: Reconstruction (U.S. history, 1865–1877) | White supremacy movements—
Southern States—History—19th century. | Southern States—History—1865–1877.
Classification: LCC E668 .D14 2022 | DDC 973.8—dc23/eng/20211020
LC record available at https://lccn.loc.gov/2021050469

CONTENTS

INTRODUCTION
The Southern Civil War
New Terms for Reconstruction 1

CHAPTER 1
The Terror Phase, 1865–1867
The Massacres Begin 20

CHAPTER 2
The Guerilla Phase, 1868–1872, Part 1
The KKK Resisted 58

CHAPTER 3
The Guerilla Phase, 1868–1872, Part 2
The KKK Triumphant 81

CHAPTER 4
The Paramilitary Phase, 1872–1877
White Supremacist Armies 102

CHAPTER 5
What Makes a War a War
Assessing Reconstruction 141

APPENDIX
Major Incidents of the Southern Civil War 153

NOTES 155

INDEX 177

The War after the War

INTRODUCTION

The Southern Civil War

New Terms for Reconstruction

Fierce rebel yells filled the air on the hot streets of New Orleans as three thousand Confederates swarmed around Union forces huddling behind barricades defended by light artillery and Gatling guns. In a rare case of urban warfare in the Civil War era, the Confederates raked the Union forces with well-disciplined volley fire, then charged. The Union forces broke and retreated in disorder, and Robert E. Lee's second-in-command, James Longstreet, was taken prisoner. The casualty count was estimated at twenty-one dead and an unknown number of wounded for the Confederates, thirteen dead and seventy wounded for the Union. The Confederates captured arms and artillery from the state armory, but Union reinforcements arrived and Confederates ceded control of the city of New Orleans. The Union victory was temporary. A larger force of Confederates would take to the New Orleans streets two years later and win back the city.

To Civil War buffs, this battle sounds imaginary, as New Orleans fell on April 29, 1861, without street fighting. But the Battle of Liberty Place just described did take place—in *1874*, more than thirteen years after the fall of New Orleans in the American Civil War and almost ten years after Lee's surrender at Appomattox. The September 14, 1874, Battle of Liberty Place involved more troops than Little Bighorn or San Juan Hill or many of the best-remembered clashes of the American Revolution and War of 1812. Liberty Place also taught white supremacists that they could take over the state with paramilitary forces: they would repeat the tactics in Louisiana and take control of the state two years later in the fall of 1876. Like the war it was part of, the Battle of Liberty Place offered dramatic action, significant casualties, and unlikely heroes.

For example, former Confederate general Longstreet, as a state militia commander, was courageously fighting for civil rights for all southerners—including freedmen—against his old Confederate compatriots. By 1874, former Confederates hated Longstreet for commanding biracial Republican state forces against them and their white supremacist agenda. After they wounded him and captured him at the Battle of Liberty Place, they attacked his reputation. Longstreet's war record would be assailed for generations because he'd had the audacity to fight for African American civil rights during Reconstruction. Longstreet was on the losing side of two wars between 1861 and 1877. First, he lost with the Confederacy in the American Civil War of 1861–1865, and then he lost the twelve-year war of the Reconstruction Era, fighting for democracy and civil rights in the South between 1865 and 1877. The Battle of Liberty Place was just the most dramatic chapter in this long war. Why are this battle and others like it almost unknown in the annals of U.S. history? Why is the twelve-year war it was part of—the Southern Civil War of 1865–1877—untaught in schools and colleges and unmentioned by Ken Burns in his nine-episode television documentary *The Civil War*? The Southern Civil War killed thousands and shaped the course of southern and national politics for over one hundred years, yet it has largely been ignored.

The Battle of Liberty Place includes enough characters and action for several books, but it was just one of dozens of battles and thousands of violent incidents in a war across the South following the American Civil War. The Southern Civil War of 1865–1877 was fought for control of local and state governments and constituted an ex-Confederate attempt to control the long-term meaning of the American Civil War, which had ended without a clear peace settlement. Ex-Confederate extremists seized the opportunity afforded them by the lack of a settlement to launch a new campaign of violence against the two chief regional results and symbols of northern victory: white unionist political organizations and African Americans attempting to live free. In a textbook example of modern terrorism and guerilla warfare, ex-Confederate extremists concentrated on attacking these vulnerable targets and then melted away on the occasions when federal forces arrived. Federal governmental action, however, was largely irrelevant in this war. These tactics guaranteed the military forces of the ex-Confederate extremists a persistent

Battle of Liberty Place, September 14, 1874, and the winning ex-Confederate charge. (*Frank Leslie's Illustrated Newspaper*)

local advantage and ensured that intermittent federal action was not a large factor in the overall course of this war. The federal failure to effectively occupy the South threw the burden of local defense onto African Americans and their white unionist allies, who were usually militarily outnumbered, outfought, and outgunned. They faced an opponent with the Confederate weapons, training, experience, and organization gained in the four years of the American Civil War and significant support of the white population. Between 1865 and 1877 the white supremacists of the South resorted to warfare in all its modern forms: terrorism, guerilla action, paramilitary action, ethnic cleansing, assassination, and political violence such as attempted coups and attacks on voters, meetings, and marches. Local African American and white unionists—and later democratically elected southern Republican governments—answered this violence, often with classic pitched battles as at the Battle of Liberty Place. By 1877 ex-Confederate extremists had retaken every southern state. Despite a few victories for the biracial coalition of unionists (particularly in Arkansas and Texas), the complete triumph of white supremacist military forces in 1877 settled many of the open issues of the legacy of the earlier Civil War and reversed the halting Reconstruction plans of the North. For all practical purposes, ex-Confederate extremists, with their military action, crippled the Thirteenth Amendment (outlawing slavery), the Fourteenth Amendment (citizenship with equal protection of the law), and the Fifteenth Amendment (voting rights for African American men) in the South.

The history of the United States from 1865 to 1877 is confused, distorted, and misremembered because the war in the South rarely takes center stage. It is rarely even called a war. The popular narrative of 1861–1865 imagines tidy outcomes where none existed. Likewise, the enormity of the American Civil War's death toll of 750,000 and the grandeur of its battlefield pageantry have helped diminish the reality of the more diffuse and episodic Southern Civil War. However, the death count in these local conflicts exceeds twenty thousand by the best modern estimates, and the incomplete catalog of battles numbers fifty. It was no small war.[1] The following analytical and narrative history examines the violence of 1865–1867 across the South before turning to the state-by-state battles of 1867–1877 when unionists controlled and tried to defend local and state governments. Arkansas, Louisiana, Mississippi, Texas, and South Carolina had the most dramatic conflicts and provide the major examples of the Southern Civil War as open warfare, but this book looks at the South as a whole and describes a regional war. Many recent studies have brilliantly described the "War of Reconstruction" at the state level, but none have brought together the military history of the whole era and the region. This is a crucial task for American popular historical memory, the classroom, and the history profession.

This book had its genesis in the problems professors face choosing a book to assign on Reconstruction. The field needed an up-to-date, short, accessible book that looked at Reconstruction from the perspective of violence on the ground in the South. Very few short, accessible books look at the era as a whole.[2] The story of Reconstruction is too often told from the federal political perspective, which obscures the most telling force of the time: white supremacist warfare locally across the South. This book is a synthesis of new Reconstruction scholarship. It advances a crucial thesis for historians and for general readers: Reconstruction was a war.[3]

This book highlights the need for a new popular understanding of the war from 1865 to 1877 and thus Reconstruction as a whole. After Reconstruction and during the subsequent era of segregation, northerners accepted the white southern narrative of Reconstruction. D. W. Grif-

Still from *The Birth of a Nation* (1915) dramatically depicting Reconstruction as a war between African American state militias and the KKK. (Alamy)

fith's film *The Birth of a Nation* (1915) and the 1939 cinematic version of Margaret Mitchell's novel *Gone with the Wind* were the most popular and powerful cultural products of America in the era before the civil rights movement. Both celebrated the story of the Ku Klux Klan and white supremacist triumph in a war after the American Civil War. *The Birth of a Nation*, particularly, unapologetically presented Reconstruction as an unconventional political and racial war won by ex-Confederate white supremacists.[4] Scenes in the film depict battles between the KKK and African Americans fighting in uniform for Republican southern state governments. The film chronicles KKK guerilla and terrorist tactics but climaxes with two daylight battles between KKK armies and uniformed forces of the Republican government. Griffith—son of a Confederate colonel—covered up the reality of the biracial coalition of African Americans and white voters that constituted the voting majority in southern states during the brief period of wide African American enfranchisement between 1868 and 1877. He likewise covered up the biracial nature of Republican state militias.

Gone with the Wind has the "moral" character Melanie (*left*) lie to stop the arrest of her husband for leading an attempted racial massacre and gun battle during Reconstruction. (Alamy)

Gone with the Wind covered the same time period from the same southern white supremacist perspective but in its own twisted way acknowledged that the enemies of ex-Confederate extremists were a biracial coalition. The Reconstruction section of the film opens with text about the horrors of Reconstruction and "carpetbagger" rule in the South and called this a "scourge" worse than the American Civil War that preceded it. The film then cuts to an African American Republican politician and an evil white ally who begin abusing kind and even saintly Confederate soldiers. This scene is a gross reversal of the actual story of violence in the era. In reality, ex-Confederate extremists engaged in rampant assassinations and brutalizing attacks on African Americans and white unionists. The scene also amounts to a lie by showing biracial unionists denying Confederate soldiers a ride in their carriage. In 1865, after Appomattox, the federal government provided Confederate forces with food and transportation home.[5]

Like *The Birth of a Nation*, *Gone with the Wind* openly acknowledges the battles of the Southern Civil War. In the Reconstruction battle scene from *Gone with the Wind*, ex-Confederate officer Ashley Wilkes and Scarlett O'Hara's new husband, Frank Kennedy, organize other ex-Confederates into a secret group to "protect" their women, this after Scarlett is nearly raped in a biracial shantytown. They launch a nighttime guerilla, KKK-style attack on the shantytown residents. A bloody battle ensues in which Ashley is wounded and Frank is killed. Though reversing historic facts, *Gone with the Wind* acknowledges that Reconstruction was a war between white supremacist aggressors and freed African Americans (and their white southern allies). Its white supremacists attack the biracial coalition's vulnerable homes at night while the federal army fumbles about on the sidelines. Faultlessly "moral" character Melanie openly lies to federal troops to cover up white supremacist mass murder.

Unfortunately, *Gone with the Wind* is still the top box office movie of all time when adjusted for inflation. Fewer people today, however, share the white supremacist beliefs or flawed education about the history of segregated America prevalent in 1915 and 1939. Many are now ready for the war that *The Birth of a Nation* and *Gone with the Wind* celebrated to be seen from the opposite perspective. Revisionist historians in the late twentieth century did an excellent job critiquing the interpretation in the old films and texts and did not ignore the violence of the era, but they left it ill defined. They rightly emphasized the wisdom and agency of African Americans in shaping laudable Reconstruction goals. They also championed northern Republicans and their wrongly maligned policies. The new revisionists rightly wanted to highlight African American achievements rather than those of the KKK guerillas celebrated in white supremacist texts and films, but they failed to highlight the war since they had a positive view of federal action. Still more recent historical work, however, keeps the insights of revisionists but highlights the war against biracial democracy in the South and the limits of federal and local Republican power that led to harsh outcomes for freed men and women.

This newest generation of historians has systematically examined Reconstruction violence in ways that lay the foundation for this book and frame its arguments. Many of these recent studies have focused on one state or one incident. James Smallwood, Barry Crouch, and Larry Peacock examined the war in Texas, and James Hogue chronicled the war in Louisiana.[6] Stephen Budiansky's innovative *The Bloody Shirt* chronicled the war in Mississippi, as did Nicholas Lemann in *Redemption*.[7] Mark Bradley focused on the military's role in North Carolina, and Ben

Severance did this for Tennessee.[8] These excellent works provide a fine-grained examination of state history, but because of their narrow focus they do not often place Reconstruction events in the larger regional context. The same goes for works that look at single incidents like the 1866 Memphis Race Massacre and the 1873 Colfax Massacre. Charles Lane and LeeAnna Keith each wrote important books on the battle at Colfax, Louisiana, as Stephen Ash did for the Memphis Massacre.[9] Several recent studies have taken sophisticated approaches to the KKK and racial violence in the era. Carole Emberton's *Beyond Redemption: Race, Violence, and the American South after the Civil War* looks at postbellum violence in general as a national struggle about race, gender, and citizenship. Elaine Frantz Parsons's *Ku-Klux: The Birth of the Klan during Reconstruction* updated the history of KKK violence in the era and placed it in a national context.[10] But Emberton and Parsons crucially do not consider Reconstruction a war. Douglas Egerton does consider it one in his masterful book *The Wars of Reconstruction*, which comes from the perspective of Washington, D.C., and African American agency, providing a different facet than my examination here of the war itself throughout the South. Several recent books that, like Egerton's, take a broader view of Reconstruction and provide important discussions of violence include Mark Wahlgren Summers's *The Ordeal of the Reunion* and Allen C. Guelzo's *Reconstruction: A Concise History*. Each of these overviews of Reconstruction emphasizes that southern Reconstruction governments did not "fail"—they were defeated and overthrown by white supremacist political violence.[11] Keith D. Dickson's *No Surrender: Asymmetric Warfare in the Reconstruction South, 1868–1877* provides an outstanding technical military history of the Southern Civil War from the perspective of southern resistance to the "dominant actor," the North.[12] This is a vital perspective that complements this book you are reading, which instead focuses on the war between southerners and downplays the federal role. A related new debate over the role of federal forces, military history, and violence during Reconstruction entails whether the Civil War ended in 1865 with a peacetime occupation of the South or continued for years into the 1870s, as seen in the competing works of Andrew Lang (taking the first position) and Gregory P. Downs (taking the second).[13] I contend that after the Civil War there was distinct new war in the South and that understanding Reconstruction as a separate war reshapes how we understand one of the most important periods in American history.

Since the history of this separate war from 1865–1877 has gone unwritten until these recent studies (except by unapologetic white supremacists), clear terms for the combat and combatants are unavailable. Borrowing from the many recent, excellent studies of the "War of Reconstruction" in the individual states, this book offers popular terms to clarify the war for modern audiences. Nearly all the familiar terms for the era come directly from nineteenth-century white supremacist southerners, and their gross distortions and outright lies still appear in popular parlance and even textbooks. I do not use the terms "carpetbagger," "Radical Republican," "scalawag," and "Negro rule" (much less the phrase from the era "nigger rule") in this book. These terms should be obliterated from responsible histories except to explicate and refute their historic use. Using them is on par with accepting Stalinist, Maoist, and fascist terms for the victims of their mass slaughters and ethnic cleansings. White supremacists in the South blamed the victims of their atrocities. They described untold thousands of butchered African Americans and their white unionist allies as malicious predators. The truth was very much the opposite. Right from the end of the American Civil War in 1865, ex-Confederate extremists launched a tidal wave of violence and torture against southern African Americans and white unionists, whom they blamed for the defeat of the Confederacy.[14] African Americans' marginal new freedoms and limited political ambitions were the chief results of the Civil War defeat of the Confederacy, and ex-Confederate extremists attacked these and eventually overturned them.

What is the best term for these vicious victors in the Southern Civil War from 1865–1877? White supremacy was the key unifying ideology and the wellspring of their pathological violence. But "white supremacist" is an inadequate term for them because the entire nation, North and South, was ordered around white supremacy, and that historical reality is one reason the ex-Confederates won so easily. White northerners were willing to fight against disunion and the emergence of a hostile new nation right at their doorstep in 1861, but after 1865 no significant number of whites were willing to fight a sustained war against white supremacy, let alone *for* African American rights.

In fact, the so-called Radical Republicans in Washington could be called "white supremacist Republicans," as most of them would eventually support complete abandonment of African American rights and the duly elected Republican governments under siege by white supremacist ex-Confederate armies.[15] So "white supremacist," though accurate in describing ex-Confederate forces, distorts the national triumph of white supremacy and the preexisting white supremacist culture shared by the North and South. The term "ex-Confederate white supremacists" is an accurate term but clunky and not specific. Why not just "ex-Confederates"? Two problems emerge with this simple term. First, many ex-Confederates did not participate in the white supremacist violence, openly rejected it, or even in a few cases fought valiantly alongside African American allies against racist terror. One ex-Confederate hero emerges particularly in this study, as already mentioned: James Longstreet. Lee's second in command during the Civil War, Longstreet headed a biracial militia fighting to preserve African American rights and the democratically elected Republican government of Louisiana throughout the 1870s, most dramatically at the Battle of Liberty Place. There he was wounded fighting beside African Americans championing voting and equal rights in 1874. He was an ex-Confederate who fought against ex-Confederate extremists. James Alcorn, a former Confederate general and Reconstruction Republican governor of Mississippi (1870–1871), also battled ex-Confederate extremists. Confederate general James Fleming Fagan of Arkansas became a Reconstruction Republican and commanded African American Republican troops in that state's infamous 1874 Brooks-Baxter War. Two famous Confederate officers, General William Mahone and Colonel John Singleton Mosby (renowned as the "Gray Ghost"), in the Readjuster and Republican Parties respectively, opposed the white supremacist Democrats. Ex-Confederate extremists especially hated and slandered Longstreet, Fagan, and Alcorn for their military support of biracial democracy after the American Civil War.[16] In a less dramatic example, Robert E. Lee himself was an ex-Confederate who declined to participate in the Southern Civil War, even taking some symbolic steps against militarism before his death in 1870.[17] Simply using the term "ex-Confederate" is a distortion and insult to ex-Confederates who took many positions, some as valiant as Longstreet's.[18] The KKK and paramilitary white armies that arose in every southern state to resist the outcome of the American Civil War were overwhelmingly ex-Confederate soldiers and politicians, and they saw themselves as a continuation of the Confederate Army and many of its goals. Therefore, for brevity and clarity's sake, I have called the southern white supremacist forces "ex-Confederate extremists."

I have added "extremist" to "ex-Confederate" to capture what distinguished the extremists from Confederate veterans and other white southerners who did not take up arms between 1865 and 1877 in defense of white supremacy.[19] This also serves to correct the mislabeling of congressional Republicans as "Radical" and properly highlights the parties from which most Reconstruction violence and virulent positions sprang. They were "extreme" white supremacists in their ideology, as distinguished from a panoply of white supremacists nationwide, including many southerners who supported the extremists' actions but did not participate in the violence. Ex-Confederate extremists also went to tactical extremes in their use of terrorism by means of assassination, torture, rape, the execution of prisoners, and attacks on innocent civilians. The original Confederates had used such tactics less frequently as means to win an independent nation, until the end of the American Civil War, when they began to pioneer them in targeting African American soldiers and civilians. All these tactics were used by ex-Confederate extremists wholesale between 1865 and 1877—and after.[20]

What about the ex-Confederate extremists' opponents and the heroes of this book—and other recent works on Reconstruction—and likely the heroes in future classrooms and public memory? Widely accepted terms for them are also complicated and as yet unavailable. There is no one widely accepted term for these antagonists. I have used the term "biracial coalition" and will continue to do so. Unpacking this descriptor reveals the complexity of the Southern Civil War. First, "biracial" denotes that the unionists and Republicans who elected local and state governments after 1867 shared many interests but not racial identity. Whites and African Americans worked together but retained a degree of separation in practice and in goals.[21] African Americans were more committed to racial equality and had much more at stake in the war. Their white allies had a mix of motives and levels of commitment—many whites went to their graves fighting past all reasonable hope of maintaining democracy and good government in their southern communities, let alone African American freedom. But when the Southern Civil War became savage, protracted, and costly, many white Unionists gave up the fight, fled, or acquiesced to the triumph of white supremacy, and some even went over to the ex-Confederate extremist cause. The term "biracial" thus hints at the weakness and division among unionist forces that led to the coalition's total and crushing defeat. "Coalition" here represents a shaky alliance of many disparate interests coming together in the face of a common enemy. In every state of the South this coalition would be shattered. The defeat of the biracial coalition should not obscure the bravery of its members and the near miracle that such a group came together at all and fought effectively on both the political and military fronts. African Americans and whites fought and died side by side for a democratic and racially just Dixie, as southerners have done in multiple eras. Terms like "scalawag" and "carpetbagger" cover up the fact that many white southerners had been willing to resist the region's racial terror for hundreds of years before and after the Civil War. The biracial coalition had an army of Atticus Finches who were not fictional and bled and died for the highest southern and American ideals.[22] Southern white unionist leaders Edmund Davis of Texas, Print Matthews of Mississippi, Powell Clayton of Arkansas, and William Holden of North Carolina deserve monuments rather than the slanderous abuse heaped on them for a hundred years. They all lost—Matthews lost his life—after giving the fight their all and winning significant military and political battles against the KKK and racial terrorists.[23] Yet, without massive federal intervention and occupation, which federal leaders seem never to have even contemplated, these men were certain to lose. But what a lost cause it was.

Most of the heroes of the biracial coalition were African Americans. Everything was at stake for them in this war, and nearly everything was lost. They died by the tens of thousands but went down fighting—to the everlasting fury of generations of southern extremists who set up a system of terror to try to ensure African Americans never rose to defend themselves again. African American political warriors such as William Ward of Louisiana, Charles Caldwell and Peter Crosby of Mississippi, and Prince Rivers of South Carolina populate this study. They fought for the Union during the American Civil War and kept up the struggle in the Southern Civil War by joining, forming, or leading African American state militia companies. Their stories all ended in tragedy and defeat, but their existence and resistance were triumphs.

African American self-defense was one of the central features of the Southern Civil War. Enslaved and free African Americans in the South had fought to end slavery and destroy the Confederacy. Over 190,000 southern African Americans joined the Union army and navy, and many more spied on and sabotaged the Confederate war effort. This military tradition carried over into Reconstruction and the twelve years of the Southern Civil War as African Americans joined and led state militias and formed their own municipal militias to combat ex-Confederate extremist terrorists, guerillas, and paramilitaries.[24] Many of the African

This 1876 cartoon, "He Wants Change Too," published at the time in *Harper's Weekly*, depicts legitimate African American self-defense but also suggests racist fears. (Library of Congress)

American militia and political leaders were Civil War veterans. Unfortunately, Confederates who had not formally surrendered were generally not disarmed, while the Union army did disarm its veterans, especially African Americans. African Americans in the Southern Civil War wanted weapons to match those of the ex-Confederates but were often left with only shotguns.[25] African Americans' courageous armed struggle for civil rights and democracy for all southerners frightened whites, including their own Republican allies. African American military self-defense was a necessity, a matter of life and death, but it was ultimately futile. Most nineteenth-century Americans, North and South, were not ready to tolerate, let alone support, African Americans armed to kill whites, even in self-defense and for a just cause.

This African American tradition of armed self-defense during Reconstruction had an underappreciated afterlife in the late nineteenth century and in the twentieth century, but it did not go unnoticed by a white South (and North) organized to terrorize and intimidate African Americans daily. The specter of African Americans standing up for themselves, let alone with guns and white allies, led white supremacist extremists to increase their efforts to eliminate the mere possibility of self-defense. Leaders of African American military self-defense like Ward, Caldwell, and Rivers came to sad ends by 1877, but their twelve-year stand is a largely untold tale of valor in the face of terrible odds. African Americans knew the biracial coalition was fragile and strove to keep it alive through wise political compromise, military service, and ultimate sacrifice.

Thus, the war was fought between the "biracial coalition" and "ex-Confederate extremists," but what about political terms? The ex-Confederate extremists were in the Democratic Party, and biracial coalition members were in the Republican Party (or in some cases independent coalition parties opposing the Democratic Party). But I use party labels infrequently in this book, in part since as the subsequent reversal of party alignment on race makes "Democrat" and "Republican" potentially confusing. Unlike today, African Americans and white progressives were Republicans during Reconstruction, and the conservative white South (and North) voted Democratic, although Republicans have always been largely Protestant and pro-business. I likewise do not frequently use the nonparty terms that southerners on the ground employed during the Southern Civil War, "Union League" and "White League." Reconstruction has too often been written about as a "political" era, with a focus on laws and policy, when it was actually war. The terms "ex-Confederate extremists" and "biracial coalition" highlight the regional nature of the war. Likewise, calling this the "Southern Civil War" highlights its regional military nature and its distinction from the American Civil War. Many of the histories of Reconstruction in the twenty-first century have called this "the War of Reconstruction."[26] This term, however, in effect wrongly nationalizes (and politicizes) the struggle. The North neither "reconstructed" the South nor fought a war of reconstruction. The term "Reconstruction" is associated with the legal, political, and economic policies of the era and with the federal government, which was secondary to the war on the ground in the South. Reconstruction and its policies were failures and irrelevant in the face of the brutal military struggle in the South, where "reconstruction" was a wish rather than a reality. Historians and nonhistorians alike are probably burdened with it as a name for the era.[27] For that reason, it should not be used as part of the name for the war of 1865–1877.

Some historians have begun to employ the term "Second Civil War" for the conflict during Reconstruction, to underscore the connection between the Southern Civil War and the American Civil War. But the wars were very distinct in their aims, even if one grew out of the other. In the first war the Confederacy sought independent status as its own sovereign nation, and it definitely lost that struggle. The Confederacy, however, was born largely of the wish to keep southern society and its powerful status in the national government unchanged. Central to this goal was preserving slavery and, even more important, the system of racial subordination it represented. Confederates really desired local racial and political control without interference from outsiders. An independent Confederate nation was a means to an end, not a long-held ideology or goal of white southerners. A key reason many Confederates deserted prior to the end of the war, or accepted defeat in 1865 and gave up on sovereign national status, was that they went home to fight the local war they actually cared more about. The willingness to give up did not apply when it came to preserving the long-standing racial order, local political control, and oversight (if not de facto veto power) on federal decisions. White southerners would engage in a long-term, total effort toward these goals and win them in a victory that would last one hundred years after 1865. This struggle remains central to U.S. politics today. In geographic, military, and political terms, the war of 1865–1877 was distinct from the American Civil War. It had uniquely southern goals and was fought at that regional level, for control of local governments, between two southern blocs, as already noted: a biracial coalition and a large body of triumphant ex-Confederate extremists.

The War after the War: A History of Reconstruction is organized into five chapters, the first four of which describe phases in the 1865–1877 war in the South. The Southern Civil War took place in three phases: the terror phase (1865–1867), the guerilla phase (1868–1872), and the open paramilitary phase (1872–1877). The war also had many aftershocks in the late nineteenth and early twentieth centuries, when the white supremacist victors continued to use their wartime tactics to terrorize African Americans. This holistic approach to the war is the first description of these phases of the conflict.

Chapter 1 examines the terror phase, when ex-Confederates were left in power in the South because African Americans did not yet vote and consequently unionist whites had little power (except in Tennessee). Ex-Confederate extremists avoided open warfare with federal forces, instead attacking the supposedly freed African Americans and their white southern political allies. The 1865–1867 terror phase was the briefest but bloodiest of the Southern Civil War. In this period thousands of vulnerable African Americans and their white allies were massacred by ex-Confederates who controlled local and state governments.

The North had lost the initiative in 1865 by failing to impose advantageous peace terms and a new political order on the South. The federal government would never regain the initiative, but northern reaction to the 1865–1867 bloodletting brought about the second phase of the war, discussed in chapters 2 and 3. After 1867—too late—congressional Republicans tried to impose a peace on the ex-Confederates by dividing the South into military districts and organizing new state governments elected by enfranchised African American voters and their white Unionist allies. With a biracial coalition of Republican southerners in charge of every ex-Confederate state government (except Tennessee, which alone had a Unionist state government from 1865 to 1868 but fell to ex-Confederates in 1869), ex-Confederate extremists took up guerilla tactics. They avoided attacking federal troops (except in Texas) and instead used classic hit-and-run tactics against the new biracial unionist state and local government forces and leaders. The Ku Klux Klan, which had successfully fought the unionist government in Tennessee (the state in which the KKK was born) inspired many localized imitators, and they collectively dominated this phase of war between

1868 and 1872. Ex-Confederate extremists hid their identities when attacking local governments and then blended back into the population in typical guerilla form. The ex-Confederate South's powerful commitment to white supremacy defined the whole era but particularly so did this move to guerilla tactics, which had been used against the predominantly white Union adversaries of the American Civil War, especially in a few key states (Kentucky, Missouri, and Tennessee) and increasingly at the end of the war in 1864–1865.[28] In 1865, when they surrendered, Confederates had been unwilling to take up guerilla action and protracted war to preserve a new independent southern government—the Confederacy. But they would fight endlessly with any tactic to preserve the racial order of the South during Reconstruction and afterward. Several biracial Republican state governments did successfully fight back and break the insurgency of the KKK and other guerilla groups. These brief biracial coalition triumphs are the subject of chapter 2. Governor Powell Clayton of Arkansas and Edmund Davis of Texas both cleared their states of KKK-style opponents using martial law and the state militia, as Governor William Brownlow of Tennessee had done earlier. In the clearest case of federal military activity in the Southern Civil War, President Grant sent in national forces and arrested many members of the KKK in South Carolina. However, Grant suffered politically for this intervention and never repeated it, and state governors in the South faced immediate backlash. Their use of arrests, martial law, and African American troops against whites angered white voters who turned southern Republicans out of office via votes, violence, and election fraud, even in Texas and Arkansas.

Chapter 3 examines the ex-Confederate extremist guerillas' insurgent triumphs against the state governments of Georgia, Alabama, North Carolina, and Virginia, though Virginia exhibited the weakest biracial political effort and therefore the least ex-Confederate extremist guerilla violence.[29] Merciless guerilla action in Mississippi, Louisiana, South Carolina, and Florida (the first three of which had African American majority populations) could not topple those state governments, so those states saw a further escalation of tactics.

In war's the last phase, discussed in chapter 4, these insurgent guerilla victories further emboldened ex-Confederate extremists and their white supporters in the states remaining in unionist hands after 1872. In these last states, ex-Confederate extremists openly took up arms in paramilitary armies that directly attacked state government forces, as at the Battle of Liberty Place. The threat of northern military intervention and ex-Confederate extremist fear of such intervention had largely evaporated in this phase. The conventional battles of this last phase ushered in the complete triumph of ex-Confederates extremists in seizing power in the last former Confederate states with biracial coalition governments. Ultimately, ex-Confederate paramilitary triumphs led to the famous Compromise of 1877 in which the North withdrew all forces from the South and acquiesced to the ex-Confederate extremists—signaling their white supremacist victory.[30]

As in most civil wars, the victorious side then launched a wave of reprisal killings: the mass lynching and massacres of African Americans in the region that lasted for generations well into the twentieth century. Also typical of the violence following a civil war was the movement of African Americans fleeing systemic terror that became known as the Great Migration, starting in 1916. Chapter 4 also recounts how the violent paramilitary warfare of the final phase of the Southern Civil War could not be turned off in 1877. The warfare in the South during Reconstruction had built up traditions of white paramilitary repression that white supremacists inculcated into the two generations after 1877, and bloody aftershocks of white supremacist paramilitary violence erupted throughout the late nineteenth and early twentieth centuries. Not just lynching but also organized attacks resulting in the slaughter of entire African American communities became commonplace in places like Wilmington, North Carolina (1898), New Orleans (1900), Atlanta (1906), Slocum, Texas (1910), Elaine, Arkansas (1919), Tulsa (1921), and Rosewood, Florida (1923). One intention behind most of these massacres was the disruption of a complementary Southern Civil War tradition in African American communities. African Americans—used to advocating for and ultimately defending themselves—fought back in all the clashes listed above. Historian George Rable, the ablest chronicler of Reconstruction violence, noted that, after 1865, "The country miraculously avoided the bloody reprisals that commonly follow civil wars." [31] The North did avoid such reprisals, but the South did not. Ex-Confederate extremist victors of the Southern Civil War perpetrated massacres into the twentieth century.

The lynching and mass attacks on African American communities after 1877 look like the bloody reprisals that victors have carried out in the generations after civil wars in subsequent generations. The book's final chapter, chapter 5, examines parallels between the Southern Civil

War and later civil wars fought with unconventional warfare over protracted periods of time and over peace settlements and occupations. Some of these international examples include the Irish Civil War, the Vietnamese Wars, and the U.S. occupation of Iraq. This chapter highlights how civil wars rarely end with clear peace settlements and usually have a protracted, on-again, off-again nature that can stretch over generations of political violence and guerilla warfare—the precise pattern that played out in the American Civil War and the Southern Civil War.

As the Southern Civil War takes its place in history books, historians are finding more cases of violent engagement between 1865 and 1877. Historians need to reinterpret the whole Civil War era in light of recent scholarship on the Jim Crow era that describes it as a new and often worse phase of slavery—best exemplified by Douglas Blackmon's *Slavery by Another Name* (2008) and Michael Oshinsky's *Worse than Slavery* (1997). The classic histories that claim the American Civil War of 1861 to 1865 ended slavery and reunited the nation are unsustainable in the face of new scholarship. The history of the Southern Civil War illuminates Reconstruction as a compelling martial story that better accounts for the continuing troubled legacy of the Civil War era.

CHAPTER ONE

The Terror Phase, 1865–1867

The Massacres Begin

The first phase of the Southern Civil War had its roots in the collapse of order in the Confederacy in the last years of the American Civil War. Guerilla fighting, local violence, assassination, racial massacre, and chaos marked the final year of the war in the South. Confederate Home Guard militias patrolled the countryside and attacked draft dodgers, deserters, unionists, and runaway slaves in small running skirmishes. Southerners were turning on each other in an anarchic power vacuum. When the federal government did not step in to fill this vacuum after 1865, the old white power structure tried to retain power, and the violence multiplied. Between the end of the American Civil War in 1865 and 1867, ex-Confederate extremists dominated much of the South. They used their control of law enforcement, courts, and militias to slaughter and intimidate freedpeople and unionists. The Southern Civil War began in earnest in 1865. No one knows how many were killed in those chaotic two years controlled by ex-Confederates. The historical evidence suggests tens of thousands, with terror visited on millions. The ex-Confederate extremist war of terror shocked Congress into action. This violence right after the war is well known, but its scale and origins need greater historical and popular attention. This chapter examines the origins of the terror phase of the Southern Civil War in the settlement of the American Civil War, the anarchic violence of the Confederate home front, and the Confederate tactics at the end of the war, as exemplified by those of Nathan Bedford Forrest and John Wilkes Booth. I attempt to categorize, characterize, and estimate the scale of bloodshed across the South from 1865 to 1867.

What was the peace treaty that ended the Civil War? This trivia question will trip up many American Civil War buffs. "Appomattox, April 9, 1865" is often the answer, but that was just the first military surrender of many. It was never a peace settlement, and the war continued in earnest for more than a month after Lee's surrender. If not then, when did the Civil War end? The Union army held a grand review parade of all its forces and then demobilized nearly all of them on May 23 and May 24, 1865, but it was not until June 23 that the last Confederate general formally surrendered. President Andrew Johnson finally declared the end of hostilities August 20, 1866, almost a year and a half later.

Prior to that declaration, on April 3, 1866, Johnson had proclaimed the insurrection over except in Texas. Unlike the other formerly Confederate states, Texas still had no state government and was rife with violence against unionists, Black and white. The violence in Texas was particularly brazen but otherwise not distinguishable from that of the other former Confederate states that had mounting body counts. Johnson sought any pretext to end reconstruction with conservative forces in control of the states and repressing freedpeople. Texas also had a particularly tense situation, as many Confederates had fled to the state and brought their slaves since the Union had little presence there. These migrations continued after 1865, and the newly liberated people became a target for the rootless white migrants as well as the local planters and ex-Confederate forces who had not experienced defeat in the isolated Lone Star State.[1] In this atmosphere, the conservative ex-Confederate general James Webb Throckmorton became governor on August 9, 1866. On August 20, President Johnson backed the new conservative Texas government that had refused to ratify the Thirteenth Amendment, proclaiming that "said insurrection is at an end and that peace, order, tranquility, and civil authority now exist in and throughout the whole United States of America." None of these were true. In Texas many reports of attacks on African Americans and unionists poured in to federal authorities. The governor, it was said, was not only failing to protect unionists' lives but also raising ranger units participating in the persecutions. Federal military commander Phil Sheridan removed Throckmorton and replaced him with a Republican governor. Similar violence plagued most other southern states at the time Johnson claimed that "tranquility and civil authority" existed everywhere.[2]

What prompted the president's declaration? Expediency. The war had been traumatic and bloody, and the North did not want to undertake a war of pacification. Imposing a peace in the South would have required acknowledging the continued state of war. Declaring the war's end, on the other hand, was comforting to northerners and played into Johnson's conservative racial vision for the South. For Johnson to acknowledge ex-Confederate extremist violence against African Americans and white unionists as a war would have been too politically compromising and alien to his southern white supremacist sympathies. Popular memory has retained his myopia, imagining a neat end to the war—when even Johnson admitted it continued through much of 1866.

Unionists then and since desperately wanted a progressive, triumphant, meaningful end to the war. Ken Burns's widely viewed PBS documentary *The Civil War* (1990) concluded in 1865 on the triumphant note that slavery was over and the nation united and modernized by this moral and splendid war. But this is like concluding that World War I ended German aggression and even war itself, which was not borne out. "The war to end war" was followed a generation later by the bloody atrocities of World War II. In the case of the Southern Civil War, its atrocities began the same year that war supposedly ended in the United States. While repressing the history of this insurrection helps paper over the regional, ideological, economic, and racial cracks in the country, it is time that Americans reckon with the Southern Civil War, the vital aftermath of the tidy "end" to the American Civil War and a peace settlement that simply did not exist.

The central problem in the American Civil War that led to the Southern Civil War was the lack of a peace settlement. Civil wars rarely end with clear, mutual peace settlements. Usually one side wins and politically represses or more often purges its opponents via reprisal killings. But many civil wars have multiple phases that continue or overturn the previous phase and have less clear winners in the long run. The American Civil War followed this pattern. It lacked a peace settlement and was followed by twelve bloody years of a new armed conflict that reshaped the meaning of 1861–1865.

Civil wars are internal political struggles, and the American Civil War, though often fought as a conventional war between two nations, began as a disputed election. Abraham Lincoln's 1860 presidential election victory was unacceptable to many in the South, and the election was refought with bullets rather than ballots. The bullet outcome was remarkably similar to the ballot outcome, with Lincoln's northern coalition prevailing with help from the border states that did not side with the Deep South in the war (though they also did not vote for Lincoln). These border states had an enormous geographic area claimed by both sides. In the Deep South, the Confederacy was a minority movement in every state, as many whites opposed secession and virtually every African American opposed continued servitude. Therefore, the American Civil War was particularly divisive in the South, and this internal southern war could not just be turned off in 1865 by president proclamation. Thus, the political roots of the American Civil War foretold the political origins of the Southern Civil War. The latter moved into the vacuum left by the lack of a political settlement, let alone a peace plan, at the end of the American Civil War. With no peace plan, the field was open for a violent contest over the meaning of the war. Instability and continued political violence were the true outcomes of American Civil War—in other words, another war.

Generals William Tecumseh Sherman and Joe Johnston appreciated this potential for chaos and continued war when Johnston surrendered to Sherman weeks after Appomattox at the Bennett Farm in North Carolina on April 26, 1865—the largest troop surrender of the war. Sherman and Johnston, two of the most thoughtful commanders of the war, drew up a document that went beyond a military surrender and took up the issues of the political, social, and economic order of the future South. Sherman and Johnston discussed the future of African Americans, but the final form of the "Sherman truce" said little about the status of African Americans. It was a very generous settlement for Confederates that would have kept the antebellum southern racial order and political elite in place and in many ways preserved a quasi-slavery for African Americans—exactly the outcome of the Southern Civil War in 1877. Far from being acknowledged for at least raising the issue and setting a precedent for clear national action and treaties, Sherman was severely reprimanded by Johnson's entire cabinet for overstepping his authority, and the settlement's terms were rejected by both Congress and the administration. The Sherman-Johnston settlement was pragmatic, appeasing racist sensibilities by continuing to deny civil rights to African Americans. Their agreement did not imagine rights of citizenship, let alone the vote, as theoretically came with the Fourteenth and Fifteenth Amendments. Fears that these rights would be granted were alive and well in southern minds, and they would be realized in 1867. In this early, terror-based phase of the new civil war, the goal was to keep these outcomes beyond imagination. Through fighting against basic rights for African Americans after 1865, many white southerners became acculturated to terrorizing African Americans, and they became pathologically racially embittered.[3] Sherman's plan of appeasing these white southerners was at least a plan, but it is not clear that if carried out it would have forestalled ex-Confederate terror.

Sherman's capitulation might have been one way to avoid the Southern Civil War, though not the victory of the ex-Confederate extremists, but the more obvious and just route to avoid this would have been a thorough federal occupation and "de-Confederatization" of the South. Immediately upon finding the mass graves of Union soldiers at Andersonville and discovering a pro-Confederate and proslavery plot to assassinate President Lincoln and cabinet members in 1865, the North could have imposed a forceful peace plan. Millions of northern men were still under arms and could have been posted in the South. Trials for treason and war crimes could have been held and mass executions of southern leaders carried out. Land redistribution to formerly enslaved people and poor white unionists could have been undertaken. And, far less importantly, new governments could have been installed that represented the majority of southerners. The African American population, who were the majority in several states, when added to the significant white unionist population, made a unionist majority in most Confederate states. These seem like an obvious set of actions that any victor in a hard-fought civil war would take. Yet, tragically, the federal government instead emboldened ex-Confederate extremists by demobilizing virtually the entire northern war machine, granting Confederate commanders and soldiers clemency from prosecution, returning confiscated land granted to freedmen to the ex-Confederate plantation owners, issuing pardons wholesale, trying only one Confederate officer for war crimes, and not providing any political settlement to the war at all. No effective occupation of the South ever happened, as northern troop counts in the region were always low after the American Civil War and generally decreased as the Southern Civil War dragged on. Traditions of northern and national racism, distaste for standing armies, and suspicions of central government action certainly undermined decisive action. In 1865 no civil or economic rights were granted to the African Americans who had destroyed the southern economy, run away, and fought by the hundreds of thousands to ensure northern victory. In retrospect, the North failed to act to preserve their victory and abandoned their African American allies. No wonder ex-Confederate extremists were emboldened and launched an all-out negation of pronouncements from Washington.

Many Confederates might have expected and even accepted a peace settlement that remade the South and eliminated the plantations in 1865.[4] But when none came forth and they still controlled the South as they always had, they used their position to attack the verdict of the war and define the postwar order in the South. This period from 1865–1867, which is called Presidential Reconstruction (or "Self-Reconstruction") in traditional histories, emboldened the defeated Confederates to escalate their violence and military actions over the next twelve years. Once the North handed them the initiative at the local level, ex-Confederate extremists never surrendered that initiative. In the terror phase of the Southern Civil War, the most obvious targets were African Americans and northerners in the region. Under Lincoln's wartime "ten percent plan," which was intended to quickly build loyal southern state governments, once 10 percent of a state accepted loyalty to the Union and the end of slavery, the state could be readmitted. Andrew Johnson continued Lincoln's general policy and directed the states to write new constitutions, which called really only for two statewide acknowledgements of defeat: the legal end of chattel slavery and the renunciation of Confederate government debts. Much has been made of the Black Codes written into most new southern state constitution between 1865 and 1867 that restricted the rights of all African Americans and often sought to require them to work under white control—even if they were not technically property. As Mark Bradley put it well, "Southern state legislatures passed so-called Black Codes to keep freedpeople in a condition as close to slavery as the lawmakers dared."[5] After news of the Black Codes and violent outrages in the South, northern voters rejected Johnson's plans in the congressional elections of 1866. The voters returned Republicans who supported the Fourteenth Amendment, which passed Congress in June 1866 and was ratified in 1868. The Fourteenth Amendment struck down the harsh Black Codes in principle, but in practice the Black Codes remained in effect via terror. The Black Codes were codified again in the Jim Crow laws of the late nineteenth century and early twentieth century and by federal court rulings in the 1890s validating segregation. Yet the racial control in the Black Codes, while a goal adhered to successfully by the ex-Confederate extremists, was not the main focus of 1865–1867. Violence was. Attacking and killing African Americans and their overt white allies came first and offered a more effective means and higher rate of success than writing laws to re-enslave African Americans. Violence kept African Americans enslaved before the Black Codes, after they were written, and especially after they were supposedly overturned by the congressional Civil Rights Act of 1866, the Reconstruction Acts of 1867, and then the Fourteenth Amendment ratification in 1868.

When Congress finally moved via the Reconstruction Acts of 1867 to grant African Americans rights, reorganize the South into military districts, and supervise elections of loyal voters, the North still did not send meaningful numbers of troops to the South or effectively prosecute, let alone punish the thousands of mass murderers and armed insurrectionists in the South. After the 1867 congressional pronouncements, ex-Confederate extremists avoided antagonizing the few, scattered, and passive federal troops in the South but went about slaughtering, with impunity, local biracial coalitions and driving them from power and into subjugation. Under congressional plans after 1866, the federal government made greater claims for itself in the region but still lacked the will to enforce its laws and amendments intended to protect African American rights. This federal failure accelerated ex-Confederate extremist disdain for the law and the turn to more open warfare.

Why did the federal government not act forcefully in its interests? One reason is that the North was severely white supremacist itself. Also it was still shocked and exhausted by the military power it had exerted at the end of the war in 1864–1865. Like white southerners, many northerners distrusted federal government power and centralization and romanticized the prewar "limited" government. The federal government's actions during Reconstruction were ill planned but also hampered by a divided electorate in the North and, in key periods, divided government. (Republicans did not control the executive from 1865 to 1869 and lost the House of Representatives in the election of 1874.) Northerners had been horrified by the carnage of the last year of the war, especially Grant's casualties, and they wholeheartedly stood down when the chance to end the bloodletting came. What to many white northerners were a few thousand dead African Americans and their white political allies compared to avoiding the horrors of the last years of the American Civil War?

The period from 1865 to 1867 was the least conventionally military phase of the Southern Civil War but it was by far the bloodiest. At the local level, the Confederates never stopped fighting after the American

Civil War. After 1865, ex-Confederate extremists remained committed to the violence of war but changed targets, tactics, and goals.[6] Attacking northern soldiers was no longer an option, but the North had made free African Americans the symbol of their victory and the main component of its plans for the future of the South. Attacks on African Americans vented ex-Confederate rage at the results of the Civil War, but they mostly had the economic, ideological, and social purpose of keeping the South unchanged. The racial control and attempted re-enslavement of African Americans depended on a new war of terror. The new war's logic was so obvious and grew so organically out of ex-Confederate frustrations that it erupted spontaneously everywhere in the old Confederacy without any central planning or coordination.

Terrorism is a tactic of warfare that generally aims violence at civilians instead of military targets but also may include attacks on military installations that avoid direct military combat.[7] The aim of the violence is to strike fear in the population in order to change their behavior or deter them from continuing to engage an opponent or enact policies the terrorists hate.[8] Terrorism often has an element of revenge driving it, and ex-Confederate extremist bitterness with defeat in the American Civil War also drove them to terroristic violence. Ex-Confederate extremists thus had multiple purposes in their war of terror from 1865 through 1867.[9] Primarily they wanted local white supremacist domination of southern communities with no input from African Americans, unionists, or the North, and they also wanted their terrorism to keep African Americans unfree and northerners out of the region. Ex-Confederate extremist terrorism was largely successful in these goals. Ex-Confederate extremists also wanted to overturn the results of the American Civil War in the region and retain full political control of the South. As is often the case with unconventional warfare, this took time. The brutality and audacity of their war of terror brought a political reaction from Congress in 1867. The ex-Confederate extremists, however, escalated their warfare after 1867 and added guerilla warfare and eventually open paramilitary warfare to their arsenal, but they never ceased using terrorist tactics. In the long run, terrorism had a crucial role in defeating biracial coalition governments in the South and driving the federal army and all federal power from the South by 1877.

The terror phase of the war through 1867 had another element that defined it and made it distinct from the rest of the Southern Civil War: state terror. Only in these two years did ex-Confederates control the state and local governments without opposition. Ex-Confederates controlled the police and militias (except in Tennessee), as they had under the slaveholding regimes they were trying to preserve. Ex-Confederates often initiated terror through the police and militias and used political offices and courts to shield terrorists, especially in the large-scale actions in places like New Orleans and Memphis in 1866.

"Asymmetrical warfare" is a modern term for a strategy used by a side in a military struggle that does not have anywhere near the resources or capabilities of the side it opposes and uses unconventional tactics like terrorism and guerilla warfare.[10] The weaker side thus does not meet its far superior opponent on the battlefield but instead chooses unconventional situations and targets that keep it from directly confronting the military strengths of its opponents.[11] So roadside bombs, attacks on civilians ("soft" targets), political murders, ethnicity-based killing, and other tactics are employed to undermine the authority and military-political control of a region by a far superior power. The far superior power, like the North, is often engaged in a limited war that plays into the hands of the weaker side.[12] The South did this to great effect between 1865 and 1867. In those years the ex-Confederates were at their weakest militarily and at the height of their fear of the North's commitment to military intervention in the region, so they hit the softest of soft targets—vulnerable African American freedpeople. After the success of this terror phase and the limited response of the North, they escalated to guerilla tactics and then, after more northern reluctance to engage in the conflict, turned to open paramilitary warfare after 1872. Union generals William Sherman and Phil Sheridan had taught the South the futility and mortal consequences of directly resisting northern armies, even with hit-and-run guerilla tactics. Ex-Confederate extremists throughout the Southern Civil War, except in Texas for limited periods, customarily never targeted or confronted the few federal troops in the South or their installations and the limited areas they directly controlled. Ex-Confederate extremists learned the effectiveness of avoiding direct confrontation with the North in 1865 and 1866 when they spontaneously slaughtered African American civilians by the thousands and probably tens of thousands. Through terrorism, slavery would not end. The North would not control the region or dictate its politics or way of life. When African Americans, white unionists, and northerners in the region remained unprotected, the North's lack of will was revealed and its limited claim to have the authority to change the

South—by ending slavery—was denied. Northern weakness and nonresponse to the war of terror between 1865 and 1867—despite thousands of terrorist killings in those two years, the vast majority of those responsible faced no punishment—taught the South that resistance was a live option. Ex-Confederates who controlled the South in the terror phase initiated and defined the terms of the Southern Civil War.

Of course, the bloodletting and chaos of 1865–1867 cannot be examined in isolation from the bloodshed and terror of 1864–1865. These were inextricably linked and grew out of the same forces of racism and social breakdown. The formal battlefield accounts of the American Civil War obscure the fact that much of the South was descending into internal civil war in the last year and a half of the war. The catalog of violence in the South from 1865 to 1867 was a continuation of the collapse of order inside the old Confederacy. Guerilla warfare, race warfare and massacre, political and economic violence, general lawlessness, and local armed struggle plagued the South in 1864 and 1865.[13]

Two examples of the Confederate precedent for the terrorism and extremity of the 1865 to 1877 Southern Civil War have always been in plain view: Nathan Bedford Forrest and John Wilkes Booth. Forrest is the better-known example of the continuity of the American Civil War's violence in the post-1865 Southern Civil War. As a legendary Confederate general, Forrest effectively used guerilla tactics from 1864 to 1865. Avoiding engaging the main body of the Union forces, he conducted hit-and-run raids against smaller detachments of Union forces as his cavalry units ranged across the western theater. His targets were often garrisons and supply trains run by southern unionists and formerly enslaved people. Forrest infamously massacred over two hundred of the African American soldiers among the more than three hundred at Fort Pillow, Tennessee, on April 12, 1864, after the Union soldiers surrendered. Fort Pillow was the most dramatic event in Forrest's race war but presaged similar massacres by later imitators at Opelousas and Colfax, Louisiana, and Hamburg, South Carolina, between 1865 and 1877.

Forrest served as the first grand wizard of the Ku Klux Klan after joining the Klan a year after its December 1865 founding in Pulaski, Tennessee, as a secret fraternal organization.[14] This first small, elite Klan group was not political.[15] Forrest helped recruit for it, spread it to other states, and helped transform it into a guerilla organization of racial terrorism.[16] The KKK thus had an unbroken connection with the guerilla operations of the American Civil War. Its night-riding forays and as-

Confederate general and first grand wizard of the KKK Nathan Bedford Forrest (1821–1877). (Wikimedia Commons)

sassination campaigns provide textbook examples of terrorist and guerilla warfare. The KKK avoided direct confrontation with federal forces and blended into the population most of the time. Then it came out in force as cavalry units, attacking, usually at night and in disguise, African Americans and white unionists, the most vulnerable representatives of federal ambitions in the region.[17] As the KKK and its imitators were composed of numerous local cells that shared goals but operated secretly and independently of each other, its diffuse operations were particularly hard to isolate and combat, anticipating the best practices of modern guerilla warfare and terrorism.[18] Forrest raised the profile of the KKK, even traveling out of state to speak and start new cells.

To maintain racial control and push for a pro-Confederate white supremacist government in his home state of Tennessee, which had a unionist government before the end of the American Civil War, Forrest simply continued his Civil War violence.[19] Unionist governor William G. Brownlow developed the biracial Tennessee State Guard militia that successfully guarded polls and let Tennessee be the first former Confederate state with wide African American voting, in the state election of 1867.[20] The State Guard kept the peace, and Brownlow and the Republicans dominated that election, but Forrest's Klan came out in force in the next year's election, which saw widespread violence. Forrest succeeded so thoroughly in Tennessee that he largely disbanded the state's Klan at the start of 1869 after Republicans lost power in the state, as the new unionist governor Dewitt Clinton Senter caved in and re-enfranchised former Confederates. Forrest had warned in a newspaper interview, "There is not a radical [Republican] leader in this town [who is not] a marked man; and if a trouble should break out, not one of them would be left alive."[21] Other intimidated unionist leaders, like Senter, retreated from Brownlow's bold action, and the State Guard was ended for decades. Tennessee was the first ex-Confederate state to reestablish white supremacist, Democratic Party control of local government after a period of biracial Republican election victories and self-defense. Forrest journeyed to other southern states to set up Klan chapters, and his example inspired spontaneous imitators in local communities across the South. Tennessee set a precedent for KKK-style violence that would plague the South after African American voting and biracial governments reached other states.

The origins of Forrest's KKK violence were directly tied to Confederate guerilla warfare, Home Guard actions, and pre-existing slave patrols. Historians who have focused on the African American experience, from W. E. B. Dubois to John Hope Franklin, Herbert Aptheker, Leon Litwack, Steven Hahn, and Douglas Egerton, have put Forrest's KKK properly in this broader context of a long-standing, white-initiated war of terror against African Americans and unionists in the South.

The other obvious example of how the terrorist tactics of the Southern Civil War after 1865 emerged from the American Civil War was John Wilkes Booth's assassination of Abraham Lincoln in April 1865. Strangely, this obsessed-about event is rarely placed into the pattern of the southern violence it helped foster. The assassination has to rate as one of the most successful and influential acts of political terrorism in history. Even though Booth and his pro-Confederate coconspirators intended to kill Andrew Johnson too, Lincoln's death made that ruthless, white supremacist southern Democrat the president.[22] Booth's act previewed, symbolized, and was the model for resistance in the South that launched hundreds of assassinations between 1865 and 1877 (and beyond) in a nation almost devoid of that tradition. Booth demonstrated the effectiveness of political assassinations of Republican politicians, which would become commonplace in the Southern Civil War. Hundreds of Republicans would fall from assassins' bullets in the South after 1865. To be a white (or, later, African American) Republican politician was to be marked for death in the former Confederate States. Booth shared ideological roots with ex-Confederate extremists of the Southern Civil War after 1865 and the strategy of undermining a peace settlement. After hearing one of Lincoln's last speeches at the White House on April 11, 1865, in which Lincoln said that the end of slavery would not be effective unless African Americans had some civil laws to guarantee their freedom, Booth commented "That means Nigger citizenship" and launched the assassination conspiracy he would develop with Confederate agents.[23] He told Lewis Powell, one of his band of conspirators, "Now, by God, I'll put him through. That is the last speech he will ever make."[24] Citizenship and then the vote for African Americans were exactly the ideas ex-Confederate extremists would resist with any tactic at their disposal. African American citizenship became a legal reality with the Fourteenth Amendment in 1867, and thousands of Booths took up the shout of the South: such a political reality had to be exterminated. The Fourteenth Amendment and African Americans' rights to life, liberty, and property were eliminated when, in 1896, the Republican Supreme Court let the Fourteenth Amendment die with its *Plessy v. Ferguson* decision. The ex-Confederate extremists had won the war.

Booth and Forrest are just the most famous individuals in a regional descent into new levels of anarchic violence that constituted a new local civil war. As noted above, civil chaos and violence had come to dominate much of the South by 1864. White unionism and desertion from the Confederate forces had also become epidemic in the South. In the last year and a half of the American Civil War numerous units of unionists and deserters clashed with the Confederate Home Guard across the region. The Home Guard, composed of impressment officers and conscription units, had met some local resistance across the South from its inception.[25] But in the last years of the war the numbers of unionist and local resisters had grown to regularly contest them in many more communities. Along roads and in villages of the South, unionists and de-

John Wilkes Booth (1838–1865) was present with a gun at Lincoln's second inauguration. (Library of Congress)

serters conducted running battles with forces of the Confederate government.[26] The chaos and violence on the Confederate home front after 1863 often fostered desertion, as desperate letters from home reached soldiers. These letters expressed the prospect of starvation and the fear of race war (engendered by rumors of African American insurrection) and depravations visited on civilians by the supposedly friendly forces of the Home Guard.[27] These local Confederate units were often organized ad hoc and used their authority to make economic raids and attack runaway slaves on the roads. These running battles and the violent patrolling of southern roads would actually increase after 1865 and degenerate into the mass slaughter of African Americans and the open assassination of white unionist leaders. Tennessee, in particular, where white unionism had always been strong, remained a theater for running battles between unionists and rebel road patrols in 1865 and 1866. Most Confederate forces were state and local units engaged in "home defense" and "keeping order." These Home Guard forces rarely formally surrendered to any Union army.[28] These forces kept their arms and their local pattern of organization. They easily shifted after 1865 to use their arms and organization to battle political foes in a new civil war.[29]

The ex-Confederate campaign of terror had varied targets and tactics, but all had the shared purpose of terrifying the agents of change in the region. All persons in the South had to submit to white supremacy; the labor, class, and gender status quo; and ex-Confederate political and economic dominance. African Americans, southern white unionists and progressives, and northerners in the region (white teachers, missionaries, and aid workers helping formerly enslaved people) all faced terror. The mass atrocities of the terror phase of the Southern Civil War had political and even strategic purposes, and these can be placed in six broad categories. One category is terrorism stemming from the violent, racist ideology of many southern whites, who wanted to exterminate freed African Americans. Reconstruction's potential for genocidal campaigns went unrealized, but African Americans faced massacres at the hands of ex-Confederate extremists that resembled incidents of ethnic cleansing. Second, and easier to document, ex-Confederate extremists used terrorist tactics to try to keep African Americans functionally and psychologically enslaved. These extremists continued to use slave patrols to restrict African Americans' movement, and they whipped, beat, and killed numerous African Americans who tried to break free of plantation work. Third, as during the era of slavery, ex-Confederate extremists carried out sexual assaults. Such attempts to rob African American women of their independence and agency terrorized entire African American communities. Fourth, many southern whites and even plantation owners accepted African American freedom and even distributed land to freedmen. Such white southerners became targets of terrorism, especially via threats and vandalism. Northerners who came south to run schools and missions for the formerly enslaved, to farm, and to run businesses were likewise threatened, shot at, and chased from the region by ex-Confederate extremists. Fifth, ex-Confederate extremists targeted African American schools, churches, and homes in a campaign of mass arson. Schools and churches constituted community meeting places, power bases, and symbols of African Americans' newfound freedom. Finally, mass killings abounded in the region, and all the above-mentioned terrorist tactics were combined in urban massacres of the Southern Civil War's terror phase in cities like New Orleans and Memphis.

Allen Guelzo, in his excellent short history of Reconstruction, reflects on the missed opportunities and potential of the era in the South: "While it is always possible to wonder what might have happened if Reconstruction's issues had been pressed more firmly, or its overthrow contested more vigorously, it also has to be admitted that it might have spiraled onward in agony and insurgency for decades, and with every chance for a far more damaging, perhaps even genocidal, outcome."[30] But didn't Reconstruction "spiral onward" in close to this manner for African Americans? The Southern Civil War and its aftermath did entail events akin to what would later be called pogroms or ethnic cleansing. Even after the Southern Civil War came to a close in 1877, African Americans faced generations of agony and terror, with tens of thousands lynched, massacred, worked to death in convict leasing, and violently intimidated in the grueling system of sharecropping. In 1865 these cruel outcomes were a long way off, and potential was seen for a positive outcome, but the South was already descending into mass slaughter. This raises the question: how many were killed during the Southern Civil War, especially in the immediate postwar campaign of terror? Surprisingly, few attempts have been made to answer this question. The challenges of counting Southern Civil War deaths are particularly difficult for 1865–1867. One very incomplete source suggests the extensive scale of African American victimization in the South: the incident reports of the federal Freedmen's Bureau in each southern state. African

Americans reported violence to the bureau on an individual and voluntary basis, so the sample size is limited, and the bureau reports were very limited geographically. Many of the most vulnerable and isolated freedpeople had no access to bureau agents even if they knew reporting was an option. And, of course, African Americans intimidated by terror and years of repression often avoided coming forward.[31] Given these limitations, though, the Freedmen's Bureau reports contain accounts of killings that, if extrapolated across unreported regions and missing data, give numbers of dead in the tens of thousands.[32] The Equal Justice Initiative, reporting only documented cases, states in its 2020 *Reconstruction in America* that "at least 2,000 Black women, men, and children were victims of racial terror lynchings" during Reconstruction.[33] This is a count of just one form of terrorism. The 2020 report lists thirty-four documented "mass lynchings" in the era.[34] By historian Eric Foner's reckoning, the area of North Louisiana (around Shreveport), East Texas, and South Arkansas had a count of at least two thousand African Americans killed in 1865–1866 alone.[35] That region did not contain a tenth of the southern African American population. Other states, like Mississippi and South Carolina, were reported to have equally high violence, and there were also uncounted white unionist victims. Historian James Hogue counted thirty-five hundred killings connected to reconstruction in Louisiana, and PBS reported two thousand killings in Arkansas connected to the 1868 elections that saw more KKK violence than those of other years.[36] Historian Dorothy Sterling did exhaustive research on KKK killings from just 1868 to 1871 and estimated twenty thousand dead, which extrapolates out to nearly sixty thousand in 1865–1877, and the bloodiest years may have been 1865–1867.[37] The years 1872–1877, however, had less bloodshed, as the war had ended in many states by then, so forty thousand may be a better estimate. No reliable numbers exist for the whole war, but twenty thousand is a low estimate, and that number establishes that it was a significant conflict.

The false pretext and impetus for a war of terror in the South after 1865 was the white fear that African Americans were organizing insurrections.[38] History is rife with pogroms and ethnic cleansings that began with such rumors driven by self-serving hatred. Many white southerners considered any act of African American independence an insurrectionary offense. After hearing that some freedmen had been shot down near her husband's plantation, a white South Carolina woman wrote: "If I could get up tomorrow morning and hear that every nigger in the country was dead, I would just jump up and down."[39] Another southerner was clear about the reality of continued war and massacre. Emma LeConte, a seventeen-year-old South Carolinian, kept a diary in 1865, and like most white southerners she had already foreseen the continuation of war in the region. "[The North's] oppression and insolence . . . may drive the people to guerilla warfare," she wrote. "[The North will] be wearied out at last." LeConte also saw that the leniency of the peace would open the way to almost any southern act against African Americans that would reduce their status to slavery in all but name: "[Every white southerner is] empowered by Johnson to act as he pleases with the exception of remanding Negroes to slavery."[40] Both the perpetrators and victims of this cruel terrorist warfare knew exactly what was happening and saw where it would lead: a postwar southern order dictated on the terms of local ex-Confederate extremists. When African Americans did organize for political action or defense, especially after 1867, or served in state militia units and federal forces, many white southerners reacted with pathological violence. This pattern emerged in 1865–1867 as ex-Confederate extremists tried to negate the changes brought by the Civil War. Between 1865 and 1867, southern states under the control of ex-Confederates formed racist state militias and then KKK bands from units of the Confederate Home Guard.[41] Their main activities consisted of "patrolling" and assaulting African Americans to forestall "insurrection."[42] This was a false, racist pretext used to justify the slaughter and intimidation of African Americans and their white allies. A Massachusetts newspaper editor, commenting on the incredible campaign of terrorist killings by ex-Confederate extremists in the South from 1865 to 1867, wrote, "There never was a people in such terrible peril as the loyal people of the South, white and black. Unless Congress proceeded at once and did something to protect these people from the barbarians who are now murdering the whites, and putting into secret graves hundreds of thousands of colored people, it would be liable to the just censure of the world for its neglect, its cowardice, or its want of ability."[43] The best evidence suggests that more African Americans were killed in 1865–1867 than in the longer and more dramatic period of open warfare that followed in 1867–1877.

The catalog of attacks listed in the Freedmen's Bureau state-by-state "Reports of Outrages, Riots and Murders" is long. As in other wars, the sheer volume of the violence makes it hard to describe with words. Again, these reports, listing thousands of deaths, are just a small sampling of the ex-Confederate extremist terror attacks in this new war. The majority of incidents overall occurred in rural areas and had their roots in ex-Confederate refusal to accept the immediate results of the Civil War: that slavery had ended and that Confederates had lost complete control of the region. So ex-Confederate extremists massacred African Americans because they were vulnerable targets. As noted, the simple act of African Americans living free triggered violent hatred in many southern whites, and a long tradition existed of patrolling and openly attacking slaves. When the strategy of attacking freedmen to reverse the apparent postwar order was added, an orgy of regional killing resulted. African Americans were shot down for simply walking the roads to test their freedom, search for loved ones, or leave their plantations. Southern whites had long maintained that, if slavery were to be abolished, a war of extermination would result in the region. In 1865–1867, ex-Confederate extremists made this a self-fulfilling prophecy.[44] They also terrorized African Americans in attempts to get them to keep working on plantations. The logic of slavery motivated this tactic. Violence against African Americans and whites who questioned slavery had been central to the social system of the antebellum South.[45] Before the American Civil War, even nonslaveholders had served in nighttime slave patrols, and the postwar terrorism was a continuation of that system that had existed for well over a hundred years. During chattel slavery, a common control tactic was to make an example of an enslaved person by whipping and even killing one in front of the enslaved community, especially after a slave revolt. The Civil War occasioned and entailed the greatest slave revolt in American history and one of the greatest ones in human history. Nearly four million enslaved African Americans broke their bonds. In response, and in attempts to maintain the status quo, ex-Confederate extremists brought forth a reign of terror in the South, raping and killing tens of thousands of freedmen and freedwomen.

In describing an event of this scale, beyond marching through an endless parade of horror stories, we need to center the strategic effect of the terroristic violence as an act of war. That said, a few cases from the Freedmen's Bureau reports serve as examples that could be multiplied by additional years, numbers in the states where they were reported, and all the states in the region. The reports in 1865–1868 catalog the torture and killing of free African American men, women, and children in the South. Many white southerners had become habituated to violently dominating African Americans under slavery and the post–Civil War years stepped up such violence to a degree that it would last several more generations. Adding to the violent legacy of slavery was the brutalizing experience of the American Civil War itself. The war was largely fought in the South and to some degree desensitized southerners to death and suffering while arousing powerful longings for revenge and violence. Historian Eric Foner noted: "In Texas, where the army and Freedmen's Bureau proved entirely unable to establish order, blacks, according to a Bureau official, [were] 'frequently beaten unmercifully, and shot down like wild beasts, without any provocation.'"[46] Bureau records provide clear insight into the political and economic reasons for the nearly one thousand documented killings of African Americans in Texas alone between 1865 and 1868. Ex-Confederate extremist violence was directly aimed against any signs of freedom or active independence. One freedman in Grayson County was shot because he didn't remove his hat quickly enough: "The freedman was in the act of raising his hat when he was shot by this Desperado just because he wanted to kill some body. Afterwards said he had a gang with him for the purpose of 'killing niggers.'" A leader of a similar ex-Confederate extremist group in Fannin County was even more explicit about actions akin to ethnic cleansing: "[They] concluded to thin the niggers out a little and drive them back to their holes as they said. Fired into a crowd of freedmen going to the show. Killed three and wounded quite a number. An effort was made to arrest the party but failed. These men are still in the County fearless of any consequence."[47] A freedman named King Davis in Brenham, Texas, was shot and killed for attempting to leave his former master because he wanted to find "employment elsewhere after learning that he was free."[48] One freed person was "beaten by her employer for 'using insolent language,' another for refusing to 'call him master,' a third 'because he whipped [his] mother.'"[49] The Freedmen's Bureau reported nearly innumerable such incidents in every southern state. The impetus for violence in 1865 in particular was to deny emancipation. An African American boy sixteen to seventeen years of age was shot in the arm and had it amputated, and a federal army officer reported "this boy was shot for asking his master if he was not free."[50] Patterns of violence from slavery and the American Civil War continued and mutated into a gruesome culture of terrorist warfare during Reconstruction.

Freedmen and freedwomen were also victims of whippings. Just living free or not being openly servile to whites in public murderously offended whites. Whipping and execution had been the traditional punishments under slavery. In 1865, a North Carolinian visited Louisiana and witnessed a number of white men whipping African American men the same way they had before the American Civil War. In a several instances, ex-Confederate extremists sought out African Americans living free in their own communities and shot them. Many raids were committed at night by groups. In some cases, ex-Confederate extremists spared African American elders' lives but whipped them and told them not to go to federal authorities. They told African American men and women to lie to authorities and say nothing violent was happening. Not doing so would put them at risk of death. The unpunished violence in Alabama included some horrific acts of cruelty intended to instill terror that would keep African Americans on plantations. As one example: "On May 30, 1866, Horace King, an ex-Confederate soldier, 'went on a murderous rampage' targeting blacks in Morgan County. According to one resident, he 'shot two freedmen through the head.' Following the shootings, King brandished his weapons, bragged about his accomplishments, and cursed and threatened the entire black race. Another observer lamented, 'the civil authorities refuse to take any notice of King or his acts except to quietly inform him to keep out of the way for a day or two.'"[51] The typical acquittals of the few ex-Confederate extremists brought to trial prompted investigations by federal authorities, but little was done. Again, in 1865–1867 ex-Confederates controlled all local and state governments in the South outside of Tennessee, and African Americans had few civil rights and no right to vote. This political reality made justice in southern courts impossible. Justice was so perverted in this era of terroristic warfare that African Americans were framed for the killings carried out by ex-Confederate extremists. African Americans did not even have the right to testify against white abusers. A Freedmen's Bureau agent recorded Maryland's 1866 Black Codes, which read: "No colored witness can testify in cases involving conflicting interests between white and black. A Negro convicted of an offense the punishment of which if committed by a white man would be imprisonment in the penitentiary may, at the discretion of the court, be sentenced to receive not exceeding forty lashes."[52] Very few ex-Confederates were tried, much less convicted for their war of terror or for their killing of the thousands of African American and white unionists between 1865 and 1867 when they controlled the courts. The rate of prosecution was little better after 1867. The state militias, like the courts, were typically under ex-Confederate control during the terror phase of the Southern Civil War, and the militias also took on the role of "disciplining" African Americans who were challenging the labor status quo. They also targeted whites who were not cracking down on African American workers or were even encouraging their new freedoms. In a case on December 25, 1865, a group of ex-Confederate extremists under command of N. Taylor's Bossier Parish Militia came to the plantation of a "Mrs. Dickerson" in Bossier Parish, Louisiana. "[They] knocked at a door of the house of Willis Dickerson, a freedman employed on the place. While opening the door, he was struck over the head with a revolver by a white man. When he started to run, he was shot by one of the attackers. Willis Dickerson died the next day from the effects of his wound."[53] Ex-Confederate extremists maintained terror tactics to keep African Americans virtually enslaved even after more effective civil rights legislation and Republican governments came to the South starting in 1867. In 1868 in Alabama, "an overseer shot an African American worker who 'gave him sarse.'"[54] Maintaining the rules of slavery motivated much of the violence in the South, but atrocities long associated with the slave system also multiplied during the Southern Civil War.

The ex-Confederate extremist war of terror indulged, on a mass scale, in brutal tactics that had been less prevalent during the American Civil War. One of these tactics was rape, which may have been more common in the American Civil War than the sanitized popular histories of the war portray.[55] Rape, however, clearly became more prevalent in the Southern Civil War and, of course, had been a feature of slavery. The position of African Americans was even more vulnerable after the American Civil War. After 1865, African Americans faced assaults from both their employers and armed gangs of whites roaming a destabilized society that was breaking down into chaos and local warfare. Rape is often weaponized in modern civil wars fought by local militias, terrorist units, and paramilitaries that also use rape to recruit and "socialize" members.[56] KKK-style terrorist and guerilla units frequently raped African American women who were now targets to an even greater range of white men than their enslavers. Essic Harris, an African American man in North Carolina, commented after the KKK raped African American women in his area: "That has been very common . . . it has got to be an old saying by now. They say that if the women tell anything about it, they will kill them."[57] Rape was also a vicious form of assault, torture, and attempted degradation that served the purposes of the ex-Confederate extremists' war of terror.[58] It proved the Union could not protect African Americans, it spread fear, and it asserted continued African American enslavement. During the mass terrorist attacks in Memphis in 1866—known as the Memphis Massacre—African Americans reported multiple rapes and sexual assaults despite the threats of reprisals.[59]

No tactic was off limits to the ex-Confederate extremists. In Perry County, Alabama, a white politician recounted how "a young girl on her way to visit her mother in a neighboring county was found 'hanging from a tree with a garment stripped off and eyes plucked out.'"[60] Assaults against women and girls rarely resulted in charges. The Louisiana Freedmen's Bureau reports from 1865 described how "Damascas D. Day attempted to kill Mary Stewart (freedwoman), cutting her on the head, side & arms with a knife, and otherwise maltreating her. Civil Authorities did nothing. Day was arrested and brought to New Orleans and then turned over to the Civil Authorities for trial. At the District Court in November no witnesses appearing against him, it being believed they were kept away by threats, he was acquitted and immediately."[61] In 1866, Rhoda Ann Childs bravely came forward to the Georgia Freedmen's Bureau about eight prominent ex-Confederate extremist men who sexually assaulted her, beat her daughters, and robbed her. She recounted how the men held her down and "applied the strap to my private parts until fatigued into stopping, and I was more dead than alive." One of them then raped her.[62] The intimidation of African American women became widely accepted in the South, and the terrorist tactics multiplied. Again, since ex-Confederates were in charge of state and local governments between 1865 and 1867, white men who assaulted women went unprosecuted. Another Louisiana Freedmen's Bureau account: "On the day of August 11, 1865– Lieutenant L. L. Butler at Alexandria, Rapides Parish, reports that a planter, Thomas Wall of Springville, Natchitoches Parish, struck a colored girl breaking her forearm and fracturing her skull and no action was taken by authorities."[63] Violence against women remained a tactic throughout the Southern Civil War, and, for generations after, white men who raped and assaulted African American women largely avoided facing justice. Despite the lack of prosecution, the courage Rhoda Childs "and so many other Black women exhibited in reporting such attacks stands as enduring evidence of the sexualized terror Black women suffered during Reconstruction and their determination to survive."[64] African American women, despite these constant attacks, remained some of the strongest supporters and "enforcers" of the biracial coalition and its political activities.[65]

Persecution of white unionists and sympathizers with Reconstruction policies became widespread as well.[66] Confederates had executed white unionists during the American Civil War, and antebellum southern whites could not express criticisms of the slave system without danger to their lives, but between 1865 and 1867 violence against white unionists reached previously unseen region-wide levels. The provisional governor of Texas, Andrew Jackson Hamilton, commenting on attacks on white unionists, reported, "Human life in Texas is not today worth as much, so far as law or protection can give value to it, as that of domestic cattle."[67] Terroristic violence in North Carolina led twelve hundred ex-Union soldiers to sell their property and flee the state by 1867.[68] Southerners occasionally took shots at federal troops, especially the few African American units in the South.[69] In Texas federal troops routinely faced violent intimidation. After murdering African American men, women, and children, ex-Confederate extremists often dumped their bodies into rivers or on open roads—a pattern that would persist through the civil rights movement killings of the 1960s. As also happened during the civil rights movement, whites were victims of killings meant to send a message discouraging interracial cooperation. In a gruesome example in Arkansas, the KKK killed the local white Republican deputy sheriff and then shot a random African American man and tied them together face to face, as if kissing. They were left in the road as a warning to the biracial coalition.[70] Ex-Confederate extremists singled out white and African American teachers from the North and the buildings where they worked for violent attacks.

Throughout the South churches and schools were particular targets of ex-Confederate extremists.[71] One of the first steps African Americans took when they were free was to seek literacy and the independent African American churches denied them under slavery. The terrorism against African American churches even spread to Washington, D.C., where many freedmen and freedwomen fled only to experience the same violence as in the Deep South. Washington was in many ways a southern city since slavery had been legal there. Reverend Dyson of the African American Union Wesley Church reported to the Freedmen's Bureau how his "church ha[d] frequently been stoned and glass broken out of the windows, and persons stoned while going to and from the Church."[72] In former Confederate states, churches and schools (often the same buildings) were torched at staggering rates since they were symbols of racial change and bases for African American political organization. Near Pine Bluff, Arkansas, in the spring of 1866, African Americans had raised five thousand dollars to build a church. Local ex-Confederate extremists burned it and several nearby African American houses. Near the torched church a freedman, William Mallet, described what he found the following morning: "a sight that apald me 24 Negro men and women and children were hanging to trees all around the Cabbins."[73] Schools, like churches, often served as community and political meeting sites for African Americans and were "frequent targets for arson."[74] Ex-Confederate extremists ostracized, beat, and killed teachers as well. About a third of teachers were African American in Freedmen's Bureau schools before 1867, most of them and the white teachers having come down from the North with idealistic hopes of helping the formerly enslaved. "'When a teacher goes to some [Louisiana] village and opens a school for colored children,' [New Orleans] *Tribune* editor Louis Charles Roudanez charged, 'he is turned out and not seldom beaten, stabbed or killed.'"[75] One such incident today could horrify an entire nation, but African Americans and their white allies faced thousands of such incidents during the terror phase of the Southern Civil War. The effects were multiplied as communities heard of horrific cases, often nearby.

Mass killings remained the main ex-Confederate extremist tactic, and these reached a frightening scale in both rural and urban areas in 1866. Alabama was typical. The state did not have as much bloodshed in the Southern Civil War as the most violent states of Texas, Louisiana, Mississippi, and South Carolina did, nor did it have the strongest Freedmen's Bureau presence as some of these states with large cities. Yet two Freedmen's Bureau reports from Alabama in 1866 are typical of the terror phase of the Southern Civil War in that they largely took place in rural areas and are a depressing litany of bloodshed:

Freedman killed in Sumter County, January.
Freedman killed in Russell County, February.
Freedman killed near West Point, March.

Freedman killed with an axe in Butler County. Three freedmen killed by two brothers in Shelby County, April.

Freedman killed in Montgomery County, April. Freedman & freedwoman killed, thrown into a well in Jefferson Co., April.

Freedman killed for refusing to sign a contract, Sumter Co., May. Freedman killed in Butler Co., clubbed, April.

Freedman found hung by a grapevine in woods near Tuscaloosa, May.

Freed girl beaten to death by two white men near Tuscaloosa, July.

Freedman murdered between Danville & Somerville.

Freedman shot dead while at his usual work, near Tuscaloosa, Sept.

Freedman killed in Pike County, Sept.

Negro murdered near Claiborne, Alabama, June.

Freedman brought to hospital in Montgomery, shot through the head by unknown parties—died in few hours, Dec.

Jan. 4—Bob Foreman cut at Union Springs.

Jan. 2—Alfred killed in Sumter County.

Febry. 14—Richard killed in Russell County near Columbus, Ga.

March—Freedman killed near West Point.

March—Bradley killed freedwoman with an axe. Montgy.

March—Guard fired on & driven off when attempting to arrest the murderer, Butler Co.

April 3—Woman taken by three men out of her house in middle of night to swamp & badly whipped—beaten on head with pistol.

April—Freedman killed near Saw Mill near Montgomery.

April 27—Freedman shot by Confed. Soldier wantonly near Livingston, Sumter Co.

May 7—Moore taken to woods & hung till nearly dead to make him tell who robbed a store, at Tuscaloosa.

May 29—Colored man killed by Lucian Jones for refusing to sign contract, in upper part of Sumter Co.

May 30—Mulatto hung by grapevine near roadside between Tuscaloosa & Greensboro.

May 29—Richard Dick's wife beaten with club by her employer. Richard remonstrated—in the night was taken from his house and whipped nearly to death with a buggy trace by son of the employer & two others.

June 16—Mr. Alexander, colored preacher, brutally beaten & forced to leave his house at Auburn, Ala.

July—Band armed men came to house of Eliz. Adams, threatened to kill her & her sister if they did not leave the county, abused & beat them. (illegible) Franklin & (illegible) started to report outrage, not heard from afterward.

July 16—Black girl beaten to death by Washington and Greene McKinney, 18 miles west of Tuscaloosa.

July 23—White man named Cook murdered a Negro between Danville & Somerville.

Sept. 14—Black man picking fodder in a field shot dead—& another who had difficulty with a white man abducted & supposed to have been murdered near Tuscaloosa.

Sept. 3—Murderous assault upon returned Black Union soldier in Blount Co.

Sept. 12—Assault & firing upon a freedman in Greenville.

Dec. 18—R. S. Lee of Butler Co. brutally assaulted a freedwoman of Sumner.

Dec. 18—Same man assaulted with intent to kill Peter Golston, freedman.

Dec. 18—Wm. Lee, son of above shot Morris Golston on 10th December.

Dec. 17—Enoch Hicks & party burned school house in Greenville in Sumner—assaulted Union soldier &c. Judge Bragg & son mercilessly beat wife & daughter of James, freedman & drew pistol on James.[76]

Again, this is just a single year in not the most war-torn of states, with an average Freedmen's Bureau presence and massive underreporting. Many of the reports came from the area around Tuscaloosa since the federal presence was strong there. For every atrocity documented by the Freedmen's Bureau, another equally gruesome one probably went unreported.

Another window into this brutal war of terror in 1865–1867 is the memoirs of African Americans who spoke of the violence and disappointment of the era when they expected their status to change and were bitterly disappointed. Historian Leon Litwack chronicled this terrible time for African Americans in his award-winning *Been in the Storm So Long* in 1979, but the most eloquent testimony came from the freedpeople themselves.[77] In December 1865 after witnessing the continuation of the war by ex-Confederate extremists, whom he called "rebel traitors," Calvin Holly, an African American former Union army soldier from Mississippi, wrote to General Oliver O. Howard, the head of the Freedmen's Bureau:

> Sir Suffer me to address you a few lines in reguard to the colered people in this State, from all I can learn and see, I think the colered people are in a great many ways being outraged beyound humanity, houses have been tourn down from over the heades of women and Children—and the old Negroes after they have worked there till they are 70 or 80 yers of age drive them off in the cold to frieze and starve to death. . . . The Rebbles are going a bout in many places through the State and robbing the colered peple of arms money and all they have and in many places killing.
>
> They talk of taking the armes a way from (col[ored]) people and arresting them and put them on farmes next month and if they go at that I think there will be trouble and in all probability a great many lives lost. They have been accusing the colered peple of an insorection which is a lie, in order that they might get arms to carrie out their wicked designs—
>
> . . . A trouble now with the colered peple on account of Rebs. after they have rendered the Government such great survice through the rebellion would spoil the whole thing—and it is what the Rebles would like to bring a bout, and they are doing all they can to prevent free labor, and reasstablish a kind of secondary slavery Now believe me as a colered man that is a friend to law and order, I blive without the intervention of the General governmt in the protection of the (col[ored]) popble that there will be trouble in Miss. before spring.[78]

Private Holly was prescient and saw the course of the Southern Civil War and the continuation of slavery. The records of ex-Confederate extremists and African Americans from the terror phase of the war echo each other. Warfare had not ended, and targeted violence was terrorizing the region.

Many African Americans felt they had no choice but to try to escape to urban areas with safety in numbers and a greater chance of being near the few federal troops in the South. Some African Americans thought they would be safer in a neighboring county or state and were already on the move before heading for the cities. When some African Americans attempted to migrate to other counties of Alabama, "terrorism against blacks grew increasingly severe, especially in certain counties in the western part of the state."[79] The ex-Confederate terrorist acts forced some freedmen to migrate with their families to other parts of the state. Often migrating African Americans found they would experience the same kind of violence in the area to which they fled. Many went to the cities that had large free African American populations even before Emancipation. The protection of being in a large city was a rational choice, but some of the most ruthless and large-scale white supremacist attacks during the Terror Phase of the war between 1865 and 1867 took place in these cities, most notably Memphis and New Orleans.

In most southern cities, ex-Confederate extremists treated African Americans as if they were still their property. In Litwack's words, "Numerous communities such as New Orleans and Savannah, often with the full support of military authorities, preferred to revive the old curfew and pass regulations, resorting at times to arrests of blacks found on the city streets after a certain hour without the permission of the employer. Faced with the possibility of overcrowded jails, city authorities happily complied with the offers of local residents and planters to pay the fines of the blacks in exchange for their employment as virtual indentured servants."[80] In the cities African Americans were also denied jobs, housing, and land, though as many as a quarter of freedmen managed to become landowners at some point in the era. In southern cities custom and law held, Litwack wrote, that "no freedman could rent or keep a house within the town limits 'under any circumstances' or reside within the town unless employed by a white person who assumed responsibility for his conduct."[81] Freedmen and freedwomen did not have the right to hold social events or public meetings. Free African Americans could not even possess a gun or purchase food without the permission of their employer. If freedpeople were caught violating these laws, they were arrested by authorities and placed in forced labor—functionally re-enslaved. A loophole in the Thirteenth Amendment that allowed slavery for conviction of a crime would grow into the massive convict-leasing system that worked generations of African Americans to death under the worst conditions of slavery. Only the federal takeover and reforms of southern prisons in the late 1960s and early 1970s curtailed this corrupt and inhuman system, which has not been fully eliminated and to which many states are increasingly returning.[82] When African Americans attempted to settle in urban communities, ex-Confederate extremists burned down their settlements. Some of the attacks were disguised in the language of urban reform. Litwack wrote, "To break up the urban black settlements, like the shanty villages appearing on the edges of numerous towns, local authorities might simply order their demolition. To justify such arbitrary actions, they would cite the outbreak of disease among malnourished and ill-clad freedmen and the need to protect the health of the community."[83] In urban areas, however, such attacks brought federal military intervention in the most large-scale disturbances.

During the terror phase of the Southern Civil War white mobs assaulted African American settlements and political meetings in urban areas. The 1866 massacres in Norfolk, Memphis, and New Orleans offer the most famous examples of white supremacist attacks on urban African American and white unionists, with arson and high body counts. All three began when white mobs and police attacked African Americans who were asserting their rights. On April 16, 1866, African Americans in Norfolk, Virginia, marched in support of the Civil Rights Act just passed in Washington. At the end of the parade speeches were planned, but the parade was attacked by white onlookers hurling bricks. When the mob reached the podium, a police officer shot a young African American marcher. Firing then commenced between whites and African Americans, and bands of whites including police roamed the streets attacking African Americans. Federal forces had to be brought in to restore order. Eight African Americans were dead. The violence had a direct political origin and goal of suppressing a movement for African American civil rights.[84]

The much larger Memphis Massacre of May 1–3, 1866, was a pivotal event in emboldening white supremacist violence across the South. Unlike many battles of the Southern Civil War, the Memphis Massacre is very well documented and has an outstanding recent history by Stephen Ash. For thirty-six hours white mobs led by the police massacred forty-six African American men, women, and children, wounded seventy-five, and burned every African American church and school in the city—four churches and twelve schools.[85] African Americans in Memphis killed no whites, though they did wound several in self-defense. Two whites died, but one was killed by another white and one by accident. This was not a riot; it was a white supremacist invasion of African American Memphis.

The main perpetrators of the massacre were the Irish American police. Other white supremacists and ex-Confederates fully supported the police and mob action, and some joined in, but working-class Irish

Americans initiated and carried out most of the violence. African Americans and Irish immigrants competed for jobs. As across the South in 1865–1866, many whites in Memphis resented African American freedom and had fears of a Black uprising that were driven by racist newspapers, town officials, and rumors. The African American population of Memphis had swelled during the war as African Americans sought the protection of federal troops and new opportunities in the city. Memphis had four thousand African American residents in 1861 and five times that number in 1866, making up half the population of the city that had grown from sixteen thousand in 1860 to forty thousand by 1866. White supremacists particularly resented the Third Colored Heavy Artillery, a unit of African American troops at Fort Pickering. The unit was mustered out in late April 1866.[86] Many of the former soldiers still in uniform were having a spirited party on May 1 just out of city limits in South Memphis when they were harassed and told to disperse by four policemen who technically had no jurisdiction there. The African American unit had been disarmed, but several were carrying their own pistols. A war of words escalated into a shootout after an African American fired into the air as the police withdrew and the police fired into the crowd.[87] The police retreated with two wounded, and the crowd dispersed, but rumors of an African American uprising swept the city, and the police force led mobs into African American South Memphis the next day. The mobs spoke the language of ethnic cleansing and said they planned to torch "every nigger building, every nigger church, and every God damn son of a bitch that [teaches] a nigger."[88] They assaulted "nearly every black person who [came across] their path, venting particular fury on those in uniform."[89] The central role of the police in the massacre also makes it a clear case of state terrorism emblematic of the terror phase of the Southern Civil War.

There were only 185 federal soldiers in Memphis, which was just a little more than the size of the Memphis police force.[90] General George Stoneman, a Democrat and critic of Reconstruction policies to extend African American rights, commanded these federal troops and was slow to respond to the massacre and deferred to local authorities.[91] The paucity of troops around Memphis and in other key areas of the South indicates the major weakness of federal policy throughout the Southern Civil War. Federal troops never effectively occupied the South. On May 3, after a request from city officials who had been drunk and negligent through the whole massacre, Stoneman declared martial law, and the massacre ended. Many African Americans and their white allies had fled the city. No one was punished or even charged for any of these atrocities, a clear signal to the white South that taking up arms against formerly enslaved people and their allies was effective and a tactic that could be safely repeated. Memphis inspired mob, KKK, and paramilitary violence across the South in the coming decade.

The New Orleans street battle and massacre of the same year, 1866, was more organized and explicitly political in its origins and results. This was a fight over nothing less than the state constitution that renewed the brief Civil War era unionist state government and a call for African American voting. James G. Hollandsworth in his excellent book on the New Orleans incident says it was to the Southern Civil War what Fort Sumter was to the American Civil War.[92] The year 1866 saw the birth of the African American and white unionist political coalition that would take state and local power across much of the South after 1867. The formation of a biracial coalition in New Orleans, as would be true across the South in the years to come, was met with well-organized and successful violent repression. The street battle in New Orleans shared the key element of those in Norfolk and Memphis: ex-Confederate extremists attacked African Americans, many of whom were union soldiers, who were attempting to assert their independence. New Orleans had a newly installed ex-Confederate government that was packing the police department with ex-Confederate extremists. The African American and white unionists in the city initiated a desperate plan to regain the short-lived political power they'd had in the last years of the American Civil War. They called the unionist state constitutional convention from 1864 back into session. In speeches leading up to the convention, white unionists openly discussed instituting African American suffrage and—more ominously for paranoid ex-Confederate extremists—asserted African Americans' right to armed self-defense. When the convention opened in the Mechanics Institute on July 30, a crowd of African Americans in Union uniforms carrying a U.S. flag marched in support. A hostile crowd of white supremacists, led by police in a planned response, fired on the African American marchers, chased them back to the Mechanics Institute, and then assaulted the audience and members of the unionist convention. Only a few of the African Americans and white unionists were armed, but they defended themselves in the street and convention hall with improvised weapons. The lopsided battle became a massacre when the ex-Confederate extremist mob broke into the building. Twenty-two policemen were injured, while at least thirty-four African Americans and three white unionists were dead. Over 130 were wounded. One "rebel" was also dead.[93] As in Memphis, no one was convicted for these atrocities. A. P. Dotsie, the white unionist who had spoken most powerfully in favor of African Americans' right to armed self-defense, was taken from police custody outside the Mechanics Institute, shot a dozen times by the crowd, and left for dead in the street.[94] Federal troops who had been deceived by the ex-Confederate local officials about the time of the convention's opening, arrived too late to stop the slaughter but did restore peace.[95] There were only 850 federal troops stationed south of New Orleans, probably fewer in number than the ex-Confederate extremist mob and police forces attacking the unionists.

The New Orleans massacre, where African Americans (and their white allies) were more organized and exchanged more fire with their white assailants than in Norfolk and Memphis, was characteristic of a political street battle. Clausewitz's dictum that warfare is politics extended onto the battlefield fits these early clashes of the Southern Civil War, as political meetings and troop deployments supplied the pretext and stage for armed assaults. New Orleans and Memphis were the bloodiest and most infamous clashes of ex-Confederate extremists and African American soldiers (and armed freedmen) and their white allies, but similar clashes also happened during the war's terror phase in Mobile, Alabama; Alexandria, Virginia; Clarksville, Tennessee; Charleston, South Carolina; and Wilmington, North Carolina. African Americans had begun military drills as soon as white violence arose in 1865. In Alexandria, Virginia, more whites harassing African Americans died than did freedmen. Three regiments of federal troops were called out to quell the violence in Virginia.[96] New Orleans, Memphis, Norfolk, and the smaller clashes in cities like Alexandria merely provide urban expressions of the wider running battle between ad hoc white terrorist groups and their overmatched African American and white unionist targets. The 1865–1867 total body count from isolated rural and small-town clashes dwarfed that of the more dramatic urban clashes of Memphis, Norfolk, and New Orleans combined.[97] Ex-Confederate extremists assassinated white and African American unionist leaders in large numbers in both cities and rural areas, usually attacking when they feared African American organization and independence. Often African Americans defended themselves and even drove off attackers, but usually the local small-scale clashes were as one-sided as the larger urban battles. The violence of 1865 to 1867 was anything but random. It was a continuation of the guerilla race war and Home Guard actions of the last years of the American Civil War. It had the direct object of limiting and or even reversing the changes brought by that conflict and maintaining the racial and political order of the Old South. As a KKK document put it at the start of the struggle: "The effort for Southern independence is still in progress. The check it received in the surrender of General Lee was hardly disastrous to our interests, because open war had then become inexpedient and profitless; but the organization of our friends is to-day more perfect than ever before, and thousands are enlisting in the cause . . . an army of such magnitude as to strike terror into the hearts of all tyrants, would spring to arms, obedient to the word, and bear down every impediment to complete success."[98] The effort attained success, in part because the federal government reacted with only a feeble effort to aid the unionists and African Americans.

General John Pope understood the war breaking out in the South between 1865 and 1867. He had been an aggressive but incompetent Civil War commander and then exterminator of Native Americans during the Sioux uprising in 1862. His condemnable, racist violence toward Native Americans, however, contrasted with his support of formerly enslaved people in the South and willingness to take the fight to ex-Confederates. Pope's unique experiences and commitment to bringing full democracy to the South let him see that the region was slipping back into violent white supremacist control. The federal government was not opposed to extreme tactics—Pope was absolutely vicious in putting down Sioux opposition, but the government would not let him do the same to white people.

Pope had commanded the Union army of Virginia in the American Civil War, famously losing the Second Battle of Bull Run to Robert E. Lee in 1862. Lincoln fired him from command of the eastern Union army but sent him on an important assignment to stamp out a Native American revolt in Minnesota. The Sioux had tired of settlers pouring onto their lands and fought back, clearing settlers out of the area around the Minnesota River, killing hundreds. Pope crushed this guerilla uprising with brutality. He conducted depopulation raids and sentenced three hundred Sioux soldiers to death after they were captured. He infamously stated to his subordinates, there "will be no peace in this region by virtue of treaties and Indian faith. It is my purpose utterly to exterminate the Sioux if I have the power to do so and even if it requires a campaign lasting the whole of next year. Destroy everything belonging to them and force them out to the plains, unless, as I suggest, you can capture them. They are to be treated as maniacs or wild beasts, and by no means as people with whom treaties or compromises can be made. Urge the campaign vigorously; you shall be as vigorously supported and supplied."[99] Pope carried out this war of extermination in 1862 as Sherman and Sheridan would with the Sioux and Cheyenne on the western plains in the 1870s. Pope interned the families of Sioux warriors in deadly conditions and held unjust military tribunals to sentence captured warriors to death. Abraham Lincoln reviewed these trials and commuted over 260 sentences, those of all but 38 Sioux men. Pope executed these 38 in a simultaneous mass hanging on December 26, 1862, in Mankato, Minnesota. To this day, it is the largest federal mass execution in U.S. history, but it was fewer than the 41 suspected white unionists hanged in Gainesville, Texas, by sham Confederate courts two months earlier in October 1862.

In Minnesota, Pope, like the Texas Confederates, committed an atrocity. He was on the wrong side in Minnesota in 1862, but when he went to Atlanta to command the Third Military District in 1867, he rightly recognized that ex-Confederate extremists were conducting a war of terror and massacres. Pope was willing to fight to promote African American rights and feared that the Johnson administration would undermine him and all generals like him who took steps to extend African American rights.[100] During the Southern Civil War, the federal government never allowed any federal officer to take a harsh line with ex-Confederate extremists, who had killed thousands more U.S. citizens, with far less justification, than the Sioux had in Minnesota. The federal government executed no ex-Confederate extremists or KKK members, and the few jailed were quickly released, most often without being prosecuted. Racism clearly explains this glaring discrepancy between the treatment of Sioux and ex-Confederate extremists by the federal government. The discrepancy lasted all of Reconstruction, as the Plains Indians were interned en masse, starved, killed in custody, and massacred by federal troops, while simultaneously ex-Confederate extremists roamed free and unpunished for their mass slaughter in the South.

General Pope did not support such leniency toward ex-Confederate extremists and protected the rights of unionists in the South, no matter their color. Pope was despised by ex-Confederate extremists in Atlanta where he made his headquarters and across the Third Military District, which included Alabama and Florida as well as Georgia. Appointed in April 1867, Pope ordered full rights and protection for African Americans, including service on juries, and suppressed all anti-unionist newspaper activity. He also postponed or cancelled elections that would have resulted in ex-Confederate supporters in office in this last period before African American voting. He promoted African American voting rights and unionist political rallies, pushing for such rights across the South. As the year before in Memphis, New Orleans, Norfolk, and smaller communities across the South, these movements toward unionists practicing civil and political rights led to ex-Confederate extremist armed attacks of unionist rallies in Pope's district. The most infamous armed clash came in the Mobile, Alabama, street battle of May 14, 1867. Pope's leadership helped this battle have a very atypical outcome: the ex-Confederate extremists were outgunned and suffered more casualties than the unionists. Unionist speaker William Kelley, who had been an abolitionist and Republican congressman from Pennsylvania, had come to Mobile to promote African American voting and civil rights. His very presence there incensed ex-Confederate extremists. He spoke to a large crowd of African Americans and white unionists in Mobile about the rights and power they should have in Alabama. Ex-Confederate extremists jeered and disrupted Kelley's speech from the back of the crowd and then fired on the biracial crowd. The biracial coalition of unionists was armed and, though casualty counts vary, they killed at least three ex-Confederate extremists. Pope's troops intervened as well, and the extremists who were not wounded or killed melted away.[101]

Pope's leadership and encouragement of biracial unionism kept Mobile from becoming another massacre as in Memphis and New Orleans, but his extension of African American rights and armed protection of them were anathema to much of the country and certainly to Andrew Johnson, who fired him in December 1867. Johnson replaced him with the more conservative George Meade, who quickly removed the African Americans Pope had placed on juries and election boards. Pope had served seven months. He understood what was happening in the South and feared what would follow over the next ten years. Pope knew ex-Confederate extremists were fighting a total war and were not being met with serious opposition. They were bound to triumph and then marginalize unionists, African American and white. Pope wanted the North to wake up and realize that there was a war in the South, but the North never woke up. Pope warned in a letter to army commander Ulysses S. Grant after being fired that his whole district was still full of the Confederate rebellion, "nearly as powerful as during the War." "You can scarcely form an idea of the spirit of malice & hatred in this people," Pope wrote. "It is a misnomer to call this question in the South a political question—It is *War* pure & simple. . . . The question is not whether Georgia & Alabama will accept or reject reconstruction—It is, shall the Union men & Freedmen, be the slaves of the old negro rebel aristocracy or not?"[102]

As it did to similar vigorous Union commanders during the Southern Civil War, the federal government denied Pope any opportunity to fight the violent white supremacist power structure enslaving the South. Pope did, however, get to return to total war, as the federal army again sent him west, this time to oppress the Apaches. The federal army knew how to fight total war in the face of terrorist or guerilla tactics but only did so against nonwhites—such as the Plains Indians and Apaches. To do this they transferred troops out of the South that could have protected African Americans and their white allies.[103] The federal army most often sided with white supremacy after the American Civil War and kept aloof from the Southern Civil War even after it turned into a more conventional war after 1867. White and African American unionists on the ground in the South would have to do the fighting. After 1867 the biracial coalition controlled southern state governments, but biracial coalition forces everywhere were inadequately armed, trained, and staffed when compared to the ex-Confederate guerillas in the Ku Klux Klan. Sometimes guerillas fight a weaker power. KKK-style guerillas would attain quick victory in most southern states after 1868, and in the states they did not take over quickly they transformed into open armies or paramilitaries, grew in power, and adopted bolder tactics, such as shedding disguises and drilling and deploying publicly.

The Reconstruction Acts of 1867, which established military districts to control former Confederate states, and the Fourteenth and Fifteenth Amendments of the next two years gave the biracial unionist coalition of the South what it had sought in the Mobile and New Orleans rallies: African American franchise and the opportunity to compete for political power.[104] But the franchise was not sufficient to turn away the power of emboldened ex-Confederate extremists or to survive a civil war. When biracial Republican state governments gained political power throughout the South after 1867, they realized their vulnerability and called on the federal government to supply military arms and forces. Neither was ever offered in the strength needed to conduct a civil war. Hastily assembled and poorly trained biracial state militias were organized by struggling biracial coalition Republican governments in the South to fill the void, and they took up the battle as best they could. But the terrorist strategy of ex-Confederate extremists had worked by 1867 and also taught them resistance techniques. Ex-Confederates extremists knew how to undermine Reconstruction policies and forestall federal intervention. They would simply ramp up their violence to full-scale guerilla war when faced with new unionist state governments they did not control, increasingly confident that the North would not enter the fray.

The violent acts toward African Americans and white unionists during the terror phase of the Southern Civil War proved that the ex-Confederate extremists launched their war long before African Americans had rights under the Fourteenth Amendment and male votes under the Fifteenth Amendment.

CHAPTER TWO

The Guerilla Phase, 1868–1872, Part 1

The KKK Resisted

The two-year terror phase of the Southern Civil War saw the ex-Confederate extremists deciding via violence who would control the region, excluding unionists from the body politic and denying agents of change a meaningful presence in the region. The second phase of the war was a guerilla struggle from 1868 to 1872, defined by the KKK and many similar local organizations in opposition to state governments elected by the biracial coalitions. To continue to overturn local governments in the South as well as the results of the American Civil War, ex-Confederate extremists turned to direct insurgent warfare. Republicans in Washington in late 1866 and 1867 reacted to the terrorism and murder by trying to impose a new peace settlement. But they did not send guns to the embattled unionists, nor did they militarily suppress the ex-Confederates. Instead they gave unionists paper rights, and ex-Confederate extremists got a scolding. The extremists had been emboldened and triumphant for two years, violently ruling the South and flouting the Reconstruction Acts of 1867 and the Fourteenth and Fifteenth Amendments. Nothing short of remobilization, invasion, and occupation was going to have effect on the ground in the South. And the federal government did not even come close to taking these steps.

The Reconstruction Acts and Fourteenth Amendment allowed for many ex-Confederates to be barred from voting or holding office. These acts with the additional Fifteenth Amendment also granted civil rights and votes to male African Americans. This strategy was cheap and convenient and did not risk the nightmare of the North getting involved in another civil war. But using policies to address a military problem was not likely to work, and it did not. Instead it upped the ante by again making African Americans the symbols of national authority. Ex-Confederate extremists, worried that the federal government was serious, escalated their military campaign to test Washington's resolve. They quickly found there would be little federal prosecution of the war and even less federal criminal prosecution of open and bloody insurrection. Southern African Americans and their white allies would be on their own in organizing political coalitions, trying to win elections, and, where successful, attempting to govern an ex-Confederate extremist population in open rebellion.

After the enfranchisement of African American males starting in 1867, a biracial coalition elected Republican or unionist governments in every former Confederate state except Tennessee. There the KKK worked to overthrow the state government. In many ways Tennessee went through an accelerated version of the Southern Civil War, as the Nathan Bedford Forrest–led KKK successfully defeated the unionist government there before other Confederate states even had Republican governments and African American voting. Tennessee also had the lowest percentage of African Americans in its population of any former Confederate state. Tennessee had already been readmitted to the union, in July 1866, so did not come under the congressional reconstruction plan and was not placed in a military district. Thus, the KKK and ex-Confederate extremists worked fastest and most effectively in Tennessee, where guerilla tactics and organizations were pioneered. In Pulaski on January 7, 1868, a KKK attack on African Americans at a local store resulted in the death of two of them and the wounding of five (shot after they agreed to a truce). The attack would typify KKK violence across the South from 1868 to 1872. Conservative Democrats would take back the Tennessee state government by 1869. In the other southern states, however, the guerilla phase of the war was just heating up in 1868 with the advent of African American enfranchisement and democratic elections that brought the Republican biracial coalitions to office. Nathan Bedford Forrest's and Pulaski's example in Tennessee would be followed in the other ex-Confederate states between 1868 and 1872.

With the dawn of the successful biracial coalition, the ex-Confederate extremists no longer attacked symbols of federal power and the results of the American Civil War as they had from 1865 to 1867. Now they were in a direct guerilla uprising against the authority of the new bira-

KKK guerillas, like these arrested in 1872, were localized and did not have standard regalia. (Library of Congress)

cial coalition Republican state governments. This constituted a direct civil war between armed parties contesting political control of a geographic region—both within each southern state and collectively across the entire South. By attacking the coalition rule, as in 1865–1867, the ex-Confederate extremists avoided confronting federal troops. Now local politicians, police, and state militias were the targets of ex-Confederate extremist guerillas and their terrorist tactics, but African American and white Republican citizens continued to be attacked too. These insurgent campaigns were a rousing military and political success in Texas, North Carolina, Virginia, Alabama, and Georgia. Arkansas's biracial coalition continued to hold power in the early part of the next phase of the war. The guerilla campaigns were successful in intimidating Republican voters and destabilizing the states of Louisiana, Mississippi, South Carolina and Florida, but these heavily African American states (the majority in all but Florida) maintained their biracial coalition governments until 1876. Their overthrow required an escalation by ex-Confederate extremists to all-out, open paramilitary warfare from 1872 until their total triumph by 1877. The biracial coalitions, however, put up their best fight in the guerilla phase of the war when vigorous and creative governors and state militias temporarily crushed the KKK on the battlefield in several states, only to be outmaneuvered by ex-Confederate extremists later. Powell Clayton, the Republican governor of Arkansas, raised and equipped a biracial state militia and cleared KKK-style guerillas out. Edmund Davis in Texas, who had fought for the North in the American Civil War after raising a unionist unit of like-minded fellow southerners, also used state forces and local unionist allies to defeat KKK-style guerillas. These and similar campaigns, like the one undertaken by Governor William Holden in North Carolina, proved temporary and in many ways backfired politically. The same limitations plagued the U.S. Army's brief campaigns against Klan-style guerillas.

The federal army used the new authority of the Enforcement Acts, of which there were three written between 1870 and 1871, to arrest KKK insurgents in those years and early 1872. These three acts were drawn up by Congress and signed by President Grant in reaction to the wave of Klan violence used to undermine elections and in response to the federal reports compiled about these atrocities. Collectively, the Enforcement Acts made such activity federal offenses and allowed the federal military to intervene in states where basic rights, like voting and holding office, went unprotected. In 1871 the Third Enforcement Act also allowed the federal government to use state militias to combat insurrection, to suspend habeas corpus, and to arrest persons for conspiracy. This final act was also known as the Ku Klux Klan Act since it criminalized most of their activities. In South Carolina the ex-Confederate extremists were so powerful that President Grant ordered federal forces to intervene, and they made hundreds of arrests in the main KKK counties of the state. Grant also authorized the Secret Service under Hiram C. Whitley to send agents to infiltrate the Klan, especially in Alabama and North Carolina, where many cells were arrested.[1] In Florida, the guerilla hotbed in and around Jackson County, which was rife with assassinations, saw a string of U.S. Army interventions and Enforcement Act arrests.[2]

But all of these state and federal campaigns backfired and emboldened the ex-Confederate extremists and undid the biracial political coalitions that supported them. Davis's and Clayton's parties, the Republican Parties of Texas and Arkansas, split over the martial law tactics and especially the use of African American troops the governors employed, and the biracial coalitions lost control of both states in subsequent elections. Grant also lost considerable political power by his action in the Carolinas and Alabama, and courts released, without significant jail time, nearly all of the hundreds of ex-Confederate extremist guerilla fighters captured in South Carolina, North Carolina, and Alabama.[3] Grant then permanently backed away from federal investigative and military action in the Southern Civil War after the brief foray against the Klan. Most southern states, however, saw little if any vigorous or sustained anti-Klan military activity by state or federal authorities. The ex-Confederate extremist guerillas undermined the legitimacy of state Republican governments, decimated the local biracial coalitions, and drove Republicans from the voting booths and political meetings by physically attacking them. By 1872 most southern states were officially in the hands of ex-Confederate extremists, so the KKK was no longer needed. The KKK victories diminished the appeal and usefulness of the Klan, which transformed out of existence in 1872 (until reviving in 1915), as Klansmen became government officials or members of new and stronger military units.[4] In states still with significant biracial coalition control, the Klan evolved into open paramilitary armies.

Like this later evolution of violence after 1872, the transition from the terror phase to the guerilla phase of the Southern Civil War grew seamlessly out of the changes in opponents, tactics, and goals of the ex-Confederate extremists. They had largely controlled the state and local governments in 1865–1867 and used this power to continue warfare, undermine unionist power, and attempt to re-enslave African American unionists. But after the biracial coalition of unionists coalesced under new federal laws and claims of military authority, ex-Confederate extremists chose more often to go underground and use hit-and-run, classic guerilla tactics against them. After 1868, the state militias and many local law enforcement officials in every ex-Confederate state except Tennessee and Virginia were under the control of the biracial coalition. Ex-Confederate extremist insurgents had the same targets as in the terror phase of the war, but those victims were now armed and organized and in control of state and local governments. The extremist goal shifted to destabilizing and overthrowing these governments and then shattering the biracial coalitions as a political force. Overthrowing the biracial coalition governments would also directly undermine federal policies for the region, just as re-enslaving and slaughtering unionists had done in the first two bloody years of the Southern Civil War. What in the terror phase was often a one-sided ex-Confederate extremist campaign against the unionists' vision of the meaning of the American Civil War became a classic two-sided civil war in the guerilla phase. Using violence and ensuing chaos to undermine the legitimacy of the new biracial governments, ex-Confederate extremists made the South ungovernable and then blamed the new coalition governments for failing to govern. The federal government threw too much of the burden of reforming the South and enforcing federal law and the settlement of the America Civil War on the vulnerable unionist government officials. When ex-Confederate extremists undermined biracial governments, they undermined federal authority and the scope of the Union victory in the American Civil War.

Prior to turning to paramilitary armies, the KKK-style guerillas in this warfare had the advantage in training, arms, and numbers over the forces of the elected state governments and local militias. The militias of the new biracial governments and spontaneous units of local self-defense were often organized and led by African Americans who had served in the Union army, but they had little access to arms. Ex-Confederate extremists were not the weaker military actors in this war.[5]

Texas provides an excellent example of the transition from the terror phase to the guerilla phase of the war. Andrew Johnson had not declared the end of the American Civil War until August 1866 largely because of Texas. The last major Confederate army to surrender, Kirby Smith's, surrendered in Texas. The state was rife with Confederate veterans who had seen little action and retained unit cohesion. Also, the bitterness of the divide between unionists, who were plentiful in Texas, and Confederates had a rival only in the bloody division between Confederate West Tennessee and the unionist East Tennessee. Texas was a hotbed of unionism, especially West Texas and the cities. Remember, Texas was where the greatest mass execution of civilians took place in U.S. history when in two days Confederates shot and hung over forty men for suspicion of Union sympathy in Gainesville, north of Dallas, in October 1862.[6] As North Texas was a unionist base, so were West Texas and Central Texas in the Hill Country near Austin, where Germans were staunch unionists. Around the same time as Gainesville, in August 1862, Confederates killed nearly thirty or more unionists of German descent fleeing to Mexico after a battle, in the Nueces Massacre, along the Nueces River. At least nine of those killed were executed long after they were captured. About as many as were killed, thirty or so, made it to Mexico. A messy and unclear dividing line between unionist West Texas and Confederate East Texas ran from Dallas to Austin and just west of Houston. Most of the slave plantations in the state were in Confederate East Texas. The bloodshed that prolonged the official close of the American Civil War came predominantly there, particularly in Northeast Texas, which had not experienced Yankee invasion and felt unconquered, with strong cohesion among its only partially disbanded Confederate units. One major area of extreme warlike violence was "the Corners" in Northeast Texas. Here Confederates never surrendered—as the war barely came to Texas—and the aptly named Bob Lee (no relation to Robert E. Lee) led a guerilla campaign against federal troops in late 1865 and then against Republican politicians after 1867.

Texas stood out for its violence in the era, and it even had attacks on federal troops, which were almost unheard of outside of the state. Local white southerners who had been unionists, however, did the bulk of the fighting against the virulently racist and violent Lee, who formed a KKK unit and spent most of his time terrorizing freedmen and trying to maintain the system of racial control from slavery days. Lewis Peacock led the unionists, and his allies in the U.S. 6th Infantry killed Lee in June 1869. Although defeating Lee in what became known as the Lee-Peacock War, Peacock, like many white unionists in the Southern Civil War, was ruthlessly gunned down by ex-Confederate extremists when Democrats reclaimed the state in 1871. Bob Lee embodied the ex-Confederate extremist campaign in Northeast Texas. Lee and others like him in East Texas had organized a KKK-style guerilla unit of ex-Confederate soldiers in mid-1865, prior to the official founding of the KKK in Tennessee later that year.[7]

Lee launched his campaign of terrorism in a typical way in the summer of 1865. He simply refused to give up his enslaved people, violently continuing to hold them and even abducting more. When Freedmen's Bureau agent and Texas unionist Hardin Hart came after Lee with part of the Twenty-Sixth U.S. Infantry to free the African Americans, Lee opened fire on them, fled to the woods with his organized band, and launched a campaign of terror against local unionists and African Americans. Earlier in 1865 Lee had organized his terrorist group and claimed to have killed Union soldiers, but once his slaves were liberated, Lee's group and associated groups in the Corners escalated their attacks. African Americans were not only killed but also tortured and their bodies mutilated—as some terrorists skinned them and nailed the skins to trees. White Texas unionists like Peacock defended and sheltered African Americans and were targeted by Lee's men in a vicious running war. Lee was attempting to overthrow the verdict of the American Civil War in his region of Texas, and he successfully initiated a new war locally.[8]

Only in Texas did ex-Confederate extremists regularly attack federal troops in addition to local unionists. By early 1868, only 1,291 federal troops were posted in the settled areas of Texas, while 2,479 patrolled the Indian frontier.[9] By comparison, 25,000 Texans joined the Confederate army in 1861. Most stayed in the state and, as noted, never became casualties and retained their arms and some unit cohesiveness in 1865 at the supposed end of the war. Perhaps 90,000 Texans served in the Confederate army at some point in the American Civil War. Texas ex-Confederate extremists thus drew on a large base of veterans to intimidate federal troops that were a thirtieth of their number. In addition, young men who missed the American Civil War and sympathized with the Confederate cause were anxious to take up arms, see some action, and take revenge on unionists of any race as the Southern Civil War stretched across a decade. Between June 1865 and August 1866 these ex-Confederate Texas forces attacked federals and controlled most of the countryside, where local unionists, not federal troops, fought them more effectively. Because Texas warfare marginally involved federal troops, President Andrew Johnson kept a state of war in place until a year and a half after Appomattox. Johnson made many mistakes, but declaring an end to the American Civil War in August 1866 was particularly divorced from reality. The war in Texas actually escalated after 1866.

The Republican governor of Texas from 1870–1874, Edmund Davis, was a Civil War military hero who bravely led forces fighting for civil rights against white supremacists in the Southern Civil War, and ex-Confederate extremists would forever after vilify him for it. The massive obelisk marking Davis's grave in the Texas State Cemetery, the tallest marker there, was erected entirely by his family. He has never been memorialized by the state he served, and in the twenty-first century he is in the center of a public battle over a historic site. Fort Davis National Historic Site and Jeff Davis County are both named for Jefferson Davis and are the only national fort (and current museum and park) and county named after the leader of the Confederacy. For a few years, however, in the late 1860s and into the 1870s, the fort was designated to be named after the Republican governor and Union military hero Edmund Davis. When white supremacists violently reclaimed Texas in 1874, they changed the designation back to Jefferson Davis. Since 2001, African American and Democratic activists in the state legislature have been trying to get the designation changed back to Edmund Davis. Davis defended African Americans personally, and he publicly befriended them as political colleagues.

Davis's case is instructive of the divisions among white southerners before, during, and after the American Civil War. Davis was in many ways typical of the whites who joined in coalition with African Americans in the Republican Party and in the Southern Civil War. Davis was born in Florida, came to Texas early in his life, and became a protégé of Sam Houston. Davis held no slaves, like 75 percent of white southerners, and he took a staunch Union stand in the crisis of secession in Texas when Governor Houston tried to keep Texas out of the Confederacy. Davis even tried to persuade Robert E. Lee to accept Lincoln's offer of command of all Union forces in 1861. Unlike Lee, Davis fought with the Union as a cavalry general during the American Civil War. Davis's unit consisted entirely of his fellow southern unionists, whom he recruited and led. Likewise, most of the white shock troops on the unionist side in the Southern Civil War came from those who had actively or passively supported the Union during the war.

After Davis led Texas's Union cavalry during the American Civil War, his military career naturally transitioned into his leading the biracial coalition in the Southern Civil War. In the first war he fought Texas Confederates and was even captured by them, and then he stayed in his home state fighting the same Confederates in the second war, those who refused to surrender. Texas's reputation for partisan violence during the Civil War was more than confirmed during the Southern Civil War. The public and even historians have misunderstood General Sheridan's famous quote from when he was military commander of the reconstruction district of Texas in 1866: "If I owned Hell and Texas, I would rent Texas and live in Hell."[10] This quote is used today as a humorous comment on Texas's hot weather, but Sheridan was referring to the inces-

Edmund Davis (1827–1883) was a southern-born Union general and the governor of Texas during the Southern Civil War. (Texas State Library and Archives Commission)

sant and vicious violence of the state. Edmund Davis was at the center of that violence. He never knew peace in Texas from 1860 until his death in 1883.

Ex-Confederate extremists in rural locales were disgusted when Davis admitted African Americans to the six-hundred-strong Texas State Police, which he created in 1869. Davis also developed the State Guard of Texas and a "reserve militia," the former of which would become the Texas Army National Guard in 1903. Unlike the elite State Police, the thirty-five-hundred-member militia was largely African American, and 40 percent of its officers were African American.[11] Davis worked closely with the African Americans in these units and with African American politicians like Norris Wright Cuney.[12] Davis's close ties to the African American community, willingness to prosecute rampant racial crimes against them that constituted a local war, and his decision to arm African Americans brought white supremacist violence to a fever pitch. Ex-Confederate extremist guerilla bands launched a campaign of lawless violence against his government and its new military units and against local African Americans and white unionists. Rather than cave in to white supremacist demands, Governor Davis declared martial law in key counties and allowed African American police to arrest whites. Davis curbed the violence in Texas, but after he was defeated in the 1873 election, the ex-Confederate Democratic Party leaders disbanded the State Police. Extremists assassinated leaders of the Northeast Texas white unionist forces that had defeated Bob Lee's raiders. Political and racial violence ran rampant in Texas after the 1873 reversal and then subsided with the total victory of Democratic ex-Confederate extremists in 1874. After taking the legislature two years earlier, they assumed the governorship and all statewide offices in 1874. They would then hold state office for one hundred years without significant Republican opposition. The ex-Confederate extremists in Texas had violently suppressed Republican votes to win and continued to intimidate their political opponents in the same ways until after World War II. Despite constant threats against his life, Davis ran for governor again in 1880 and stayed in the state, running unsuccessfully for office as a Republican.

Davis put the state on a war footing in 1870 and had the numerical forces in the militia and a crack unit in the mounted State Police to take the battle to the KKK-style guerilla fighters. Davis was methodical. He waited to see if local authorities could handle the violence. When they could not, he declared martial law in a county and sent in state forces. He armed them well with artillery, thousands of Winchesters, and over a million cartridges.[13] In the next year, 1871, they would make nearly six thousand arrests and halt the guerilla activity. Davis first ordered the militia into Liberty County in August, but the first clash came in Madison County in November 1870.[14] Madison County, in effect, revolted against the state and attacked State Police in both guerilla and mob action. The leaders of the uprising threatened to kill every "Radical in Madison County and then go down and clean out Grimes County," as reported in a Galveston newspaper at the time.[15] This quote reveals the standard procedure for guerilla ex-Confederate extremist groups throughout the South: identify the supporters of the biracial coalition in a local setting removed from the reach of state power and then drive them out of the voting booth, out of the county, or to the grave. The tactic was remarkably astute politically and militarily. Small, dispersed, but viciously violent groups were highly effective but hard to hunt down and combat. The terror they spread drove voters away from taking stands in favor of the biracial coalition and made such stances the choice of a brave but dwindling minority. Equally important, such attacks and assertions of ex-Confederate extremist control delegitimized and destabilized the biracial coalition governments and national authority in the South. The biracial governments clearly did not govern in the countryside, and federal authority did not extend into most southern communities. Edmund Davis understood the ex-Confederate extremist strategy better than almost anyone in the South because it was amply displayed in Texas. He had been combating these same forces politically before, during, and after the American Civil War and recognized their purpose in the Southern Civil War.

Davis received desperate letters from rural Republicans about the terror they faced. One citizen from Liberty County described attacks on a white unionist's wife and children and ended with the plea: "Save our state from the hands of the Traitor's rule."[16] With such pleas coming to Davis, when he took up the battle in Madison County he took it up fiercely. Three hundred troops and the adjutant general of the state, James Davidson, went into the county and subdued it almost immediately. Next, in January 1871, in Hill County, ex-Confederate extremists killed several African Americans, and when the State Police went after the guerillas, the policemen were captured by the guerillas. After escaping, they called in the adjutant general who had Davis declare martial law and send in the militia. By these first demonstrations of state military power, Davis was asserting his authority to govern the state and protect all its citizens and serving notice to all insurgents of what would happen in violent regions.

Davis would need that power because the guerillas were not yet learning from the examples of his actions. Later in January 1871, Walker County exploded when Sam Jenkins, a prominent African American, was killed by ex-Confederate extremists. A unit of State Police led by the future Texas Ranger legend Leander H. McNelly went into the county to track down the insurgents. McNelly arrested four but, as happened throughout the Southern Civil War, local courtrooms (and later state and national ones) were fixed against the biracial coalition. When ex-Confederate extremists lying under oath and jury tampering did not work, guerillas in Walker County smuggled arms into the courtroom for the defendants. Then townsmen and the defendants started shooting the State Police and officers of the court, with McNelly himself wounded. Virtually no white townsmen would help in identifying or chasing the guerillas, who melted away into the friendly and armed crowd.[17] Again, Davis declared martial law and sent in Adjutant General Davidson with the militia. He started arresting townsmen and set up a military tribunal, putting over twenty on trial, including one of the original prisoners, aptly named Nat Outlaw, who had fought his way out of court and had been killing African American supporters of Davis.[18] Martial law lasted sixty days, and Davis made the county pay for the upkeep of the militia troops during the period. Davis also had to declare martial law on January 31, 1871, in Mason County.[19]

In September 1871, an uprising took place in the town of Groesbeck. There an ex-Confederate extremist crowd attempted to capture and try African American State Police working in the area and in surrounding Limestone and Freestone Counties.[20] Davis declared martial law in both counties, sent in the militia, again set up military commissions to try suspected insurgents, and fined the counties for the cost of the soldiers stationed there.[21] Many of these militia troops and their officers were African American. Their use by the state government brought a visceral wave of racial resentment that drove indifferent whites and even supporters of the Davis government into the opposition camp, but the wave of arrests and show of force made the swelling anti-Davis forces think twice about open warfare. Davis took an even bolder and more effective step with the militia and State Police by using them to guard polling places. This tactic anticipated, and in fact went beyond, the 1965 Voting Rights Act. Guerillas targeted African American voters and their white Republican allies in order to keep them from the polls. In the 1871 election, Davis used the state military to guard voting places and forbid firearms and demonstrations near them.

Davis's forceful military stance worked in 1871 but his military victory backfired politically, as happened in all the southern states where biracial and even all-white militias took the battle to KKK-style guerillas. In 1872, largely with an antimilitia stance and the help of violent intimidation and fraud, the ex-Confederates won at the polls and took back the Texas State legislature. One of their first acts was to repeal the State Police law over Davis's veto and to rewrite the Militia Law to take the power to declare martial law away from the governor. The legislature also demobilized the militia units.[22] But many largely African American military units continued to drill and mobilize in favor of Governor Davis. Davis still had fight in him, but that fight came in a new context for the Southern Civil War as Texas ex-Confederate extremists no longer needed guerilla tactics and fielded open paramilitary armies in Texas and other states after 1872. Davis was driven from office in the next election. In 1872 the ex-Confederate extremist paramilitary Travis Rifles faced off against the African American remnants of Davis's militia who were protecting the governor.[23] President Grant refused to aid Davis and ordered him to have his militia stand down.[24] Davis famously refused to leave or unlock his governor's office until driven out by force in 1874 since he knew the vote had been fraudulent and backed by paramilitary violence.[25]

Like Texas, Arkansas, of all the southern states, produced the Republican government that best defended itself and its African American citizens with military force during the Southern Civil War. Like Davis, the biracial coalition governor of Arkansas, Powell Clayton, could have provided a model military strategy for the biracial coalitions elsewhere in the South, but, also like Davis, his successful repression of KKK violence and employment of African American troops alienated white voters. Initially Clayton was as successful as Davis in combating ex-Confederate extremist guerillas in his state using the state militia (in his case the Arkansas State Guard). Arkansas, though, saw more open warfare than Texas did. Clayton would militarily subdue the guerillas, but, as in Texas, Arkansas turned against the use of African American troops and martial law. Nineteenth-century white Americans saw armed African Americans as taboo and certainly worse than any problem they were called on to solve, especially when that problem was a slaughter of African Americans. Centralized government power and use of the military at the local level, despite the American Civil War and in reaction against it, was almost as alien and anathema to Reconstruction Era white Americans as were armed Blacks in their community. Thus, Clayton's military victories were followed by electoral defeat and emboldened white supremacist violence. Clayton's and Davis's examples were not widely copied in other states, and the militarily victorious Republican regimes of both Arkansas and Texas abandoned the battlefield and fell into political disarray.

Powell Clayton was the greatest military leader of the biracial coalition in the Southern Civil War. Like Davis, his war against the KKK guerillas was a direct continuation of his American Civil War service as a general and even his pre–Civil War activities. Clayton, who was born in Pennsylvania, was in Bleeding Kansas in 1855 and an early Republican, so he had been in the struggle against proslavery forces since that time.[26] Clayton was then the Union general stationed in Arkansas, defending cities like Helena and Pine Bluff against Confederate guerillas in 1863 and 1864. He married a young woman from Helena and settled in Pine Bluff in 1865, after almost two years vigorously defending the city and nearby areas.[27] He immediately had to defend his farm and then region and then state against ex-Confederate extremist guerillas. His involvement in politics grew organically from his local experience trying to control recalcitrant and openly violent ex-Confederates. As governor of Arkansas, he had the political will to do what the ex-Confederate extremists most feared and fought to prevent. Clayton armed African Americans and organized them into the militia, doing so before Davis did in Texas.[28] Other Republican governors, such as Adelbert Ames in Mississippi, contemplated the use of African American troops, which aroused such ex-Confederate extremist violence, but backed off from employing African American militia for fear of inciting a "race war." On the other hand, Clayton understood that firm action and direct confrontation of the KKK offered the only chance to stop a race war already initiated in 1865 by the forces of white supremacy.[29] Their cruel guerilla actions infuriated Clayton, and he commented, "I am convinced that open warfare would have been preferable to the stealthy method of murder employed by the Ku Klux Klan."[30] Clayton called the Klan actions a "second rebellion" and "war, with all its horrors."[31]

In a mass employment of night riding and hit-and-run tactics, the KKK in Arkansas killed over two hundred African Americans and white unionists between July and October 1868.[32] Some very prominent assassinations took place in this reign of guerilla terror.[33] One was an ex-Confederate who was not in any way an extremist and publicly and bravely supported African American rights and voting, Thomas Hindman. A former Democratic congressmen and Confederate general, Hindman was assassinated in September 1868 after attending a meeting in support of the African American vote, and the perpetrators and motives for his death remain a mystery today. Equally prominent and better understood was the case of James M. Hinds, a Republican congressman who was assassinated on October 22 by ex-Confederate extremists.[34] Following the nearly universal pattern of the Southern Civil War, no one was brought to justice for these assassinations. Clayton, however, could meet warfare with warfare and root out the sources of

Arkansas governor Powell Clayton (1833–1914) was one of the most aggressive leaders of biracial coalition forces. (Library of Congress)

the guerilla violence. Guerilla warfare was concentrated in the most heavily African American southern and eastern regions of Arkansas but also present even in the largely white northern part of the state. First Clayton sought overwhelming force. Clayton asked for help from fellow Republican governors across the country and called for federal troops but was refused. Nonetheless, Secretary of War John Schofield understood the necessity of fighting back and wrote to Clayton:

> Where the Civil authorities and entire communities are so paralyzed and helpless as to allow half a dozen outlaws to stalk through the Country in open day and deliberately murder whom they please with impunity, it is clear that a radical change in the local government is necessary. The Military force at my command, or even a larger one, could not protect the lives of citizens in such helpless communities without the exercise of absolute martial law.[35]

After the presidential election in November, Clayton declared martial law in fourteen counties, calling up the biracial state militia.[36] Clayton sent the militia of over four thousand into KKK-infested counties where he estimated the Klan had fifteen thousand armed Arkansans and help from ex-Confederate extremists forces from Texas and Louisiana.[37] The federal government refused to supply arms to Arkansas's government, so Governor Clayton had to make a purchase of arms on the open market backed by his own money. As unbelievable as it now seems, that a governor, facing an armed insurrection that had already killed hundreds, had no aid and had to resort to private arms purchase, this federal inertia was typical of the Southern Civil War. In a coordinated attack in Memphis, KKK forces seized Clayton's first arms shipment, bought in New York. Klansmen dumped the arms—about four thousand rifles and ammunition—in the Mississippi River after an armed steamboat attack on the ship carrying the arms.[38] Undeterred, Clayton made further purchases, some with his own money, and effectively armed the militia by November 1868.[39] In several pitched battles in northeastern Arkansas, the militia defeated the forces of the KKK.[40] Ad hoc African American forces even entered the fray, ambushing the Klan and defeating it between Lewisburg and Plummerville.[41] In most cases, however, the KKK melted away before these state forces. Yet the Arkansas militia was firm and creative, even when arresting suspected Klan members. In the Southern Civil War and during its aftermath in the lynching era of the 1890s and beyond, ex-Confederate extremists killed African American and white unionists with impunity—rarely being brought to trial and virtually never convicted, sentenced, or imprisoned for any significant time. Clayton's militia, however, was different. It summarily executed a number of suspected Klansmen after quick ad hoc military trials. A few were even shot while "escaping."[42] A repetition of this example in the remainder of the Southern Civil War or, even more importantly, at the end of the American Civil War, might have changed the character of the peace to the benefit of unionists. The tactics certainly worked in Arkansas.

Like Davis in Texas, Clayton was methodical. He was well aware of the warfare ripping through several regions of his state, but he bided his time. Although a man of action, Clayton had to draw on the calculating patience he had shown as a Union officer at Pine Bluff. He waited for the completion of the federal elections of 1868 before striking against an enemy apparently holding a strategic advantage. Clayton stated, "In view of the fact that an election is pending and from motives of public policy, I do not wish to use a military force if it can be avoided. The whole principle of the ballot is a free expression of the public will and the use of a military force, either at the registration or election is not desirable."[43] Two weeks after these comments were published, Clayton informed the state legislature that he would declare martial law in the counties which had seen the most violence.[44] Clayton minced no words about civil rights, declaring: "The colored man possesses the same rights, privileges, and immunities—civil and political—that the white man possesses."[45] Defending African American rights and securing them for the future would take both a war and a transformation of Arkansas's government and political culture.

Clayton began by declaring that the Arkansas counties of Ashley, Bradley, Columbia, Lafayette, Mississippi, Craighead, Woodruff, Greene, Sevier, and Little River were all in a state of "insurrection." Clayton stated that the Ku Klux Klan had been attempting to subvert the electoral process and overthrow the state government:

> Now, therefore, I . . . do hereby proclaim martial law in the aforementioned counties. All unlawful organizations will, upon receipt of this proclamation, or notice of same, at once disband and abstain from all illegal and violent acts. All who fail to do this will be treated as outlaws, and not entitled to the protection of the Government, and will certainly be brought to a speedy and merited punishment; and all bodies of armed men (not organized in pursuance of the laws of the State and the United States) will at once disperse and return to their homes; and I hereby call upon and request all law-abiding citizens to use their influence to prevent disorder and to preserve the public peace. Citizens of the counties not under Martial Law are requested to abstain from all unauthorized military organizations or from any interference in the affairs of other counties. Unless this is done Martial Law will be extended to them, and war, with all its horrors, may be precipitated upon the State, which is still suffering terribly from the former rebellion.[46]

Clayton understood that he was not taking his state into war but that a war was already under way.

Clayton divided Arkansas into four military districts. He assigned command of the North Eastern District to General D. P. Upham, the South Western District to General Robert F. Catterson, and command of the South Eastern District to Colonel Samuel Mallory. The North Western District in the Ozarks had long been unionist and was not assigned a commander as no significant ex-Confederate extremists operated there. Each of the commanders had the power to draft a militia in addition to the Arkansas State Guard. The commanders were to report to Adjutant General Keyes Danforth, as the Texas militia had been under Adjutant General Davidson.

Catterson's men engaged in some of the first action of the operation. After finding no insurrectionary forces at Murfreesboro, they moved on to Center Point, where 400 ex-Confederate extremist fighters assembled, with more on the way, including 150 men under the command of the notorious outlaw and mass murderer Cullen Baker. On November 14, Major Josiah H. Demby, under Catterson's orders, orchestrated a pincer movement. Demby sent units on either side of the town in order to surround the enemy as he began a frontal assault. Demby outmaneuvered the force gathered at Center Point and quickly defeated them. The militia took several guerillas prisoner. In addition, ample evidence was found indicating that Center Point was a site from which the Klan conducted meetings and planned much of their activity.[47] Clayton's orders to Catterson included that he "select the worst" to stand trial in military courts. At first, Clayton insisted on personally authorizing instances of capital punishment. Later, as the operation gained momentum, Clayton eased that qualification. He wrote to Catterson, "all desperate characters that fall into your hands, you had better deal with summarily."[48] The declaration of martial law allowed Clayton and his commanders to use military discipline against captured insurgents, who were considered ununiformed enemies that could be dealt with summarily.

Clayton designed his actions to secure justice for the victims of terrorists and to punish anyone who took action to threaten the very existence of the state government. He declared martial law to secure a republican form of government, open to all eligible voters in Arkansas as the Constitution and Reconstruction laws and later Fourteenth and Fifteenth Amendments demanded. Clayton was not fulfilling any personal vendettas; he was hunting guerilla insurrectionaries who had perpetrated atrocities in an attempt to overthrow the state government and subvert the political process to further their extremist agenda. Clayton's aggressive use of force was the only method by which all eligible voters in Arkansas could take part in the political process free of intimidation.

Upham's northeastern district was the area in which subduing organized insurgents was the most difficult. Upham faced two ambushes designed to assassinate him. On October 2, 1868, Upham and county registrar F. A. McClure were both wounded in an ex-Confederate extremist guerilla ambush. Upham was a target not just because of his role as a militia commander but also because he was a successful local businessman tied closely to the African American community, which had helped elect him to the state legislature after they could vote in 1867. He was an outspoken advocate for their rights and Clayton's efforts to secure a truly republican form of government in the state. Upham set up headquarters near federal troops in Batesville where over one thousand African American and white volunteers signed up for the militia. Upham then invaded his home county of Woodruff and, to forestall racial backlash, took a crack force of over 120, largely mounted, white militiamen into a series of seven or more counterguerilla hit-and-run engagements. Upham knew counterguerilla warfare meant throwing out the rulebook, and he fought ex-Confederate extremist KKK forces using their same tactics—mobile mounted units hitting and running quickly and willing to take hostages and summarily execute unarmed opponents when they could be found.[49] Melting back into civilian life did not protect ex-Confederates extremists from Upham's forces. Ex-Confederate colonel A. C. Pickett (no relation to George Pickett of Pickett's Charge) led the local Klan in Woodruff. Pickett and his men captured and ransacked Upham's own farm, but Upham's militia stopped them from capturing the town of Augusta by taking several ex-Confederate supporters hostage. Upham promised to execute them if the ex-Confederate guerillas did not leave the field of battle. In a classic guerilla move, the KKK appeared to disperse under this creative threat but then reassembled in the hundreds and assaulted Upham's forces. In a succession of running battles, the biracial coalition militia defeated Colonel Pickett's forces. Upham had cleared the county and was later appointed as a federal marshal in Fort Smith, Arkansas, and served with distinction the famous "hanging judge" Isaac Parker. After ex-Confederate extremists purged the state of Republicans between 1875 and 1890, Upham became an object of abuse and slander in all state histories. He died peacefully in 1882 in his native state of Massachusetts after being driven from the U.S. Marshals Service by Democratic enemies in Arkansas.[50] Had he reentered Republican politics in Arkansas he might have suffered the fate of Powell Clayton's brother John who ran for Congress as a Republican in Arkansas in 1888. He was assassinated while disputing the fraud and voter intimidation in the election of his Democratic rival Clifton Breckinridge, former Confederate officer and virulent white supremacist. Breckinridge was the son of John C. Breckinridge, the former vice president of the United States, proslavery candidate for president in 1860, and then a Confederate general and secretary of war under Jefferson Davis. As with almost all Republican supporters of the biracial coalition assassinated in the Southern Civil War, no one was tried or punished for the assassination of John Clayton, though he was declared the winner of the congressional election as voter fraud was proved. A key incident documented in the election investigation after Clayton's assassination included masked white men breaking into an African American precinct at gunpoint and stealing and destroying the ballot box.

That violent day for his brother lay far in the future for Powell Clayton who on November 24, 1869, addressed the state's General Assembly and extolled the success of the Militia Wars and his maintenance of martial law. He affirmed that "the policy of the United States Government in withdrawing its support and protection from us has had the effect to some extent of placing us in a situation of great peril and difficulty."[51] Clayton insisted that the federal government's refusal to provide assistance in suppressing insurrection in Arkansas emboldened the state's ex-Confederates extremists to organize and institute a "program of assassinations, robberies, threats, and intimidations."[52] Clayton refused to yield until his forces secured the state and then cleared out the last counties dominated by ex-Confederate extremists.

In December, an escalation of violence compelled Clayton to extended martial law to include Conway County (where just two months before he had so clearly expressed his determination to uphold the law). Clayton's forces also declared martial law in Drew and Crittenden Counties. The extreme methods of the Klan, such as widespread arson, cost them support and hastened their downfall in Conway County. However, Crittenden County was the most difficult area to bring under control. Crittenden's proximity to Memphis became an obstacle. Memphis was a base of operations for displaced ex-Confederate extremist forces from Arkansas who had found a safe haven there. These Memphis-based Arkansans had a hand in destroying Clayton's original arms shipment. In Crittenden County the militia's fortification, expertly constructed by African American veterans of the American Civil War, was the target of snipers every night for almost a week until a company of Missourians arrived to assist in finally subduing resistance there.[53]

Clayton lifted martial law in the embattled counties once insurrectionary forces were suppressed. In most of the thirteen affected counties, Clayton lifted martial law by January 1869. Martial law was lifted in Drew County on February 6 and from the last county, Crittenden, on March 21. By that point, ex-Confederate extremist activity had subsided significantly, and Clayton determined that all of the guerillas of the previous summer and fall that could be captured either had been brought to justice or had fled the state. On rare occasions, however, fugitives returned to settle old scores. Such was the case with Clarence Collier. Collier was a former Klansman who returned to Marion, Arkansas, in July 1869. He shot and killed Captain A. J. Haynes in retribution for an incident that had occurred during the militia occupation the previous winter. Despite the presence of ample witnesses, Collier rode off unpursued. The *Memphis Public Ledger* proclaimed Collier a returning hero.

Despite such continued assassinations, in March 1869 Clayton toured the former occupied counties. He later recalled being greeted cordially and respectfully on these visits and, in an address to the state legislature, claimed the operation as a success. He noted that only five guerilla assassinations had occurred in the first three months of 1869 and recalled that nearly two hundred people had been killed in guerilla acts throughout the state in the months leading up to the November elections the preceding year. Clayton had defeated the KKK and other ex-Confederate extremist guerillas by early 1869. Yet, like Texas, Arkansas experienced a collapse of biracial coalition power after Clayton's considerable military success. That story centers around a named war in Arkansas: the Brooks-Baxter War of 1874 which will be covered in the next chapter.

Arkansas had named wars during Reconstruction besides Powell Clayton's Militia Wars and the Brooks-Baxter War. The Chicot County War of 1871 revealed a great deal about the Southern Civil War since it was an exception to some of its patterns.[54] Chicot County is in the extreme southeastern corner of Arkansas bordered by the Mississippi River and the state of Mississippi to the east and Louisiana to the south. African Americans made up the majority of the population of around nine thousand prior to Reconstruction. Powell Clayton's vigorous campaign against the KKK encouraged militia building and active self-defense by Chicot African American leaders, like James W. Mason, who was the first African American postmaster in the country and served at every level of state and local government.[55] Mason's militia numbered in the hundreds by the summer of 1871.[56] Another local leader, Wathal G. Wynn, who was a graduate of Howard University, a member of the bar, and may have been Mason's brother-in-law, was assassinated in December in a local store by the white storeowner and two other white men, all of whom had a history of attacking African Americans and Freedmen's Bureau workers. Chicot County African Americans believed the three men, John W. Saunders, Jasper Dugan, and Curtis Garrett, were leaders of a local KKK unit. Mason helped assure the arrest of the three assassins and suspected Klan members. The African American militia then marched to the jail, seized the three men, took them to the woods, and shot them dead.[57] Conflicting documentation by biracial coalition newspapers and the ex-Confederate extremist press obscure what happened next.[58] The latter claimed that the militia then went on a rampage against local whites, but the much more credible Republican press and a state inspection showed these to be racist rumors intended to incite white vengeance.[59] Sporadic fighting clearly broke out between the militia and local ex-Confederate extremists, who fled the county over the Mississippi River.[60] When Arkansas's biracial coalition government collapsed and white supremacist Democrats regained the state after the Brooks-Baxter War in 1874, Chicot County remained under African American political control, with nearly all the elected positions in the county held by African Americans. In 1884 white Democrats began to undermine African American political leadership in Chicot, but its history of organization and self-defense had let its African American leaders survive six years after the end of the Southern Civil War. Chicot was not the only local area where African Americans retained some political power after the Southern Civil War, but these were few, and ex-Confederate extremists systematically eliminated them all by 1900. The ex-Confederate extremists, unlike northern leaders, knew how to consolidate power after a victory in a civil war. Much of the South had fallen to ex-Confederate extremist guerillas by 1872.

CHAPTER THREE

The Guerilla Phase, 1868–1872, Part 2

The KKK Triumphant

Outside Arkansas and Texas the guerilla phase of the Southern Civil War was more of a one-sided slaughter, except briefly in South Carolina with federal action and in North Carolina where governor William Holden tried to emulate Davis and Clayton. A series of battles in Opelousas, Louisiana, beginning on September 28, 1868, typified the guerilla warfare. The Klan triumphed in Opelousas as it did across the South. Opelousas may have been the bloodiest engagement of the war. The ex-Confederate extremists did not take over all of Louisiana or the state government in this phase of the war, but, as Opelousas shows, they were well on their way to eliminating political and military opposition. They were emboldened and, starting in 1872, switched to open paramilitary armies that would conquer Louisiana by 1876. Similar KKK guerilla attacks worked in some counties of Florida, Mississippi, and South Carolina, which also fell to paramilitary armies in 1876. KKK tactics had total success in Alabama, Georgia, North Carolina, and Virginia where state governments were in ex-Confederate extremist hands by the end of 1872.

The Opelousas warfare is infamous, but there were likely similar, if smaller, unreported, and covered-up clashes across the South in the second phase of the war. The KKK-style guerillas in Opelousas killed hundreds of African Americans and several white Republicans over weeks after an incident of armed resistance by the biracial coalition there on September 28, 1868. The biracial coalition's acts of political independence and self-defense triggered hundreds of less dramatic and bloody but still deadly KKK-style attacks across the region. The Opelousas battles began with African American steps toward political power and support by whites working with the Freedmen's Bureau to help with liberation and education in Louisiana. African Americans were never tools of Republicans or whites in the era but independent actors in their own liberation. For example, several African Americans around Opelousas wanted to join the Democratic Party and traveled to Washington, Louisiana, in St. Landry Parish, the same parish as Opelousas, to take part in a Democratic rally. The Seymour unit of the Knights of the White Camellia (KKK imitators) came out in force to stop the African Americans from integrating the Democratic Party. Across the South, local and decentralized guerilla units of white supremacy went under many names despite their shared purposes and tactics. The Seymour Knights unit even used KKK calling cards after they stopped African Americans in Washington. A white Republican newspaper editor in Opelousas, Emerson Bentley, who was only eighteen years old, merely wrote an editorial documenting what the Seymour Knights had done in Washington to block African Americans from attending a Democratic Party rally. Bentley pointed out that this incident illustrated why African Americans should support the party of Lincoln and the biracial coalition.[1] The guerillas hated exposure, truth, and resistance, so the Seymour Knights put a threatening note on the schoolhouse door where Bentley taught African American children, a warning that had the letters "KKK" alongside a skull, coffin, and bloody knife. The next day prominent ex-Confederate and civic leaders in the Knights savagely beat Bentley in front of his terrified young students, who ran for their lives. Bentley literally ran for his life as well after the Knights left him for dead on the schoolhouse floor. He traveled for three weeks and made his way back to the North and safety, but his African American Republican allies did not know he had made it to safety. They reasonably assumed that the white supremacist guerillas had murdered and disappeared Bentley, as they had so many biracial coalition leaders.[2]

The Opelousas African Americans raised a poorly armed spontaneous search party and marched toward Washington, Louisiana, where they knew the Knights of the White Camellia were based. The African American forces marching toward Washington were met by a trained force of white supremacist guerillas armed with excellent Confederate rifles. The ex-Confederate extremists also outnumbered the African Americans at least four to one. The biracial coalition search party had mostly shotguns or no arms at all. The Seymour Knights quickly defeated the search party and seized twenty-seven prisoners. Among the prisoners were twelve of the leading Black Republicans of St. Landry Parish. The Knights of the White Camellia summarily executed all the African American captives.[3] In a typical act of bald-faced lying central to the erroneously labeled "race riots" for the next one hundred years, the Knights spread the alarm of a "Black uprising" intended to massacre whites after they had just massacred African Americans.[4] This lie formed the basis of further massacres and battles. The ex-Confederate extremists stalked St. Landry Parish for weeks, slaughtering African Americans on sight. African Americans hid and fought back as best they could, killing some ex-Confederate extremists. As many as three hundred African Americans died, as did perhaps a dozen ex-Confederate extremists. This was war, as horrific and politically consequential a war as has ever been fought on the North American continent.

The ex-Confederate extremists aimed their violence primarily against supporters of African American rights, but their efforts also constituted an assault on the free press, truth, and memory, as well as civil rights and democracy. The assault on editors and educators continued after Bentley escaped after his schoolhouse beating. Other white Republicans fought alongside African Americans in St. Landry Parish. The French editor of Bentley's Republican newspaper, C. E. Durand, fell to the Knights' bullets early in the ex-Confederate rampage, and they displayed his body outside the Opelousas drugstore. As many as thirty white Republicans died as Durand did. During the Southern Civil War, it is documented, ex-Confederate extremists assassinated hundreds of biracial coalition leaders in the South, and certainly many more assassinations went undocumented. Two hundred fifty federal troops did come from New Orleans to Opelousas but not until May—months after the rampage. Part of the U.S. Army Twenty-Fifth Colored Infantry Regiment were attacked and harassed by the same ex-Confederate extremists who led the massacres and assassinations across the region and went unpunished.[5]

One conservative count by a white supremacist paper had one hundred killed in just one month leading up to the 1868 election in St. Landry.[6] Political assassinations, like those in Opelousas, were common in the South across every phase of the Southern Civil War. The most African American and white unionists were likely killed in the terror phase of the war, but ex-Confederate extremists carried out most political assassinations during the guerilla phase, when Republican politicians most often held power. Only three assassins were ever prosecuted. A *New York Times* article on October 20, 1868, stated, "Political murders seem to be the order of the day, not in any one State or any one section, but throughout the entire South."[7] Two weeks earlier, on October 6, 1868, the *Times* had called for one of two actions: either the military should reoccupy the South, or the government needed to administer the region in order to stop the violence.[8] Biracial coalition judge Albion W. Tourgee of central North Carolina witnessed twelve murders, nine rapes, fourteen arsons, and over seven hundred beatings, including the whipping of a woman 103 years old.[9] Emanuel Fortune was driven from Jackson County, Florida, where there was a wave of KKK assassinations and ambushes, and said, "The object of it is to kill out the leading men of the Republican Party."[10] The KKK killed three Republican members of Georgia's legislature and drove ten others from their homes.[11] Historian Steven Hahn summarized the vast scale of assassinations of local biracial coalition officials: "Although the toll is impossible to calculate with any precision, it must have run into the many hundreds if not thousands."[12] No concerted federal military action was taken to end the assassinations and guerilla violence in the southern states, only a brief and localized period of arrests under the Enforcement Acts.

KKK guerillas and their supporters typically covered up their assassinations and warfare and blamed violence on the biracial coalition. In Opelousas, after winning militarily, the ex-Confederate extremists began their propaganda war right away and denied the violence except to bemoan African American "rioting."[13] The tactic worked, and history books repeated KKK lies about the whole Reconstruction Era. Until the last thirty years most historians labeled this battle the "Opelousas Riot" and said that only a handful of Republicans died. Modern historians believe the higher numbers above, but, given the nature of this local, scattered, and intimate warfare, no accurate casualty counts are available, just as there are not for the whole Southern Civil War.[14] This is a reason to suspect an even higher toll than can be found in conflicting contemporary newspaper reports by Democratic and Republican presses. Given the pattern of Opelousas and other such clashes, the biracial coalition numbers are much more reliable. Most historians are confident that the death toll was above 150 in the Opelousas battles. Given that the ex-Confederate extremists continually covered up all such events, the biracial coalition account of three hundred African

American and between thirty and fifty white deaths is much more responsible. The high casualty rate also aligns with oral history of the battles.[15] The extremists accomplished their political goal. In the election of 1868 following the battle, the parish and four other KKK-dominated parishes recorded no votes for Republican Ulysses S. Grant, despite massive Republican voting in previous elections. Fraud and warfare carried the election for Democrats. Grant also lost the state of Louisiana as the KKK drove the biracial coalition from the polls or sent them to their graves. The pattern of Opelousas was repeated across the South between 1868 and 1872. The biracial coalition held on to the Louisiana state government until 1876, but that was not the case in other states under KKK guerilla attack. Alabama, Georgia, North Carolina, and Virginia all witnessed guerilla triumphs and takeovers of the state governments by 1872.

Alabama had one of the quickest triumphs of KKK-style guerillas.[16] The Klan and its imitators in Alabama had strong ex-Confederate leadership. James Clinton, who had been a general in the Confederacy, was the first "grand dragon" (highest-ranking Klansman in the state), but he was murdered, so future Democratic senator John Morgan, an even more renowned Confederate general, took over. He was followed by Edmund Pettus, for whom the bridge was named on which civil rights movements marchers would be attacked on Bloody Sunday, March 7, 1965. This 1965 event in Selma resembled attacks of the Southern Civil War, and the rebel yell can be heard in the television coverage of Bloody Sunday as the white supremacist cavalry charged. That temporary defeat for the civil rights movement followed ninety years of white supremacist terror and lynching in Alabama, but it took just two years, from 1868 to 1870, for Alabama ex-Confederate extremist guerillas to drive the biracial coalition from political power in the state.

As everywhere in the South, the Alabama Klan targeted African American churches and schools for burning and African American homes for night raids of murder, torture, and sexual abuse. With these assaults, African American and white Republican voting plummeted, and Democrats took back the governorship and legislature in the 1870 election. Congress documented over one hundred murders and thousands of violent incidents and certainly missed a great many in the state.[17] Republican governor William Hugh Smith, a former slaveholder and staunch southern unionist during the American Civil War, refused local unionist pleas for a militia.[18] Naturally, none of the very few arrested served significant sentences for this bloody insurrection. In Cross Plains, the ex-Confederate extremists killed six, including a teacher. African Americans identified the perpetrators, but they were not even charged, let alone tried. Unionist Henry Smith of Dekalb became so frustrated with KKK attacks and Governor Smith's refusal to use a militia in the style of Texas's Governor Davis and Arkansas's Governor Clayton, that he started killing Klansmen on his own.[19] Eutaw, Alabama, saw one of the most violent clashes. The seat of Greene County, Eutaw had a white Republican prosecutor who, like white members of the biracial coalition across the region, was marked for assassination by the KKK in July 1870. When the KKK shot him in the head, it was only the beginning. Gillford Coleman, an African American leader of the biracial coalition, was also shot and had his corpse desecrated by the Klan. Other lynching and assassinations took place around Eutaw as the election season neared. A few months later, on October 25, 1870, Republicans rallying near the courthouse in Eutaw were attacked by the KKK. Racist taunts escalated into a gun battle when ex-Confederate extremists opened fire on the Republicans. African Americans and a few white Republicans rallied to the site, at least two African Americans were killed in an armed clash with the KKK, and at least fifty-four white and African American unionists were wounded.[20]

Alabama powerfully illustrates the strategic logic of the evolution of the Southern Civil War and ex-Confederate extremist tactics. The guerilla phase of the war had been a success in Alabama, and KKK-style terrorists had driven the biracial coalition from the polls in 1870. The war in Alabama and Reconstruction would have ended there, but democracy reemerged after violent intimidation of voters subsided and the biracial coalition won elections in the state in 1872. That coalition was defeated by paramilitary armies, and its story is in the next chapter, on the final phase of the Southern Civil War.

The Klan and similar groups armed to fight the biracial coalition government also operated in Virginia, which quickly fell back into ex-Confederate extremist hands by 1870. From 1868 to 1870, Virginia saw less terror and guerilla activity than other southern states, but its violence was significant and crucial to the fall of biracial government and voting. The Virginia KKK received endorsement from key newspapers and advertised across the state. The *Richmond Daily Enquirer and Examiner* ran an editorial on March 26, 1868, as the KKK began to organize in Virginia, extolling the organization in typically deceptive terms. The

KKK, it said, would "not permit the people of the South to become the victims of negro rule. It is purely defensive, and for the protection of the white race."[21] The KKK had thousands of members in Richmond alone and launched campaigns of violence in counties such as Rockingham, Fauquier, and Lee. In 2020 the Equal Justice Initiative documented "more than 120 incidents of Reconstruction-era racial violence in 40 Virginia counties—even more than the number of racial terror lynchings documented in the state between 1877 and 1950."[22]

The most dramatic clashes took place in Richmond in 1870 when ex-Confederate extremists violently drove the Republican mayor George Chahoon from office. Chahoon had been appointed by federal district military commander John Schofield and had the support of the city's African Americans and their white allies. However, in the spring of 1870 Henry Ellyson was elected mayor by a new city council appointed by Governor Gilbert Walker, who had won election as a Democrat in 1869 (after previously serving as a Republican) and empowered ex-Confederate extremists. Chahoon's term was not up for several months, so he refused to step down. Ellyson deputized a police force of white supremacists, and Chahoon retained the loyalty of many of the biracial coalition police, largely African Americans commanded by the African American police official "Colonel" Ben Scott. Ellyson brought back ex-Confederate extremist police chief John Poe Jr., whom Chahoon had fired for his drunken assaults on biracial coalition officials. Thus Richmond had two police forces and sets of officials battling each other on the streets.[23] Chahoon's forces lost control of most city buildings and were under siege in the Old Market House police station.[24] A gun battle broke out on March 17, 1870, and Poe's men killed at least one African American and wounded several. With that success, Ellyson's forces cut off all Chahoon's supplies on March 18, 1870, and more street battles broke out.[25] Poe's forces tried to clear the streets and killed at least one African American and shot many others. A detachment of federal cavalry arrived to break the siege at the Old Market House, and the biracial coalition crowds attacked the retreating white supremacists, wounding several, but Poe's police force fired back, wounding many. Governor Walker ruled that the federal forces had exceeded their authority, and they were immediately withdrawn from action for good. On March 20, Ellyson's white supremacist forces tried to capture Ben Scott, and an exchange of gunfire left many wounded and at least one white supremacist in Poe's police dead.[26]

At least five men had died in the street fighting at this point when Richmond's "Municipal War" took a surprising turn. The fighting reached a stalemate, and the contest between mayors Chahoon and Ellyson went to federal court. The city was on edge, and on April 27 both sides packed the courtroom gallery above the House of Delegates in the Virginia State Capitol to hear the verdict. As the judges were about to enter, the gallery balcony gave way and crashed through the floor and onto the floor of the House of Delegates twenty feet below. At least 62 men died and 251 were injured, including both Chahoon and Ellyson.[27] Triumphant ex-Confederate extremists romanticized this event as they did their seizure of power throughout the South via violence and intimidation. Many histories extolled how the city then came together in the face of this tragedy and rallied to old order Democrats taking power. This is a false narrative.

Violence typical of the elections of 1868 and 1870 across the South also plagued the two mayoral elections in Richmond after the statehouse tragedy. Gun battles broke out around police stations and polling places, especially in Richmond's heavily African American wards of Jefferson and Jackson.[28] In the first election between Chahoon and Ellyson, ex-Confederate extremists made a daylight attack on the ballot box in the Jackson ward and destroyed all the ballots. Ellyson refused election under these circumstances and withdrew. In the next election, marked by the usual white supremacist fraud and violence, the former Confederate soldier Anthony M. Keiley defeated a new biracial coalition candidate, closing the Municipal War and indeed the Southern Civil War in Virginia. Chahoon did not run again, since he had run into a typical ploy of the white supremacists as they took back southern states: he was arrested and threatened with significant jail time and then pardoned by Walker on the condition that he leave the state.[29] African Americans in the state were offered no such options as ruthless ex-Confederate extremists took over the state and turned Richmond into a shrine for white supremacy and the Confederate cause.

Like Alabama and Virginia, Georgia had a quick triumph of ex-Confederate extremism by 1871. Georgia had not created Black Codes as harsh as some southern states, nor had it had a particularly high casualty rate in the terror phase of the war from 1865–1867, but when faced with the challenge of a biracial Republican coalition taking power, Georgia turned to KKK-style guerilla tactics just like other states. The KKK got off to an infamous start in Georgia after Nathan Bedford

Forrest visited the state to help set up the organization there. Georgia unionist and Grant's attorney general Amos T. Akerman instantly recognized the horror and import of the KKK. "These combinations," he said, "amount to war and cannot be effectually crushed under any other theory."[30] Akerman was prescient, but Georgia did not take the steps to crush the KKK guerilla war.

One of the first KKK chapters started in Columbus, Georgia, on March 21, 1868. On March 30, five formally attired men in masks assassinated Republican judge George W. Ashburn in the living room of the house where he was staying. Ashburn was a typical biracial coalition white unionist but a particularly active and antiracist one. Born in North Carolina in 1814, he had lived in Georgia since 1830. He had opposed the secession of Georgia, fought for the Union as a colonel, then been appointed a judge after the American Civil War. The KKK particularly hated him because he aligned with prominent African American politician Henry McNeal Turner, the future leader of the African American separatist movement in the 1880s and 1890s. Ashburn even lived among Georgia's African American community.[31] The immediate cause of Ashburn's assassination was the political formation of the biracial coalition in Columbus and Ashburn's support for the laws that would allow African American suffrage in the state. Ashburn had been a leader of the Georgia Constitutional Convention in 1867 that provided African American suffrage. Republicans led similar conventions across the South in the wake of the federal Reconstruction Acts of 1867. Ashburn wrote the sections of the Georgia Constitution that protected African American civil rights. Henry McNeal Turner had just spoken at a large biracial Republican rally in favor of the constitution, with Ashburn in attendance, on the night that Ashburn was assassinated. The message of the first KKK killing in Georgia was clear. Ex-Confederate extremists would resist with total measures all biracial cooperation and political power. It was only the start in Georgia. The constitution passed, and the biracial coalition won the governorship and senate (and later the house). Ex-Confederate extremists now had clear targets and a government to overthrow. They quickly did just that. Leading Confederate general John B. Gordon served as Georgia grand dragon of the KKK and from that powerful military platform would go on to be the governor (and U.S. senator in terms before and after his governorship). He has a U.S. Army installation named after him. What else is there to know about the Southern Civil War in Georgia? The Gordon-led

KKK and its imitators carried out 336 documented cases of assassination and attempted assassination of African American citizens in Georgia in 1868.[32]

Voter intimidation and fraud had done their work by 1870. The bloodiest clash in Georgia during the guerilla phase of the Southern Civil War came on September 19, 1868, in Camilla, the seat of Mitchell County. As with the battle in Eutaw, Alabama, Camilla started as a biracial coalition rally and parade in election season. The state legislature had purged twenty-eight newly elected members of the biracial coalition in September because they were "disqualified" from holding office on the flimsy racist pretext of being more than one-eighth African American, as the state constitution did not explicitly state that Blacks could hold office.[33] One of the expelled representatives, Phillip Joiner, led a twenty-mile march to Camilla from Albany, Georgia (which would be the site of a significant civil rights movement campaign about one hundred years later). Ex-Confederate extremists posted themselves hidden in houses and stores in Camilla lining the parade route, and then they began sniping at the Republican march. Twelve marchers fell dead, and thirty or more were wounded as the biracial coalition tried to rally a response, though they were largely unarmed. The marchers turned away from Camilla, returned some gunfire, and retreated back toward Albany, while taking fire from the obscured ex-Confederate extremists most of the way.[34] Alabama's Eutaw battle was largely lost to history, but the Camilla Massacre became national news. The attention did little good on the ground in Georgia as the ex-Confederate extremist white minority took the election via fraud and violence that surrounded Camilla in 1868.[35] Their guerilla tactics, disguises, and ability to disappear into the civilian population also worked. In any case, no one was prosecuted for the slaughter.[36] The town of Camilla did not acknowledge the event until 1998 when it finally commemorated the victims and not the Klan perpetrators of the clash, as most southern monuments and public history have from Reconstruction until today.[37]

North Carolina fell to the ex-Confederate extremists during the guerilla phase of the war in much the same way as Alabama and Georgia, though Republicans held on to the governorship longer in North Carolina. Ex-Confederate extremists took back most of the state in the election of 1870 after a brief biracial coalition period in power from 1868 to 1870. Republican governor William Holden, however, like Clayton in Arkansas and Davis in Texas, formed and used state militiamen to fight the KKK in North Carolina. Holden actually took inspiration from Powell Clayton's defeat of the KKK in Arkansas.[38] For his use of state troops to fight and arrest the KKK and support African American civil rights, Holden became the first governor impeached and removed from office in U.S. history. This, of course, happened when ex-Confederate extremist Democrats took over the legislature in 1871. The North Carolina Senate would finally pardon him in 2011. Holden was born in North Carolina and voted for secession but became an early Republican. Though a strong advocate of peace during the American Civil War, he knew when to turn to war in the face of KKK guerilla terror in 1870. Several particularly savage assassinations of members of the biracial coalition inspired his formation and deployment of a state militia. First was the Klan assassination, really an execution, of State Senator John W. Stephens. Like Ashburn in Georgia, Stephens was a white man who strongly supported African American rights. He had served the Confederacy during the American Civil War, yet after the war he became a Freedmen's Bureau agent and then a Republican and member of the Union League. Serving in the Freedmen's Bureau appears to have raised his consciousness about African American rights, but his biography is obscured by slander from ex-Confederate extremists then and since. All sources agree that he worked around Yanceyville, North Carolina, to organize the African American majority in the region. In North Carolina, as in Alabama, most of the Republican officeholders were local white members of the biracial coalition. African American voters around Yanceyville recognized an ally and elected Stephens to the state senate in 1868. Ex-Confederate extremists in Caswell County expelled him from the Methodist Church and openly hated him. Stephens knew this all too well and always armed himself. The local KKK "tried" him in absentia and sentenced him to death in one of their secret meetings. On May 21, 1870, they arranged to execute him in a backroom of the Caswell County Courthouse. A newspaper from the time reported that

> a public Democratic meeting was in progress in the court-house at Yanceyville, the county seat of Caswell; that Stephens was in attendance on that meeting; that a prominent Democrat of Caswell approached Stephens with a smile, and asked him to go down-stairs with him. Stephens assented, and they went into a room formerly occupied by the Clerk of the Court of Equity; that as soon as they entered the room the door was locked; that there were in the room

> eight white men and one negro. Stephens was surprised to find the room full of men, and was struck with horror when a rope, fixed as a lasso, was thrown over his neck from behind, and he was told by the spokesman of the Kuklux crowd that he must renounce his Republican principles; that he believed they were right, and that the Republic would prosper if they were carried out; that he could not leave the country and State, because his all was there; that the colored people looked upon him as a leader, that they depended on him, and that he could not desert them. Stephens was then told that he must die. He then asked to be allowed to take a last look from the window of the office, at his home and any of his family that might be in view. The request was granted, and when Stephens stepped to the window he beheld his little home and his two little children playing in front of his house. He was then thrown down on a table, two of the Kuklux holding his arms. The rope was ordered to be drawn tighter, and the negro was ordered to get a bucket to catch the blood. This done, one of the crowd severed the jugular vein, the negro caught the blood in the bucket, and Stephens was dead. His body was laid on a pile of wood in the room, and the murderers went up-stairs, took part in the meeting, and stamped and applauded Democratic speeches.[39]

As with almost all such incidents of the Southern Civil War, elements of this account were disputed by both the KKK and Stephens's allies, but it is likely an accurate account. The Klan was a secret terrorist organization that deliberately lied under oath to cover up its activities and kept few records. Most of its attacks were common knowledge and as subsequent generations of southern and indeed northern whites took pride in its acts, violent acts were recorded and celebrated—sometimes with public historical plaques.

Stephens's assassination received much publicity because he was white, but numerous African American leaders in North Carolina also fell during the guerilla phase of the Southern Civil War. Wyatt Outlaw, who went from slavery to service in the Union army, had been politically active in North Central North Carolina. The KKK lynched him in February 1870, almost three months before the Stephens killing. The North Carolina KKK campaign of terror against African American churches, schools, and communities looked depressingly like the rest of the South and suppressed the vote by the fall of 1870.[40] Ex-Confederate extremists celebrated a military and political triumph. At least history knows the year 1870 as a year of war in North Carolina, though few Americans are aware of the event. The conflict was named the Kirk-Holden War.

The clash between the Klan and the state militia in the Kirk-Holden War included at least one small battle with significant bloodshed and several minor clashes, totaling about a dozen casualties on each side. Governor Holden organized a militia of about six hundred. The soldiers were almost entirely white, but a few active troops were likely African American.[41] A force of three hundred went into the field to crush the KKK in Alamance and Caswell Counties. Each of these counties had experienced a virtual KKK coup d'état after the murders of Outlaw and Stephens. Holden in his letters to the chief justice of the North Carolina Supreme Court, R. M. Pearson, said he planned to use martial law and suspension of habeas corpus to defeat "insurgents" and "suppress insurrection." Holden specifically mentioned that regular courts did not work in KKK trials because whites always came forward to commit perjury unblushingly.[42] These were exactly the tactics and causes Clayton cited in Arkansas and Davis in Texas when they took the war to the KKK. Holden's formation of the militia and sending them into the field under martial law frightened ex-Confederate extremists, but not as much as the man he put in command: George W. Kirk—the other half of the Kirk-Holden War. Colonel Kirk was in some ways the anti–Nathan Bedford Forrest of the biracial coalition. His service in the American Civil War made him the perfect instrument to crush the KKK in North Carolina. Like Nathan Bedford Forrest, Kirk was a tough white Tennessean, but he had signed up for the Union cavalry in a unit with other hardscrabble East Tennesseans and Western North Carolinians called the Third North Carolina Mounted Infantry. He actively recruited local unionist guerillas and Confederate deserters and went after Confederate guerilla units, who often had Cherokees in their cavalry. A vicious war of hit-and-run raids broke out in Western North Carolina, and Colonel Kirk fought a total war. In the last years of the American Civil War, guerilla and even brutal neighbor-on-neighbor partisan fighting broke out all over the Confederacy as they did in Western North Carolina. Even in this context, Colonel Kirk's two mobile regiments became famous for hard fighting. They burned Confederate Camp Vance in Morganton, which housed a large cache of Confederate supplies. Kirk raided the towns of Warm Springs and Mars Hill, North Carolina. Most spectacularly, in February 1865 he burned and pillaged Waynesville. The Southern Civil War constituted a continuation of this harsh warfare inside the South and between southerners at the end of the American Civil War. In North Carolina, as across the South, the combatants themselves were often the same as they had been in the American Civil War. Colonel Kirk was a prime example of the continuation of Civil War service, as Holden called him back to North Carolina from Tennessee to crush the KKK in 1870. Kirk recruited men from his old units for the state militia and rode with them to protect democracy and suppress insurrection.

In July 1870 Kirk and his men descended on Yanceyville and arrested all the leading ex-Confederates, commonly known to be in the KKK. Sheriffs, lawyers, ex-congressmen, military officers, and the wealthiest leaders of the town were all rounded up and detained for weeks. Over the next few days as many as one hundred were jailed. In a familiar tale, the use of militia and meeting guerilla tactics with strong counterinsurgency measures backfired politically, though it worked militarily. Kirk's forces had victories in several small battles with KKK allies who rode into towns near Yanceyville in counterraids. Most of the KKK riders got away. Likewise, local courts released all the detained ex-Confederate extremists without trial or punishment, and instead they pushed for the arrest of Kirk and Holden.[43] Ultimately, Kirk and Holden could not protect voters in the 1870 election, so their war was little more effective than the performance of less combative state governments. Democrats won the legislature in August via intimidation. Victory came also by arguing that a mixed-race militia and suppression of rights by state military forces was unacceptable and a greater threat than white vigilantism aimed at African Americans and their white allies. Kirk, the ultimate survivor, fled back to Tennessee and, in appreciation of his service, won appointment by Republicans as a police officer in Washington, D.C. Holden, after his impeachment and removal, also moved to Washington, and Republicans rewarded him with the federal office of postmaster in North Carolina. The election of 1872 saw little violence in the state, and the Republican candidate and acting governor after Holden's removal, Tod Caldwell, retained the governorship although the Democrats controlled the legislature.[44] After Caldwell died, his lieutenant governor Curtis Brogden took the post, but in the election of 1876 the former Confederate governor and Democrat Zebulon Vance came back into office, dramatically signaling the end of Reconstruction, though the Democrats had controlled of most of the state after 1871. African Americans in the state received no federal sinecures and were removed from office and excluded from public ceremonies and forced into a new period of subjugation.[45] North Carolinian George H. White was the last African American in the House of Representatives from the South, leaving office in 1901. As the next chapter will note, the 1890s saw a resurgence of African American political participation in North Carolina and white supremacist violence to repress it.

States not retaken by the ex-Confederate extremists in the guerilla phase of the Southern Civil War also saw triumphs of guerilla warfare in this period. Mississippi was very bloody in all three phases of the war, and it saw one of the most audacious KKK-style actions during the guerilla phase. The massacre in Meridian in East Central Mississippi in March 1871 is worth a book of its own. The ex-Confederate extremist attack on the courthouse in Meridian helped push the transition from the guerilla tactics of the second phase of the war to the open paramilitary actions of the final phase. The Meridian attack was brazen and violent yet met with no federal military or legal response. This lack of response led ex-Confederate extremists to realize that hiding their identities and employing hit-and-run guerilla tactics were unnecessary. Complete disrespect for legal and political authority also inspired the battle at Meridian. Anti-Klan strictures in the Civil Rights Act of 1866 and in the Enforcement Acts of 1870 and 1871 (often called the Klan Acts) had made violence carried out in disguise a federal crime. Despite their intended purpose to suppress the KKK, these laws were used against African Americans in Mississippi who were accused of violence in disguise. The white Republican mayor of Meridian, William Sturgis, had many African American protégés, including preacher and state legislator J. Aaron Moore, who helped organize voters in the region, and political aides Warren Tyler and William Clopton. After the Klan assaulted Joseph Williams, an African American on the Lauderdale County board of supervisors, at his home, Tyler and Clopton held a protest rally. African Americans also armed and organized self-defense units more intensely after the rally, though they had been organizing militia-style units for months by the time of the rally. Another impetus for organizing self-defense units was the predation of quasi-slave catchers in the areas.[46]

Meridian was near the Alabama border, and African Americans had been moving from that state into Lauderdale County, where Meridian was the county seat. A push-and-pull migration was under way from western Alabama to Lauderdale County, as African Americans tried to escape the atrocious conditions in Alabama. Lauderdale offered a bastion of hope with its politically powerful and organized African Americans bolstered by the strong Republican biracial coalition. The Klan leader and deputy sheriff of Livingston, Alabama, Adam Kennard, was hunting Alabama African Americans who fled coerced work and debt contracts that were evolving into the neo-slavery of sharecropping and convict leasing. Daniel Price had tried to lead African American self-defense and political organization in Livingston and encouraged migration across the river to Lauderdale, where he himself had to flee after being attacked by the KKK for teaching school for formerly enslaved people and their children.

Deputy Kennard, who was in effect a KKK bounty hunter—a Reconstruction continuation of a patroller for runaways, crossed into Mississippi with a KKK detachment to detain and return several Alabama African American workers, but the biracial coalition government of Meridian refused to cooperate. After Kennard and his men refused to leave the area and continued to harass and intimidate African Americans, Price ambushed Kennard with a group of armed, masked African Americans, beat him, and transported the bounty hunter out of the area. Price was then arrested under the clause of the Civil Rights Act intended to combat the Klan. To this point, no ex-Confederate extremists had been arrested under this act in Mississippi. African Americans around Meridian were irate at this imbalance of justice and stepped up their military training and organization of armaments, which too often were just swords and shotguns. Ex-Confederate extremists also armed (usually with military rifles) and organized. Price's sensational arrest and trial, which ran for weeks, laid the groundwork for a bloody courthouse battle on March 6, 1871, as tensions increased and an arms race escalated. Both sides vowed not to let the court verdict keep them from rescuing or killing Price. Price's trial would have become a battle between the two armed camps but for the wise leadership of Republican mayor Sturgis. Sturgis knew that dozens of KKK murders and assaults of the biracial coalition in the area had gone unpunished and that African American grievances were valid. He also despised Kennard and the Klan that came into his city from outlying areas and from Alabama. He also knew that Price was defiant and that local African Americans were not bluffing. Of course, Sturgis knew that the same was even more true of the more heavily armed white supremacists who were scandalized by the very existence of Price and the example of armed African American self-defense he embodied and inspired. Ex-Confederate extremists from Alabama made a battle more likely when around sixty crossed state lines to "witness" Price's trial. Mayor Sturgis postponed the trial twice, and during a delay the Alabamians carried out Kennard's mission and grabbed several African Americans they claimed were "escaped" Alabama workers. African Americans around Meridian became angrier and more organized at this outrage. At this point, Sturgis agreed to let Price go free if he left the area. Ex-Confederate extremists were apoplectic at this and especially angry with Sturgis.[47]

The hostilities simmered and would boil over in a courthouse battle on March 6, 1871. With Sturgis under pressure from white supremacists, both local and those coming from Alabama and surrounding counties, he called for federal troops. A detachment arrived, but, in classic guerilla fashion, the armed ex-Confederate extremists did not come out into the open. They waited. When the federals went back to Jackson, the state capital, Aaron Moore came to Meridian from Jackson where he was a state legislator. He had helped organize African American voters when suffrage came to Mississippi, largely organized at the African American church where he was a preacher. He came to Meridian to build the morale of the African American community and support Mayor Sturgis. Moore joined Sturgis's African American political aides Tyler and Clopton in organizing a massive biracial coalition political rally at the courthouse on March 4. They also continued to organize African American armed units and self-defense. Armed ex-Confederate extremists decided that all these Republican representatives of the biracial coalition should be forced to leave the county or be killed. They burned the store owned by Mayor Sturgis's brother, Theodore, which caused most of the business district to burn. As with all KKK-style guerilla and terror activities, their tactics and secrecy made it hard to prove they set the fire. The proof that an active ex-Confederate extremist conspiracy was underway in this string of events was in what they did next. They raised the false alarm that African Americans were going to burn down the town and carry out an armed massacre of whites. They had the white sheriff arrest Moore, Tyler, and Clopton for "inciting riot," set up a committee to expel Mayor Sturgis from the region, and even bothered to press charges again against the long-gone Daniel Price.[48]

In even more conclusive evidence of an ex-Confederate extremist orchestrated stratagem, they made a surprise attack on the trial of Moore, Tyler, and Clopton. When the trial began on March 6, the ex-

Confederate extremists, in a clearly premeditated plan, brought guns into the courtroom packed with Republicans and white Democrats from outlying regions. There they shot dead the white Republican judge, E. L. Bramlette, and an African American policeman. They then went after Tyler, Clopton, and Moore. Armed whites were also waiting outside the courthouse. Clopton and Tyler were wounded in the courtroom. Tyler jumped out a window, was hunted down, and shot multiple times as he lay injured from his jump. Clopton was wounded in the courtroom shootout and could not move, so the ex-Confederate extremists threw Clopton out a high window, let him linger in agony for hours, and then cut his throat. State legislator Moore was reported dead in newspaper accounts.[49] Yet as with so much in the Southern Civil War, records are hazy and conflicting when not just deliberate white supremacist falsehoods.[50] Moore lay in the courthouse feigning death, then snuck out along the railroad tracks back toward Jackson. The KKK chased him for forty-five miles but never caught him. The ex-Confederate extremists spread out over the area, slaughtering the town's prominent African Americans and engaging in running gun battles with the biracial coalition. The number of dead reached thirty African Americans in addition to Judge Bramlette, but more dead probably went uncounted.[51] Federal troops returned a few days too late. The KKK guerillas again melted away. Mayor Sturgis, like Moore, hid, was captured, and then, as a condition of release, fled all the way to New York City. From there he wrote an account of the massacre for the *New York Daily Tribune*. He denounced the KKK and rightly warned the North that a war, like Clayton's, Davis's, and Kirk and Holden's, needed to be fought against ex-Confederate extremists everywhere in the South. He wrote: "I am much a sufferer in pain and feeling, but I believe that the State of Mississippi is able to indemnify me. Let me urge the necessity of having martial law proclaimed through every Southern State. The soldiery to be sent there should be quartered on the Rebels. Leniency will not do. Gratitude, they have none. Reciprocation of favors they never dream of."[52] Of course, no such thing happened, and no KKK members faced charges, let alone trial, for the Meridian Massacre. Ex-Confederate extremists were emboldened across the South and especially in Mississippi where the Meridian example of forming white "militias," paramilitaries really, expanded everywhere they had not retaken state and local governments.

Like Mississippi, Louisiana would make it through the guerilla phase of the Southern Civil War with its biracial government still intact, but that did not mean it was spared KKK-style guerilla horrors between 1868 and 1872. Klan imitators in Louisiana went by many names, including, as at Opelousas, the Knights of the White Camellia. Their tactics hardly varied from those throughout the region. They came out in force before elections to suppress the vote of the biracial coalition and met African American armed self-defense with pathological brutality. Journalist Charles Lane described the violence in parts of Louisiana in just a few days around the election of 1868:

> In the second half of 1868, white terrorists tried to prevent the Republicans from winning the November presidential election. Over three days in September, they killed some two hundred freedmen in St. Landry Parish. Later in the month, in Bossier Parish, just across the Red River from Shreveport, a drunken trader from Arkansas shot an elderly black Republican. When men of color organized a posse to capture the gunman, the "Negro revolt" electrified whites, who killed and wounded several colored men. The Negroes fired back and killed two whites. Hundreds of armed whites poured into Bossier Parish, scouring the countryside for armed Negroes—which soon turned into an all-out "nigger hunt," complete with bloodhounds. The killing lasted through October and the death toll reached 168. Later a congressional investigation counted 1,081 political murders in Louisiana between April and November of 1868. The vast majority of the victims were Negroes. Some 135 people were shot and wounded; 507 were whipped, clubbed, threatened or otherwise "outraged." The terror was so intense that the Republican Party stopped campaigning in the final week of the race and all but conceded the presidential vote to the Democrats.[53]

Even though Louisiana Republicans held on to state power until 1876, they hung on under a state of war and tremendous political losses in parishes, towns, and municipalities attacked by guerilla insurgents. The violence showed the potential for KKK-style guerilla and terrorist tactics to transform into open paramilitary action. South Carolina, like Louisiana and Mississippi with an African American majority and a Republican state government that held out until 1876, also saw intense warfare in the guerilla phase of the war that began to transform into the open paramilitary warfare that would characterize the final phase of the war in these three states (and to a lesser extent in Florida) in 1868–1872.

The transition took place as ex-Confederate extremists became more confident that they would not be prosecuted or hunted down and killed by local biracial coalition governments or the federal government. The disguises came off, and assassination and hit-and run-tactics, while not abandoned, were less necessary when ex-Confederate extremist armies could make quick work of Republican militias, repress unionist meetings and voting, and overturn governance. South Carolina, which had an even larger African American majority than Mississippi, saw this transition take place in the towns of Laurensville and Chester. The Laurensville clash, after the election of 1870, anticipated larger battles in Hamburg, South Carolina, and Colfax, Louisiana, in the next phase of the war as the African American militia in the town was ambushed by KKK snipers and took refuge in the local armory. The Klan then assaulted the armory and took the building, killing nine.[54]

Chester County, South Carolina, was a Klan hotbed too, but the town of Chester had a biracial coalition government and an effective militia led by Captain James Wilkes. The KKK attacked the home of an African American militiaman, Jim Woods, with a typical nighttime terror raid, but they were driven off. Captain Wilkes instituted patrols for the KKK along the town's roads. After the attack at Woods's home, Wilkes went to the armory in Chester for more munitions and men. The sight of the almost entirely African American militia on the streets brought white supremacist panic and rumors of race war. KKK members poured into town by train from the heavily ex-Confederate extremist town of Rock Hill and its surrounding rural areas, including neighboring North Carolina. Although they were not as trained or as highly organized as paramilitary ex-Confederate extremist armies would be after 1872, on March 4, 1871, an ex-Confederate extremist army had mobilized by rail in the open, undisguised in daylight. This would become a common sight in the coming years. In a preview of battles in the paramilitary phase of the war at Liberty Place, Colfax, Hamburg, and elsewhere, the biracial coalition militia met the trains at the rail station and were defeated by Confederate training. Volley fire was exchanged at the center of town, and, after a brief truce, the biracial coalition militia retreated to an African American church near Chester and dug in. The ex-Confederate extremists flanked their lines and scattered the militia, which carried out a disciplined retreat for a mile and then scattered. Ex-Confederate extremists were emboldened by the political outcome of the Chester battle. South Carolina Republican governor Robert

Scott, a former Union general from Pennsylvania and a Freedmen's Bureau agent in the state since 1865, had organized twenty thousand African Americans into local units to guard ballot boxes for the election of 1871. Although only half were armed, they faced the KKK in many skirmishes. After the Laurensville and Chester battles and a similar battle in Unionville, Governor Scott ordered all local militia companies disbanded and disarmed.[55] Ex-Confederate extremist paramilitaries would swell across South Carolina and the other southern states in which they had not triumphed by 1872.

CHAPTER FOUR

The Paramilitary Phase, 1872–1877

White Supremacist Armies

The permanent defeat of five of the biracial coalition state governments during the guerilla phase of the Southern Civil War opened the way for the third phase of the war from 1872–1877. In this phase, ex-Confederate extremist hit-and-run tactics were no longer necessary since prosecution and federal intervention had proven unlikely. Ex-Confederate extremist insurgents thus escalated to open paramilitary warfare using organized statewide armies. In two states, Alabama and Arkansas, defeat came early in this phase. Alabama was unique in that the KKK had triumphed in the guerilla phase, but then the biracial coalition regained wide state power in elections. In 1874 large ex-Confederate extremist paramilitaries would come out to defeat them for good. Arkansas had a paramilitary civil war in the state, the Brooks-Baxter War, which would end with the triumph of white supremacist forces in 1874. The states in which ex-Confederate extremists were denied power the longest were those with the largest African American populations and the largest federal installations and troop numbers (though these were low everywhere). In these states—Louisiana, Mississippi, South Carolina, and Florida—biracial coalitions hung on to the state governments and some county-wide power, at least in name, until 1876. Most counties even in these states were effectively under ex-Confederate extremist military control by 1872 (from which political control would soon follow). Louisiana, Mississippi, and South Carolina saw the worst and most extended conventional military violence in the Southern Civil War and the most conventional battles in this phase. Especially in Louisiana and Mississippi, open battles between ex-Confederate extremist paramilitaries and biracial government forces raged. Famously, in the election year of 1876, all these last bastions of democracy and attempts to follow civil rights laws were utterly defeated in the face of ex-Confederate extremist armies and national betrayal.

With the Compromise of 1877, the federal government and national Republican Party abandoned these last biracial coalition governments. This sad bargain constitutes the settlement that ended the Southern Civil War. Northerners got a bearded Republican midwestern Rutherford B. Hayes, acknowledged as the president by the South in a close election, as they had failed to do in 1860 when much of the South would not accept Lincoln. But the ex-Confederate extremists got complete control of the South in exchange, without federal interference, and an agreement that all federal troops would be withdrawn from the South—where they were symbolically protecting the last democratically elected governments of the region. Southern unionists and their biracial coalition got nothing. The northern Republicans in exchange for this capitulation to ex-Confederate extremists received the disputed Electoral College votes of Florida, Louisiana, and South Carolina. These electoral votes gave the Republican candidate, Hayes, the presidency by a single vote. The South would no longer dominate the federal government as it had much of 1789–1860, but neither would the federal government control the South. A local, violent, white supremacist minority would rule this nondemocratic region for one hundred years. In 1877 the North retreated from the South. The side that retreats from the battlefield, even in a largely stalemate battle like Antietam, is deemed the loser of the battle. At the end of the Southern Civil War in 1877, the North retreated from the South, so in a very real sense the South won the concluding portion of the civil wars of 1861–1877. It is an open question as to who won the wider multiwar conflict as a whole. No one, really.

This chapter will look at the paramilitary phase of the Southern Civil War on a state-by-state basis, rather than strictly chronologically, since its battles were to control state governments. Alabama and Arkansas, however, come first both chronologically and in the catalog of states since the battles were over first and most quickly in these states. Alabama and Arkansas also had unique stories. The chapter then examines Louisiana, which had the largest battles, South Carolina, and then Mississippi. The Compromise of 1877 and the end of the Southern Civil War bring all the state stories together. The Compromise of 1877, however, is not the end of the story of white supremacist paramilitaries. The Southern Civil War invented traditions of racial terror, and white supremacist paramilitary attacks on African American communities would continue into the late nineteenth century and early twentieth century. As the story of the Southern Civil War demonstrates, brutal civil wars are not easily ended.

Alabama alone switched back to a biracial Republican government after the initial triumph of the KKK in 1870. KKK insurgents helped deliver the state to the Democratic Party and white supremacy that year. But Democratic governor Robert Burns Lindsay discouraged warfare and terror upon taking office in 1870. Without KKK terrorism in force, the Republicans came back to the polls in 1872. The election reversal was unique in the Southern Civil War, but otherwise things went similarly to how they went elsewhere. Alabama's ex-Confederate extremists raised paramilitary armies, abandoning the guerilla tactics of the second phase of the war, just like all southern states not already under ex-Confederate extremist control did in 1872. White unionist David P. Lewis won the governorship, and white southern officeholders like Lewis dominated Alabama's biracial coalition, as in most states, but Alabama also elected three African Americans to Congress and many to the state legislature. This bright moment lasted but a single term as massive ex-Confederate extremist paramilitary forces arose just as the Panic of 1873 and subsequent depression decimated the economy and unfairly discredited biracial coalition leadership. At the same time, most of the semblance of federal military force abandoned the field, or their leaders lost the will to use the few troops that were in southern states.[1] This was especially true in Alabama, where the paramilitary had an enormous advantage in arms, supplies, military experience, numbers, and morale. The ex-Confederate extremist White League paramilitary particularly targeted the election of 1874 and came out in full force. In Eufaula, a biracial coalition stronghold, the White League attacked polling places on Election Day, November 3, and in a lopsided battle inflicted at minimum eighty casualties on African American voters and skirmishers. In Spring Hill the paramilitary even killed the teenage son of the white Republican town judge. The battle around Eufaula resembled the earlier clash at Eutaw in the guerilla phase of the war that had led to the ex-Confederate extremist triumph via violence in the election of 1870. Barbour County, which had an African American majority, was taken over in 1872 by the White League. The ex-Confederate extremist paramilitary declared Democrats the victors for every office in the county, and the votes of African American and white Republicans not driven from the polls by force were simply destroyed. The election of 1874 after the Eufaula battle went the same way, but this time the ex-Confederate extremists made sure to keep election terror in place. Two-party biracial democracy would not visit the state again until the 1960s.

Arkansas also turned into open paramilitary war after ex-Confederate extremist insurgent guerillas were defeated by Powell Clayton in 1869. Militias were engaged on both sides of the infamous Brooks-Baxter War of 1874. In the statewide elections in Arkansas that year, Joseph Brooks and Elisha Baxter, both running as unionists, each claimed to have been elected governor. Baxter was a Clayton ally and had been inaugurated as governor in 1872, but he had quickly turned conservative and appointed ex-Confederates to office and started to re-enfranchise them.[2] In 1874 a court ruled that Brooks, who continued to be a solid Republican, unionist, and advocate of civil rights, had won the governorship. His forces, which were largely African American, seized the arsenal in Little Rock and marched through the statehouse. Brooks's forces installed artillery at their positions throughout the city, including the arsenal and the statehouse, and on April 20 general fire was exchanged. Brooks's biracial militia captured Baxter but inexplicably let him go, and he then organized ex-Confederate extremist resistance. A serious battle took place in Pine Bluff, and in Little Rock street fighting exploded. Baxter's forces quickly became the shock troops of conservativism as Baxter supported and brought about ex-Confederate political rehabilitation. When the war heated up in 1874, most of his forces were white supremacist Democrats. Most of the African Americans in Arkansas thus supported Brooks, and African American militias eventually made up almost all of his troops. The events of the war were incredibly complex, but the fighting ended where all the warfare of Reconstruction did, with Baxter's forces solid white supremacists and Brooks's forces supporting African American rights. Not surprisingly, due to better resources and numbers and eventual federal legal support, Baxter's white supremacists won.[3]

Befitting the Southern Civil War's phase of open paramilitary warfare after 1872, both sides had well-armed armies numbering in the thousands, and both obtained artillery. Baxter, famously, had a cannon installed in Little Rock that is still there. Both sides used steamboats and railroads to move troops, and both had ex-Confederates commanding their militias. The clashes are underdocumented, but the number killed over the whole course of the Brooks-Baxter War reached two hundred—there were certainly that many total wounded, likely triple that number. Baxter forces killed at least nine and wounded three times that number in a one-sided battle at New Gascony. On May 4, a more even firefight in Arkansas Post killed and wounded about the same number. On May 8, Brooks's forces lost a steamboat at the most famous battle, the Battle of Palarm, which had total casualties of nearly one hundred killed and wounded.[4] On the last day of the Brooks-Baxter War, a four-hour battle raged in the capital. The next day the Grant administration ended the warfare by declaring the ex-Confederate sympathizer Baxter the rightful governor.[5] As happened across the South, national Republicans realized that supporting African American rights brought ceaseless warfare, while capitulating to the ex-Confederate extremists brought stability. This stability came via the silence of the grave for the biracial coalition. Arkansas had thus passed into conservative control in 1872 when Baxter had taken office, though no one knew it at the time, and in the next election, in 1874, it passed into Democratic control. Clayton, by then a U.S. senator for Arkansas, naturally supported Brooks, and the vast majority of African Americans eventually supported him. Clayton even continued the fight after Grant assured Brooks's defeat in 1874. Clayton remarkably did not leave the state, where threats from local guerillas in 1866 had driven him into politics, until 1912, two years before his death at the age of eighty-one. He remained a staunch Republican and advocate for fair elections and African American rights and lived under constant threat of assassination. These were not idle threats, given his brother's assassination in the state in 1889 and an earlier attempt on Clayton when he was governor. Clayton does not even have a controversial memorial or statue in Arkansas but was buried with full national honors and a prominent marker in Arlington National Cemetery.

A misremembered war is not likely to produce figures that become part of the popular historical memory and are marked with monuments. The Ku Klux Klan and its leaders, like Nathan Bedford Forrest, are far better remembered and memorialized than the heroic white and African American southerners who fought for democracy and racial justice. Forrest has more markers and monuments commemorating him in Tennessee than any other person in the state, including Andrew Jackson.[6] Perhaps this memorialization of white supremacist southerners is not surprising. Victors write history, and the ex-Confederate extremists were the decisive victors of the Southern Civil War of 1865–1877. But Confederate monuments have been removed throughout the South, especially since the Civil War sesquicentennial, and monuments to real heroes would more appropriately commemorate the Southern Civil War. Governor Edmund Davis of Texas, Governor Powell Clayton of Arkansas, Governor Adelbert Ames of Mississippi, and James Longstreet, military commander of Louisiana, provide powerful case studies of how southern unionists lost the Southern Civil War but also how their efforts deserve a more prominent place in textbooks and popular memory. All four men were decorated generals in the Civil War and then led the forces of their respective states in the open warfare against white supremacist guerillas and paramilitaries between 1868 and 1877. Yet their names and the names of the battles they fought are largely lost to history even in their home states, where none of them are memorialized by major historical sites.

Longstreet may not appear to fit on a list of forgotten military leaders, since he was Lee's second in command, but his role at the center of the paramilitary phase of the Southern Civil War in Louisiana is less well-known. When the American Civil War was over, Longstreet was singled out by President Johnson, along with Lee and Jefferson Davis, as one of the three men so important to the Confederate cause that he would never receive a pardon. Longstreet fought three years and ten months for the Confederacy, but he would then fight for thirty-nine years against the forces of white supremacy and oppression in the aftermath of the Civil War. For this, he was vilified by his former Confederate cohorts.[7] He was one of the few major Confederate field officers who joined the Republican Party and took up arms against ex-Confederate extremists.[8] His Civil War record would be distorted because of this civil rights stance, and his military reputation in that conflict has only been restored in recent years. Not until 1998 was a statue of Longstreet placed on the Gettysburg battlefield site even though he gave the final order for Pickett's Charge. Dozens of Confederates were memorialized at Gettysburg before him. Only since the late 1990s have historians sympathetically chronicled Longstreet's military leadership in protecting civil rights after 1865. Longstreet's role in Reconstruction is a more amazing story than his American Civil War career.

Like Robert E. Lee, Longstreet was a reluctant Confederate and an opponent of secession at the start of the Civil War. Longstreet was born in the Edgefield District of South Carolina, a hotbed of racial violence

Former Confederate general James Longstreet (1821–1904) commanded biracial coalition forces in Louisiana during the Southern Civil War. (Library of Congress)

that produced Preston Brooks, the man who caned William Sumner on the floor of the Senate in 1856. Edgefield had a long, bloody history of slavery, dueling, feuds, and white supremacy. In the twentieth century, ultraconservative U.S. senator Strom Thurmond's family lived there.[9]

As a child, Longstreet was sent to Gainesville, Georgia, to attend school and live with his uncle's family. After his father's death, Longstreet lived permanently with and was raised by his uncle Augustus Baldwin Longstreet, an author and minister who propounded the southern argument that slavery was ordained by God.[10] Despite this condemnable tutelage and an equally condemnable period of enslaving a few African Americans himself prior to the Civil War, James Longstreet grew to dislike slavery. His experiences at West Point and in the army were much more formative than his deep southern roots. At West Point he was popular and friendly with several of the future leaders of the Union war efforts, including George Thomas, William Rosecrans, John Pope, and, most importantly, Ulysses Grant. Longstreet was stationed with Grant shortly after graduation from West Point, and the two friends became closer when Grant courted and married Longstreet's cousin Julia Dent. Debate has ensued in historical circles over whether or not Longstreet was Grant's best man at his wedding, an ill-defined role at the time anyway, but Longstreet was at the wedding as Grant's principal friend, and "the two men considered each other kin."[11] Longstreet's closeness to both Lee and Grant put him in a vital position as the American Civil War drew to a close. He, like Lee, discouraged calls from Jefferson Davis and many in their army to "take to the hills" and start a guerilla war, and urged surrender to Grant.[12] When the KKK did initiate guerilla war, Longstreet would instead lead biracial armies of unionists against ex-Confederate extremists as major general in command of all Louisiana militia and state police forces.

In 1865 Longstreet joined the Republican Party and relocated to New Orleans to reform the South in the hotbed of Reconstruction and the war that would accompany it. Of all the states engaged in the Southern Civil War, none had larger or more dramatic battles than Louisiana.[13] Louisiana's population was evenly divided between African Americans and whites. Louisiana also had a strong history of African American military participation and a long federal occupation of the state during the American Civil War. Longstreet helped marshal these forces by organizing a biracial state militia. From 1867 to 1871 he faced scattered guerilla action and small-scale urban sniping by local groups like the Knights of the White Camellia. However, the Louisiana forces of white supremacy pioneered the switch from KKK guerilla tactics to White League military organization and open paramilitary violence after 1872. The two most famous battles of the Southern Civil War took place in Louisiana in this period, the Battles of Colfax and Liberty Place, but they were not isolated engagements. Longstreet was centrally involved in the Battle of Liberty Place as described at the beginning of this book, but local African American forces fought alone at Colfax in 1873. Unfortunately, Longstreet could not get state forces to the aid of African American forces at Colfax before ex-Confederate extremist paramilitaries massacred them.

Louisiana offers the best case study of the paramilitary phase of the Southern Civil War. The Battle of Liberty Place in 1874 was the largest engagement of the Southern Civil War. As described in the introduction, the battle took place on the streets of New Orleans on September 14, 1874, and engaged forces that numbered in the thousands. The highest estimate has the ex-Confederate paramilitary at nine thousand men and the state police and militia at thirty-four hundred.[14] In an orchestrated attack, the ex-Confederate extremists who dubbed themselves the White League devised barricades along Poydras Street and armed behind them. The White League had openly protested the biracial coalition government of Governor William Pitt Kellogg, whose election and legitimacy they disputed, and they intimidated and attacked voters who supported Kellogg before resorting to open warfare. Now the ex-Confederate extremists faced Longstreet, the ex-Confederate turned biracial coalition opponent. Longstreet led the combined forces of state government—the biracial militia of New Orleans and the city's biracial police—against his former Confederate compatriots. The outnumbered biracial coalition army, fighting for fair elections and civil rights and led by one of the most famous Confederate heroes, were well equipped with Gatling guns and artillery pieces. But the more battle-hardened ex-Confederate extremists brought expert volley fire to bear on the police. The volley fire displayed their Confederate training. More dramatically, as the government forces broke and retreated, the ex-Confederate extremist paramilitary launched a disciplined charge as they screamed the rebel yell. The biracial militia, like the police, were overwhelmed and retreated in disorder, leaving the ex-Confederate extremists to rule the city. The casualties were estimated at thirteen dead and seventy wounded for the biracial coalition and sixteen dead (plus six bystanders) and an unknown number of wounded for the White League paramilitary.[15] Both General A. S. Badger of the Metropolitan Police and General Longstreet were wounded and captured. Even when federal troops negotiated a march into the city as a show of force to support the duly elected Republican governor Kellogg and his biracial coalition that numerically dominated the state, the White League paramilitary remained in control of the streets of New Orleans and hauled off thousands of arms and some artillery from the state armory.[16] Federal forces protected Governor Kellogg and his key state buildings while the ex-Confederate extremist paramilitary dominated the city and countryside. Subsequent ex-Confederate extremist paramilitary violence in the next election season, in 1876, would not be met by a state government or federal counter force, not even one as meager as that of 1874.[17] Using the arms captured after the Battle of Liberty Place, ex-Confederate extremists would sweep to power in the 1876 election and impose white supremacist, nondemocratic rule in the state for almost one hundred years.[18]

The Battle of Liberty Place had the most troops involved of any clash in the Southern Civil War, but an earlier pitched battle in Louisiana had more casualties, perhaps the most in one day of the Southern Civil War.

The battle in Colfax in 1873, when acknowledged in public history, is remembered as a massacre, but it began, as did similar battles in Mississippi and South Carolina, as an example of African American self-defense in an open battle with an ex-Confederate paramilitary army.[19] Colfax was also a dramatic example of African American military leadership, embodied in William Ward. Ward had fought for the Union in the American Civil War, serving in a cavalry unit made up mostly of formerly enslaved African Americans, like himself, who had no opportunity to become officers. Ward was brash and defiant, a rugged individual who did things his own way. His confidence and boldness infuriated ex-Confederate extremists, but he enjoyed defying them. Ward was elected to the Louisiana State Legislature from the newly formed Grant Parish. He also commanded Company A, Sixth Infantry Regiment, of the Louisiana state militia. He was the white supremacists' worst fear. He took the fight to the KKK and ex-Confederate paramilitaries and inspired other African Americans to do the same.[20]

When in 1871 white supremacist paramilitaries headed by Sheriff Christopher Columbus Nash began threatening Grant Parish, Ward led the defense of the biracial coalition. His unit of African American Union veterans—still wearing old Union uniforms—cornered Nash's band in a gunfight that killed two ex-Confederate extremists.[21] A local judge, in a typical move, blocked a federal marshal from seizing Nash and five other ex-Confederate extremists. Ward ordered his African American militia unit to take them at bayonet point. Ward told the exasperated judge that his forces had superior jurisdiction, saying "Damn the court!"[22] Ward then shipped the ex-Confederate extremists to jail in New Orleans. Nash held a grudge when the courts released him and increased his raids on Grant Parish. Grant Parish Republicans were overwhelmingly African American, but they had key white allies. Under the threat of the paramilitary White League, Ward wrote to the governor for more troops and sent the message with a sympathetic prominent white local planter, William Smith Calhoun. Ex-Confederate extremist paramilitaries captured and severely beat Calhoun. Ward then set out for help himself, so he missed the Battle of Colfax that followed.

Colfax was the parish seat of Grant Parish. The parish had a geographical racial division, with African Americans along the Red River and whites in the hills. When the election of 1872 resulted in rival parish governments, African Americans came into Colfax to defend Republican office holders and drove off armed ex-Confederate extremists

This soldier, like William Ward, escaped slavery and served in the Union cavalry as a sergeant. (Library of Congress)

on April 1 and April 3. African Americans in Colfax improvised two cannons. Five hundred strong and trained by William Ward, they built trenches and barricades around the courthouse. When ex-Confederate extremist paramilitaries attacked again on April 5, they were driven away. As they retreated, the ex-Confederate extremists, led by Nash, killed African Americans outside the protected perimeter of Colfax. They also called up more paramilitary forces from neighboring white-dominated parishes. On April 13 an ex-Confederate paramilitary skirmish line of perhaps four hundred attacked an equal number of African Americans who were behind the trenches. Fighting continued for three hours, and then the ex-Confederate army gave the rebel yell as they fired and charged through an opening in the trenches. The African American lines broke, and the defenders fled into the courthouse. Exactly what happened next is uncertain. African Americans in the courthouse likely tried to surrender, but certainly the ex-Confederate paramilitaries shot unarmed African Americans who were leaving the building and then set fire to the building, chasing the African Americans and killing them as they ran. The ex-Confederate extremist paramilitaries slaughtered at least thirty African American prisoners under guard right away and many more later that night. The number of casualties from the Bat-

COLFAX RIOT
On this site occurred the Colfax Riot in which three white men and 150 negroes were slain. This event on April 13, 1873 marked the end of carpetbag misrule in the South.

This infamous Louisiana historical placard marks the location of the Battle of Colfax. (Richard E. Miller, 2010)

tle of Colfax, like so many statistics from the Southern Civil War, is unclear. A minimum of 62 African Americans and three ex-Confederate extremists died, with dozens of ex-Confederates and African Americans wounded. As many as 100 African Americans were massacred after they surrendered, with possible total dead around 150.[23] Federal forces did not arrive in Colfax until April 21. By then the ex-Confederate paramilitary forces had dispersed.[24] Despite seventy-two indictments, only nine ex-Confederate extremists were brought to trial. The U.S. Supreme Court would overturn the convictions of the three found guilty. The prosecutions of the ex-Confederate extremist killers led to the *Cruikshank* Supreme Court ruling that gutted the Fourteenth Amendment and validated ex-Confederate tactics in the war by only outlawing state violence, not "private" violence to deprive citizens of life, liberty, and property. The Supreme Court's decision made ex-Confederate extremist paramilitaries nearly immune from federal prosecution.[25] The example of Colfax and the effects of the court decision encouraged open "rifle club" and White League paramilitary violence in Mississippi and South Carolina.

The immediate effects of Colfax, however, were in Louisiana. In St. Martinsville in 1873 a White League paramilitary force of six hundred with two cannons clashed with the Metropolitan Police and disappeared when federal troops arrived to protect African Americans, though eleven eventually surrendered to federal forces and were released.[26] In the town of Coushatta, when African Americans defended themselves with effective rifle fire against armed ex-Confederate extremist scouting parties, over a thousand White League paramilitaries from the surrounding regions poured in.[27] An African American woman, Mathilda Floyd, testified to this invasion after ex-Confederate extremists came to kill her husband.[28] They rounded up Republicans and, as at Colfax, massacred them and mutilated the bodies of six captive white biracial coalition political leaders.[29] Lynching and assassinations followed in Coushatta, and the White League killed as many as twenty-five African American witnesses.[30] The most dramatic example of White League boldness in engaging in open military action came a month later in the battle of Liberty Place on September 14, 1874 as already described.

Longstreet was depressed by his capture and the triumph of ex-Confederate paramilitaries. He was so appalled at the violent backlash he faced that he fled New Orleans in 1875 and moved back to Georgia, but he did not drop his Republican activism. He served every Republican president through Theodore Roosevelt in varied posts such as railroad commissioner and ambassador to Turkey. He never stopped defending his positions in person or in print, dying in 1904 at the nadir of race relations and his own reputation. Although a statue of Longstreet was erected at Gettysburg in 1998, Louisiana did not memorialize Longstreet in any way, not even with a plaque. Instead, the City of New Orleans in 1891 placed a white supremacist monument to the forces that defeated him at Liberty Place. The public removal of that racist obelisk and its plaque honoring those who died for "white supremacy" may open the way for recognition of Longstreet's role.[31] In the 1980s the monument was a rallying point for the KKK and neo-Nazi groups and protested by African Americans and some city leaders. A building project allowed the city to "temporarily" remove the marker from Canal Street, but protests by neo-Confederates led to a compromise: reinstalling it at an obscure location on Iberville Street near a parking garage.[32] The obelisk was once at the center of city civic events and wreath displays for the white supremacist casualties, but in its obscure locale at the start of the twenty-first century it was known largely as a target for anti-KKK vandals. The city finally removed the monument in 2017 and

Antiracist slogans and symbols covered the Battle of Liberty Place monument prior to its removal in 2017, 126 years after its unveiling. (Matt Toups)

put it in storage. The Liberty Place obelisk story was only the beginning. New Orleans removed its Confederate monuments in 2017. Other cities removed Confederate monuments that year and in the wake of mass protests in 2020, though many remain in prominent locales across the South.[33]

Like Longstreet, William Ward fought ex-Confederate extremism in Louisiana long after any of hope of victory, if there ever was such hope. After the Colfax Battle and Massacre, Ward was elected as a Louisiana state legislator. When he first ran unsuccessfully for the legislator seat of Grant Parish, a white rival shot him three times, but he returned fire and hit his foe twice, recovered, and returned to New Orleans, where he won his seat. Subsequently, the state legislature expelled Representative Ward for waving his pistol during a legislative session. But Ward was a survivor, and when ex-Confederate extremists took over Louisiana and eliminated much of their political opposition, Ward became a Democrat and promoted the ex-Confederate extremist version of Reconstruction.[34] It is easy and appropriate to criticize Ward's choice today, but ex-Confederate extremists killed other African American leaders of the biracial coalition, such as Charles Caldwell of Mississippi, who continued the fight for civil rights. Prince Rivers of South Carolina, as the next section describes, went from being a soldier and influential judge to being a servant in the 1880s. Ward had always been a maverick, wild card, and survivor. Accommodation, many would say betrayal, kept him from Caldwell's and Prince's fates.

Unlike Louisiana, South Carolina had a large African American majority and the strongest federal military commitment in the Southern Civil War. The ex-Confederate extremist forces of South Carolina faced a long struggle to take back the state government.[35] African American organization was particularly strong in the state, but the pattern of ex-Confederate paramilitaries crushing African American self-defense also had one of its most dramatic examples in South Carolina. The Hamburg Battle in July 1876 in South Carolina, like the Battle of Colfax in Louisiana, arose from bold African American political and military leadership. Hamburg lay across the Savannah River from Augusta, Georgia, in Aiken County in the infamous Edgefield District. Like Grant Parish, Louisiana, Aiken County was a mainly African American area with a strong ex-Confederate extremist paramilitary in the surrounding white regions. South Carolina's white paramilitaries usually called themselves Red Shirts. To oppose the Red Shirt paramilitaries, Hamburg had an African American militia that was functionally a branch of the state national guard.

The town of Hamburg had largely been abandoned by the time of the American Civil War, but in the 1870s it was repopulated by freedpeople under the leadership of savvy local African American and Union soldiers. Prince Rivers was a community leader who had fought as a runaway slave for the Union. He became a sergeant in the First South Carolina Volunteers. He had taught himself to read while enslaved, and he became a leader of the Republican biracial coalition in South Carolina. He helped found Aiken County in 1871 after first serving at the South Carolina Constitutional Convention in 1868. Rivers helped pick the site of the courthouse, encouraged militia organization and enlistment, and served as a state legislator and then as a judge. He was typical of the thousands of freedmen and freedwomen who fought to free themselves during the American Civil War and then effectively seized the opportunity for political leadership and military self-defense after the war. He was exactly the kind of leader that aroused hatred and pathological vi-

Prince Rivers (1824–1887) is pictured on the right, holding the U.S. flag and wearing his Union uniform on the occasion of Emancipation Day in South Carolina, January 1, 1863. (*Frank Leslie's Illustrated Newspaper*, January 24, 1863)

olence from ex-Confederate extremists, but Rivers was coolheaded, realistic, and judicious. Besides organizing the town of Hamburg politically and militarily, even serving as a justice of the peace, Rivers was at the center of the start of the battle in Hamburg.

On July 4, 1876, the African American militia of Hamburg was parading. In what was surely an act of deliberate provocation, local white farmers, with no apparent business in the town, drove their carriages into the militia parade and then claimed they were blocked and harassed by the militia. Judge Rivers bravely heard the trial case against the militia for assaulting the white carriage drivers as ex-Confederate Red Shirt paramilitaries came armed and packed the courthouse by the hundreds. The white men's lawyer insisted that the African American militia be disbanded. Rivers took the moderate and reasonable position that both the Red Shirt paramilitaries and the African American state-authorized militia be disarmed. He met outside the court with both groups, promoting his plan, but the ex-Confederate extremist paramilitary swarmed the area and the African American militia retreated to its armory in Hamburg.

Rivers was not the only courageous African American leader in Hamburg. D. L. "Doc" Adams, a local African American, helped organize the militia to defend the Hamburg biracial government. Although federal forces had battled the KKK in South Carolina under the 1871 Enforcement Act, by 1876 African American and white unionists had to fill the void created when federal power was withdrawn. Historian James Sefton described the withdrawal of forces from the South: "In 1867 there had been one [federal] soldier in former Confederate states for every 708 civilians, by 1876 the ratio would be one for 3,160."[36] Prince Rivers and Doc Adams's organization of a local African American militia immediately brought out mass white supremacist paramilitary companies. Matthew Butler, a Confederate veteran, led hundreds of white troops into Hamburg on July 8 to protest at the trial. He demanded that Hamburg's African American militia disband. When the African American militia took refuge in its armory, white forces fired cannons at the building. After exchanging fire with the ex-Confederate paramilitary forces and killing one of the attackers, Adams ordered his men to abandon the building as artillery hit it. Ex-Confederate extremist forces chased the African Americans and attacked adjacent homes of unionists. Adams and the African American town marshal and several other leading African Americans were killed, but the battle gained notoriety for the violence that followed. Ex-Confederate extremists seized twenty-five African American prisoners and executed several of them, mutilating their bodies.[37] An African American militia extracted a measure of revenge in Cainhoy on October 16, when they outgunned a boat filled with of ex-Confederate extremists. At least five white supremacists and one African American died in the exchange of fire, and as many as fifty ex-Confederate extremists were wounded.[38] More typical of the final round of fighting that brought ex-Confederate extremists back into power was the five-day running battle in Aiken County between Black militias and ex-Confederate paramilitaries that climaxed in the town of Ellenton.[39] The ex-Confederate paramilitary rifle and saber clubs of the state had over fourteen thousand members by 1876 and could call up significant local armies.[40] In the Ellenton battles and massacres, from September 16 to 21, over one hundred African Americans and six whites died before federal troops arrived. The cessation of the bloodletting did not end its intimidating effect on African American voters in the forthcoming election. Ex-Confederate paramilitaries openly patrolled most communities, and Democrats won the statewide elections.[41]

After the Battle of Hamburg, but before those at Cainhoy and Ellenton, the Red Shirts went after Prince Rivers and looted and burned his home. The paramilitary went on a rampage against all African Americans in the region, killing hundreds and burning homes and churches. The African American vote was repressed in 1876, and the Red Shirts won their war in South Carolina and took over the state. Rivers, unlike many African American leaders, survived, but his fate mirrored that of African Americans all over the South after 1877. After having been an officer, conqueror, and statesman, he was functionally re-enslaved. His menial position in 1880 as a coachman and house servant to whites was virtually the same as it had been in 1858 during slavery. Rivers died at age sixty-five in 1887.

Mississippi's story in the paramilitary phase of the Southern Civil War was as dramatic as Louisiana's and South Carolina's and also featured brave African American leadership and a white Republican military leader in the tradition of Powell Clayton, Edmund Davis, and James Longstreet. No Republican governor was more outgunned than Adelbert Ames of Mississippi, but, like Longstreet, Davis, and Clayton, that did not stop him from putting his life on the line for years. Charles Caldwell led African American resistance in Mississippi, as Prince Rivers and William Ward and countless other African Americans had in their states, but, unlike Rivers and Ward (and Ames), Caldwell gave his life in the struggle.

Caldwell had grown up an enslaved blacksmith around Clinton, Mississippi. He was educated and politically astute and was one of the few African Americans to be a delegate to the Mississippi Constitutional Convention of 1868 that enfranchised African Americans. He also supported women's rights and educational and property equality for all. In 1869 he became one of only five African Americans to serve in the Mississippi State Senate. He organized the September 4, 1875, Clinton Republican rally that became the so-called Clinton Riot, a four-day battle with the white paramilitaries. Four whites and four African Americans died in the initial clash, but then white paramilitaries fanned out throughout Hinds County, killing African Americans. They raided Caldwell's home in his absence and vowed to assassinate him. Governor Ames briefly organized five African American companies for the state militia and made Caldwell a captain, but white horror at this step was so great that Ames disbanded the units immediately. The battle of Clinton proceeded with no state or federal military assistance to the biracial coalition or to leaders like Caldwell.

Clinton lay near the state capital, Jackson. As with so many clashes in the Southern Civil War, the battle began when ex-Confederate extremists attacked a Republican meeting. In Clinton, when firing began after an African American policeman tried to control rowdy ex-Confederate extremists, armed African Americans drove off the ex-Confederate attackers, killing at least four. Four African Americans also died, and many were wounded. Ex-Confederate paramilitary companies composed of Democrats poured into Clinton by train from Vicksburg. Eventually federal troops arrived from Jackson with Governor Ames commanding, but at least thirty African Americans were dead, the full number never to be known, as the battle became a massacre.[42] In 1876 these same White League paramilitaries purchased cannons and let out rebel yells as they aimed their fire at Republican meetings. Governor Ames briefly raised an African American militia and called for federal aid.[43] But aid did not come, and the African American militia was not employed, as Republicans retreated into passivity and were swept from office.

With militia protection gone, the subsequent election in November 1875 became an occasion for white paramilitary revenge on African American voters. The U.S. Senate was investigating the battle at Clinton and preparing to hold hearings with Caldwell as a star witness, but the ex-Confederate extremist paramilitary made good on its vow. A white supposed friend invited Caldwell for a drink, and, at a signal, a hidden assassin shot Caldwell in the back of the head.[44] His body was then mutilated by a series of white supremacist volleys. Several other nearby African Americans were fatally shot, including Caldwell's brother.[45] At least Charles Caldwell has a name and historical legacy, but he could stand in for the thousands of anonymous African Americans who asserted their and others' rights and were slaughtered by ex-Confederate extremists in the Southern Civil War. Governor Ames regretted not giving more aid to Caldwell and the biracial coalition forces in Clinton, but he directed all his efforts in a desperate battle to save his own life and political position. His story had more twists and turns than Caldwell's but fit many patterns of the Southern Civil War.

Ames shared much in common with Longstreet, Davis, and Clayton. He was the most decorated Civil War general of them all and, like all but Longstreet, his battles and service as governor in Reconstruction were a direct continuation of his American Civil War service. He fought the same enemies and protected the same white southern unionists while allying with and promoting the interests of southern African Americans. Exactly like Longstreet, Davis, and Clayton—and possibly in the face of even greater need—his calls for military aid from the Grant administration were rebuffed. Longstreet was Grant's friend, and Clayton and Davis were very highly connected, but Ames was all these things and more. He had been in nearly every major battle of the American Civil War, won the Congressional Medal of Honor, been promoted to general by Grant, was one of the youngest generals on either side, and was a politically connected, East Coast West Pointer from a Republican and abolitionist family. Unlike the other three biracial coalition leaders, Ames at first received a congressional appointment to be provisional governor (in Mississippi in 1868–1870) and was not a local figure. He subsequently was elected to serve Mississippi in the U.S. Senate 1870–1874 and was then elected governor, serving from 1874 to 1876. Unlike Clayton, Ames did not marry into a southern family and move there before the end of the American Civil War. While serving as senator from Mississippi in 1870, he married the daughter of Massachusetts congressman and Civil War general Benjamin Butler. Butler was hated in the South for his early calls for emancipation and arming African Americans (he came up with the strategy of not returning slaves to their masters by keeping them as "contraband") and for his effective military occupation of New Orleans, for which Confederates labeled him Beast Butler in 1862. Butler may have been more hated by ex-Confederates than Sherman, Sheridan, and even Longstreet after he became a member of the biracial coalition. Like his father-in-law, Ames faced virulent vilification even longer than Longstreet did in the generations after Reconstruction, and not just from racist southerners. Ames's daughter Blanche criticized John F. Kennedy for slandering Ames as corrupt in his *Profiles in Courage* (1955), and Ames did not have an accurate depiction of his governorship until journalist Nicholas Lemann's *Redemption* (2006).[46] White supremacists' gross distortion of Ames's record began in Mississippi in 1869, and it only grew in fervor and accompanying violence until he was driven from the state in 1876. Ames escaped assassination perhaps only because, unlike Longstreet, Davis and Clayton, he fled the South, never to return. Even that did not save him from reprisals. In 1876 Jesse James's ex-Confederate and white supremacist guerilla band rode out of Missouri and targeted Ames in Northfield, Minnesota, where Ames had briefly settled. They killed several but missed Ames and failed to rob his and Benjamin Butler's bank. Ames was brave but no fool. He fled to New York City, then Massachusetts. His instinct for self-preservation alone should put him in more history books; he fought as a general in the Spanish-American War and finally died at ninety-seven in 1933—the last Civil War general officer to die from either side.

Ames's life reads like a screenplay, but his tenure as military governor and then elected governor of Mississippi was a horror show. Unlike Davis and Clayton, Ames could not draw on a large contingent of white unionists in his state. Like Longstreet, Ames operated in an African American majority state, but Mississippi, although nearly 60 percent African American, had no long history of African American sociopolitical and military organization as Louisiana did. Mississippi also lacked the long period of Union Civil War occupation and organization of unionists forces that took place in southern Louisiana from 1862 to 1865. The state also had far fewer white unionists than Louisiana. For all these reasons, Ames's military attempt to combat ex-Confederate extremist violence in Mississippi was doomed. His experience best typifies how Reconstruction failed. Without a strong and active federal military occupation and an economically independent and armed African American community, ex-Confederate extremist warfare overwhelmed democracy and civil rights in the South. Ames was acutely aware of these odds and sought federal military aid and African American empowerment, while attempting to preserve lives and forestall full-scale warfare.[47] His ex-Confederate extremist opponents had no such scruples. As they were willing to fight an all-out war, they gained an advantage, even though more than 60 percent of the population of Mississippi opposed them. (According to the 1860 census, African Americans made up 55 percent of the state's population, and white Republicans can be added to this figure.)

Ames faced a full-scale paramilitary insurgency in Mississippi. These forces were not the guerilla and KKK bands that Davis and Clayton defeated but openly armed and warring paramilitary units, like those Longstreet faced in the streets of New Orleans. Their violence rivaled Texas's but was even more concentrated on vulnerable African Americans, who were even less likely to be armed in Mississippi than in other states. Ames also had few resources.[48] Despite ex-Confederate extremist claims of a "military occupation" of the South, at the height of paramilitary violence in 1875, when ex-Confederates were slaughtering hundreds of African Americans and had over 10,000 trained, armed men in

Adelbert Ames (1835–1933) was governor of Mississippi and the longest-lived full general of the American Civil War. (Library of Congress)

the field, there were only 248 federal troops in Mississippi, centered in Jackson.[49] In other towns and the countryside, open warfare raged between the White League paramilitary forces and improvised biracial coalition forces. In 1875 and 1876, President Grant turned down Governor Ames's requests for federal troops, famously saying, "The whole public are tired out with these annual autumnal outbreaks in the South and the great majority are ready to condemn any interference on the part of the government."[50] The "autumnal outbreaks" were White League paramilitary assaults on Republican voters and biracial coalition attempts at self-defense. The open battle for Mississippi began in 1874 when, in Republican-controlled Vicksburg and surrounding majority African American Warren County, rival African American militias and white paramilitaries started to drill. On July 4, white paramilitary forces attacked an African American holiday celebration and initiated a massacre.[51] African Americans subsequently organized around the county sheriff, Peter Crosby, a thirty-year-old Union veteran who had escaped enslavement to serve. Ex-confederate extremists won elections in the town of Vicksburg via intimidation in August and tried to get rid of African American county government officeholders such as Crosby. They briefly imprisoned Crosby and forced him to resign. Tensions and brief clashes followed throughout the fall before exploding in the Vicksburg battle and massacre of December 7–9, 1874. Sheriff Crosby came back to Vicksburg to restore his office on December 4, and African American militias marched toward Vicksburg to protect him and preserve their county power won through fair elections in which they were a large majority.[52] When the rival forces first clashed on December 7, over five hundred armed men on each side were involved. However, in a familiar pattern, ex-Confederate paramilitaries outgunned African American militia forces, and they flooded Warren County from surrounding counties and states. After the initial militia battle, the rampaging ex-Confederate extremist armies slaughtered as many as three hundred African Americans, though the official death toll was twenty-nine killed.[53] Crosby appealed to Ames, and this time his calls for help were answered. Phil Sheridan and federal troops came to Vicksburg and reinstalled Crosby to office before the county fell to white supremacist election violence and control in 1876.[54]

In a similar battle involving a Republican sheriff, Yazoo County, Mississippi, exploded in 1875 when ex-Confederate extremists spread a rumor that African Americans had ordered thousands of rifles.[55] Yazoo had a strong biracial coalition political administration led by Sheriff Albert T. Morgan, a white man who had married an African American teacher, Carolyn Victoria Highgate. This marriage made him a special target of ex-Confederate extremist armies that openly deployed in Mississippi after 1872.[56] On September 1, 1875, ex-Confederate extremists disrupted a Republican meeting where Morgan was speaking. The two sides exchanged gunshots, and Morgan fled for his life as his African American deputy was killed. An ex-Confederate paramilitary army then roamed the county, hunting other members of the biracial coalition. On September 7, African Americans managed to ambush some paramilitary bands that had been killing Blacks on the roads. When the successful act of self-defense raised more rumors of an African American uprising, Red Shirt paramilitaries flooded the county, lynching Republicans.

A. B. Frost cartoon showing the rampant violence and voter intimidation during the Southern Civil War. (*Harper's Weekly*, October 21, 1876)

Morgan and his wife managed to escape to nearby Jackson and Ames's protection and then fled the state, but the work had been done.[57] Solidly Republican Yazoo County recorded almost no Republican votes that fall. In this context, Ames pleaded for troops from Grant and received his famous rebuff.

The bloodletting in Vicksburg, Clinton, and Yazoo discouraged African American military self-defense in Mississippi, but African Americans did return fire in Rose Hill and Coahoma County in the 1876 election season. Following the pattern of Vicksburg, Clinton, and Yazoo, African American forces were overwhelmed by ex-Confederate paramilitaries, with a wave of revenge killings ensuing.[58]

In a fraudulent election in 1875, ex-Confederate extremists gained both houses of the Mississippi legislature, and they impeached Ames and every other Republican state official in 1876. This time Ames appealed to Congress for political reprieve and election monitoring and was refused. He left office under threat and won only an agreement that charges against him would be dropped if he left the state. This political and violent intimidation of an elected official was not the last act of resistance in Mississippi but was the last statewide act. Slowly, ex-

Confederate extremists killed, cowed into inaction, or drove from the state the last biracial coalition politicians, including former slaveholder Print Matthews. Matthews had founded a local Independent Party after the war and led the nearly all–African American Copiah County in the hinterlands. Although Matthews was the duly elected leader of Copiah County and white, ex-Confederate extremists assassinated him in front of the whole town of Hazlehurst when he attempted to vote in 1883. His assassin, Ras Wheeler, then became marshal of the town where the terrorized African majority would not be able approach the armed courthouse to vote for generations.[59] Print Matthews's son John attempted to carry on his father's political career as a Republican and advocate for African American rights in Carrollton, Mississippi. He suffered the same fate as his father in 1890, and his assassins too went on to become prominent Democratic politicians. Ames's fate would have been similar to that of Matthews if he had stayed in the state. Ames's two tenures as governor of Mississippi and service as political boss and senator for the state for four years are entirely unrepresented by marker or memorial in the state, but Print Matthews's cemetery obelisk in Hazlehurst has become a growing attraction for African American historical tours.[60] Ames did not even receive the national burial and acclaim that Clayton received at Arlington. He was buried near "Beast" Butler at the Hildreth Family Cemetery in Lowell, Massachusetts.

Given national historical, cultural, and political trends, Ames will likely be rehabilitated and honored, including in Mississippi. Moves are already underway to honor Clayton, Davis, and Longstreet in the capitols of Arkansas, Texas, and Louisiana. The history of Reconstruction has been rewritten, and schools and popular history are catching up to academic history as this most lied about and misunderstood era in U.S. history gets accurate and racially sensitive treatment. The current trend of describing Reconstruction as a civil war inside the South makes the era more visible in the popular culture as it is directly linked to the ever-obsessed-about American Civil War. The Southern Civil War was in many ways the American Civil War's sequel.[61] The careers of Longstreet, Davis, Clayton, and Ames highlight this, as they easily transitioned from leadership in one war to leadership in the next. The same is true for African American leaders like Prince Rivers, Peter Crosby, and William Ward, who fought for the Union in the American Civil War (though were barred from being officers) and then had leadership positions in the Southern Civil War. Rivers, Ward, Crosby, Clayton, and

Davis simply never stopped fighting, in one and then another war in the same location. Longstreet, in contrast, switched sides and was one of the few prominent men on the losing side of both the American Civil War and the Southern Civil War. Ames did not have the roots in the region that Clayton, Crosby, Davis, Ward, and Rivers did but like them fought for the same cause in both wars.[62] Ames had always been fighting for African American freedom and Republican triumph and was a far-seeing liberal on this issue, while Davis and Longstreet took up the cause of emancipation and civil rights more slowly or as a military necessity. All seven leaders, however, starred in the civil rights cause of the Southern Civil War, which has been ignored by the public, so their lives have been ignored as well. When it is understood that two distinct military conflicts were fought in 1861–1865 and 1865–1877, these men take center stage.

The Southern Civil War would close dramatically in 1877. By 1875 the Republican governments of Mississippi, Louisiana, Florida, and South Carolina, while still clinging to nominal power in their capitals, had lost control of their states and the ability to defend themselves against ex-Confederate extremist paramilitary armies. Also, after the national elections in 1874, the new Congress seated in 1875 had a Democratic majority for the first time since before the American Civil War. Republicans still held the Senate but had lost their electoral power with the economic decline after the Panic of 1873 and a northern populace weary of the problems of Reconstruction. The weakened national Republican Party would abandon the last biracial coalition governments at the next election with the Compromise of 1877.

The paramilitary phase of the war ended with the infamous Compromise. This was not an official act but a backroom agreement among northern and southern leaders in Washington to settle the issues of the disputed presidential election of 1876. Because of its unofficial and secretive nature, some historians argue that no such deal ever occurred. The Compromise's origins and outcomes, however, are well documented, and most historians agree it was a seminal event.[63] It certainly fit into the patterns of the Southern Civil War. As had been true throughout the Southern Civil War, violence climaxed around election time, especially in the run-up to them when rallies multiplied and voters could be intimidated easily. This pattern held spectacularly in the presidential election of 1876. Tens of thousands of ex-Confederate paramilitary soldiers were out in force in South Carolina, Florida, and Louisiana, and they had already seized Mississippi before the election and were still in the field in that state.[64] Of course, in the other southern states the apparatus of voter repression and terror were supported by ex-Confederate extremist state and local governments that no longer needed to field guerilla or paramilitary power to control elections. For these reasons, the national election is mischaracterized in textbooks, as really are all federal elections before the civil rights movement of the 1960s. Textbooks often describe the presidential election of 1876 and certainly subsequent ones without emphasizing enough that Republican voters could not go to the polls or have their votes counted in a vast swath of the country. So, about 1876, textbooks say that the Democrat Samuel J. Tilden won the popular vote without highlighting that the Republican Rutherford B. Hayes could have won the popular vote with hundreds of thousands of votes of African Americans and white Republicans had they lived in a democratic society rather than under regimes of terror. In 1876 Mississippi, South Carolina, Louisiana, and to a lesser extent Florida there were insurrectionary armies on the streets and in the countryside repressing votes and intimidating, indeed overpowering, the last democratically elected state and local governments the South would see for nearly one hundred years. These biracial coalition bastions of democratic government in the South would be abandoned in Washington backroom deals after being exploited to give Hayes the election.

Given the atmosphere, it is not surprising that a national election, let alone state elections, ended in chaos and corruption. Tilden won the popular vote, but the returns from the states of Louisiana, Florida, and South Carolina were contested—as all southern state counts should have been contested in 1876 and in every federal election until the 1970s. The electoral votes of these three southern states were just enough to give the election to the Republican Hayes. Congress did not certify the votes of these three states, and a political crisis ensued. The Compromise of 1877 later became the name for the deal struck by congressional leaders and representatives of each campaign that settled the presidential election. Although the exact mechanisms are obscure, the results were obvious and gave a great victory in the Southern Civil War to ex-Confederate extremists. They conceded one thing. Hayes was awarded all the electoral votes of Florida, Louisiana, and South Carolina and won the presidency, as he likely would have if there had been a free and fair election in the South. But the ex-Confederate extremists had not been fighting the Southern Civil War for the presidency or federal power, which their actions had proved were both weak anyway. Ex-Confederate extremists wanted absolute power on the ground in the South. This they obtained, along with federal acknowledgement of their power and military victory. National Republicans agreed to remove the few remaining federal troops from the South. These had been mostly guarding Republican governments in Louisiana, Florida, and South Carolina, the only states ex-Confederate extremists had not completely conquered.

In effect, northern Republicans guaranteed that they would not take any more role in southern warfare and politics. They also sweetened the deal by giving southern conservatives cabinet posts in the Hayes administration and railroad and economic development funds to the new ex-Confederate extremist governments. The federal withdrawal from the South, the policy of noninterference, and the nonenforcement of the Constitution in the region would all be codified by the Supreme Court, which had already gone a long way in this direction. In 1896 and 1898 in the *Plessy v. Ferguson* and *Williams v. Mississippi* cases, the Supreme Court ruled that the Fourteenth and Fifteenth Amendments would not be enforced in the South. *Plessy* allowed southern governments to deny African Americans civil rights, and *Williams* allowed them to deny African Americans (and many poor whites) the vote. Without the Fourteenth and Fifteenth Amendments, as Lincoln foresaw in his last speech, the Thirteenth Amendment would have no force, so the national government had also signed off on neo-slavery and terrorism, as it would prove by not passing antilynching laws in the next century. Textbooks misleadingly describe *Williams* as being the mechanism that denied African Americans the vote via "poll taxes," "literacy tests," and "grandfather clauses." While it is true that these were technical features of southern voting law and the *Williams* case, they were just legal cover for long-standing practices of violent intimidation and fraud that were the primary way votes were denied. Local terrorists, often in the guise of sheriffs and officials, had long prevented votes. They had blocked whom they wished from voting directly via violence for two generations by 1898. They denied would-be voters access to the courthouse to register, via the threat of lynching, the chain gang, a bullet to the head, and torture. *Williams* and *Plessy* gave retrospective legal cover to this established violent tradition. Ex-Confederate extremists, like Ras Wheeler who assassinated Print Matthews on the courthouse steps in Copiah,

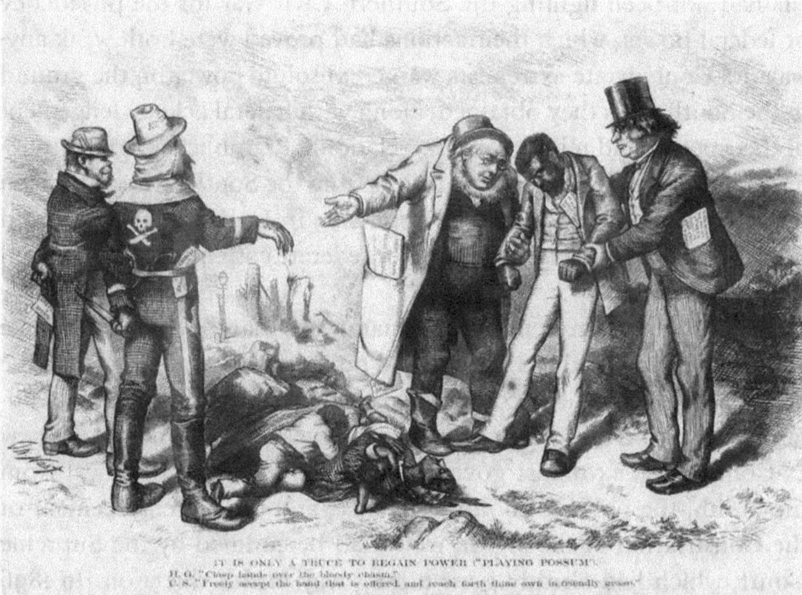

IT IS ONLY A TRUCE TO REGAIN POWER ("PLAYING POSSUM").
H. G. "Clasp hands over the bloody chasm."
C. S. "Freely accept the hand that is offered, and reach forth thine own in friendly grasp."

Thomas Nast cartoon depicting the northern complicity in forcing blacks under the control of ex-Confederate mass murderers. "H. G." is said to represent Horace Greeley. (*Harper's Weekly*, August 24, 1872)

Mississippi, were the sheriffs and local election officials. They fought a war to preserve their local power, and everyone under their authority knew the violence of which they were capable. As their violent white supremacist control became ingrained in the culture, open warfare was generally no longer needed as their system of terror ruled.

The Compromise of 1877 was a large step in ex-Confederate extremist warfare transitioning into custom. It constituted the "peace" treaty that ended a long era of war. The North retreated from the South, but the ex-Confederate extremist South acknowledged the legitimacy of a Republican northern president who would leave them alone. In 1860 they had not believed Lincoln when he pledged to protect slavery in the South and leave white southerners alone. The South had more ambitious goals in 1861, but in 1877, after a generation of war, it had diminished, if fiercely held, ambitions. Sixteen years of two civil wars had taught these lessons. The white South could keep its racial and social system but not its national power let alone its own national government. The Compromise of 1877 was a tragic bargain, but it was a real regional compromise, which the country failed to devise in 1861 or 1865. That said, the Compromise of 1877 was also a compromise between white elites for white elites, over the bodies of dead African Americans and white unionists. The Compromise of 1877 assured that future generations of southerners would live under neo-slavery, terror, and a nondemocratic regional political system.

The violence of the American Civil War could not just be turned off. Its aftershocks fed into a new war that rumbled on for twelve years. So too the violent traditions of the Southern Civil War lingered into the next era. White supremacist southerners had become conditioned for a generation from 1865 to 1877 to terrorizing African Americans and organizing systematic violence to deny them all rights but especially voting and economic rights. White supremacists kept up the tradition of lynching and other terrorism to keep African Americans down but also turned to local paramilitary attacks in bloody rampages. In the twentieth century, a new KKK arose after 1915, and virulent white supremacy and lynching had its heyday everywhere in the nation. At the end of the nineteenth century and in the new century, the South had the most dramatic white supremacist attacks in Wilmington, North Carolina (1898), New Orleans, Louisiana (1900), Atlanta, Georgia (1906), Slocum, Texas (1910), Elaine, Arkansas (1919), Tulsa, Oklahoma (1921), and Rosewood, Florida (1923). This followed generations of violent oppression during the Southern Civil War and its Jim Crow system aftermath, but African Americans continued to fight back. The white supremacist assaults of this era were horrifically one-sided, but African Americans briefly engaged again in armed self-defense, eventually futile, especially in Wilmington, New Orleans, Atlanta, Elaine, and Tulsa.

Wilmington, North Carolina, signaled this important trend after Reconstruction. African Americans returned to the polls in 1894 when the Populist Party in the form of the "Fusion" movement—fusing Republicans and Populists—won elections. Fusionism was a new biracial coalition, and it gained control of North Carolina from 1894 to 1898. Such evidence of democracy was as intolerable to the white supremacist minority as it had been during the Southern Civil War, and they struck back with the same violent tactics they had mastered and built into their culture then. Armed attacks combined with race-baiting rhetoric undermined the new biracial coalition, and in Wilmington in 1898 a full-scale armed clash erupted. Before the election that year, white supremacist Democrats in a deliberate strategy revived KKK-style "riding" to stop African American voters from reaching the polls. They attacked political meetings and polling places and suppressed the Fusion vote. After these white supremacists won the election, they attacked African Americans and their white allies in Wilmington. White supremacist forces burned prosperous African American businesses and slaughtered African Americans in armed clashes, with at least sixty African Americans and three whites killed. Much of Wilmington's African American population fled the city and the South. North Carolina then passed Jim Crow laws to ensure that the government permanently repressed African American votes and freedom.[65] The federal government ignored pleas for justice, and no one was arrested for the Wilmington clash and massacre.[66]

The New Orleans clash two years later originated in a bold example of African American armed resistance. The New Orleans massacre is often called the Robert Charles Riots. Robert Charles was a politically astute African American who practiced armed self-defense. Charles came from Copiah County, Mississippi, and had likely witnessed the aftermath, if not the events, of Print Matthews's assassination and the repression of the county's African American voters. Charles fled this repressive county and moved to Vicksburg, where he always carried a gun after seeing more ex-Confederate extremist warfare there.[67] Like many late nineteenth-century African Americans, he was radicalized by his experiences. The records are sketchy, but he clearly became an advocate of African American separatism and emigration to Liberia. He also preached self-reliance and self-defense. African Methodist Episcopal bishop Henry McNeal Turner, who had served as a state legislator from Macon, Georgia, during the Southern Civil War and had been involved in trying to combat KKK-style guerillas, was the leader of the back-to-Africa movement in the era. Charles espoused Turner's ideas.

Charles had seen in Copiah County and Vicksburg how white political oppression was accompanied by violence intended to teach African Americans the new rules and to stay in their place. Charles spectacularly refused to stay in his place. He had moved from Mississippi to New Orleans, where the preconditions for a massacre were brewing. New Orleans had an active and growing African American elite and a resentful white community that was ready to pass new oppressive laws and longed to destroy African Americans' limited autonomy. Charles was an intensely aware civil rights activist and knew this wave was coming since he had seen it his whole life.[68] Historians will never know, but certainly he decided he was not going down without a fight. On July 23,

1900, when a group of three policemen harassed him on the street and began to assault him, he drew his pistol to defend himself. He shot an officer in the leg, likely after the officer shot him in the leg. Charles fled home and gathered his Winchester rifle and ammunition. When police came to his house, Charles killed two officers and pinned down the rest. Lurid racist newspaper accounts of Charles spread throughout the city. Charles's isolated act was blown into a racist witch hunt. Whites armed by the thousands, assaulted African Americans, and burned their property all over New Orleans.

For four days armed whites rampaged throughout the city, killing African Americans in their search for Charles, until a tip led them to Charles's hiding place. The African American who offered the tip was shot dead on a public street a few days later by Lewis Forstall, an African American avenger who supported Charles.[69]

Charles made an even greater statement with his rifle. Charles gave the armed white crowd a gun battle for the ages as he shot an additional twenty-four whites, five more fatally, including one more policeman. Most of the crowd were "militia" police or "volunteer" citizens. After hours of gunfire, the police and "militia" burned down the house Charles was defending and shot him dozens of times when he emerged. Then the crowd mutilated his corpse. The white "militia" continued killing African Americans and burned African American schools and businesses. The mayor had to bring in the state militia to quell the five days of violence. Casualties were uncertain, but at least thirty were dead and over fifty wounded, and millions of dollars' worth of property had been destroyed.[70] New Orleans then passed more restrictive and permanent Jim Crow and voter repression laws. Historian William Hair wrote an excellent history of Charles in 1976, but, like the Southern Civil War itself, Charles's important and dramatic story has little place in American popular memory. As the Southern Civil War acculturated whites to slaughtering African Americans as they did in New Orleans, Charles was also an echo of the organized but outgunned military traditions of the biracial coalition in the same conflict.

Charles orchestrated most of the African American self-defense in New Orleans, but the 1906 Atlanta massacres saw more organized and widespread African American armed defense.[71] The Atlanta clash, like the New Orleans one, was driven by increasing racism, newspapers printing racist rumors as news, and white plans to crack down, violently and via new laws, on prosperous African Americans. Louisiana passed its key Jim Crow voting statues just before the white paramilitaries hunted down Robert Charles, and Georgia passed its in 1908 following the Atlanta massacre. Yet, like in New Orleans, white supremacist politics pushed and preceded the Atlanta conflagration, which may have been planned. The 1906 governor's race was obscenely racist, and candidates, especially former Atlanta newspaper editor Hoke Smith, demanded final disenfranchisement of African Americans by law. In his campaign speech, Smith, the eventual victor, called African Americans "savage, vicious, inhuman" and asked his audience "Shall it be ballots now or bullets later?"[72] Smith said he favored a constitutional amendment that would "insure a continuation of white supremacy."[73] He and his followers also called for Atlanta's growing African American elite to be put in their place. Atlanta newspapers, in what looks like deliberate incitement to attack the African American community, printed false stories of African American men raping white women. Robert Charles at least existed, though papers lied about him. In Atlanta a coordinated press campaign simply fabricated African American fiends for armed mobs to hunt. The attack came in late September, the very same election season time of so many of the bloodiest battles and massacres of the Southern Civil War.[74]

On Saturday, September 22, thousands of armed whites gathered in the center of the city.[75] In an example of the real purpose of this paramilitary gathering, the whites went after African American political leaders and the most prosperous and respected Black businesses. The whites shot and beat to death African Americans and destroyed their stores. The all-white state militia was called out by the governor, but it went into Atlanta to protect white neighborhoods. Whites kept invading African American neighborhoods unchecked and even were emboldened by the militia. Many of Atlanta's African Americans armed themselves and drove off the attackers through Saturday night and into Sunday. African Americans in the elite suburb of Brownsville, which as yet had seen no attacks, organized a well-armed militia of their own. As in the Southern Civil War, this taboo act brought an invasion of Brownsville by white police and militia aiming to disarm and abuse the Black community. A gun battle ensued, and one white policeman was killed. The white militia then arrested 250 African Americans and disarmed them. No one knows how many died or were wounded in the massacres and the four days of sporadic fighting, but at least thirty African Americans were killed along with the one white police officer. The injured went uncounted, and property damage was massive.[76]

Tulsa, Oklahoma, in 1921 was the scene of perhaps the greatest bloodshed and property damage of any civic disturbance in American history, which is a long and continuing list. Tulsa had the most prosperous African American community in the nation in 1921, just fourteen years after Oklahoma statehood, but the June "riot" there exterminated the prosperity.[77] Rumors and lies in the wake of generations of race-baiting and resentment of wealthy, independent African Americans, just as in New Orleans and Atlanta, led to the violence.[78] Tulsa was very much a southern town and had been a part of Indian Territory, where slavery was legal, and its residents had most often fought for the Confederacy. The spark for the "riot" was so inconsequential that only a populace itching for a massacre could have blown it into the gore that followed. An African American, named Dick Rowland, apparently tripped in a store elevator and startled the elevator operator, a young white women named Sarah Page, who screamed.[79] A store clerk saw she was distraught and called the police. Rumors spread that she had been assaulted, even though no record remains of what was said to the police in the store.[80] Racist newspapers spread false accounts of the nonincident. Rowland was arrested the next day, probably for his own protection, but this pattern of false accusation and arrest was usually followed by the prisoner being turned over to a mob for a ghastly lynching. Twenty-five armed African Americans, therefore, went to the courthouse to protect Rowland. A lynch mob was also assembling. On May 31 an armed white mob attacked the African American defenders of the courthouse. Shots were exchanged, and the armed whites went on a citywide rampage, burning, looting and murdering their way through Tulsa's thriving African American community. Whites bombed the African American business district from private planes, dropping dynamite and incendiaries.[81] On June 1 the governor ordered in the Oklahoma National Guard. They proceeded not to protect African American victims of the violence but to arrest Tulsa's African Americans. African American oral histories tell of the National Guard firing machine guns at African Americans in the wealthy Greenwood district, where the plane attacks had been reported the previous day. For over a week, as many as six thousand African Americans were interned at the city fairgrounds.[82] As with all these white supremacist–initiated clashes in the twentieth century (and as in the Southern Civil War), numbers are hard to come by, and the event itself was covered up and kept out of the history books until recently. As many as three hundred African Americans or more died, and a thousand were wounded.[83] The Oklahoma Commission to Study the Tulsa Race Riot of 1921 estimated in 2001 that forty city blocks—virtually the entirety of Tulsa's African American residential district—were burned by the white mob.[84] African Americans fled the city in the aftermath. The Tulsa Massacre began to enter the history textbooks in 2001 and has been featured in documentaries and HBO's series *The Watchmen*, but the educational system has not placed it in a meaningful context. The term "race riot" alone is grossly misleading to describe this orchestrated white supremacist attack in the tradition of Reconstruction. The context of the Southern Civil War reveals events like Tulsa to be premeditated, part of a tradition of political warfare, and a step toward ethnic cleansing.

The 1923 massacre at Rosewood, Florida, like Tulsa, has at least entered the popular imagination with film and television coverage. Rosewood was a prosperous African American town that neighboring white supremacists burned to the ground, displacing the entire African American population.[85] As with most of these violent twentieth-century incidents (and those during the Southern Civil War), "mystery" surrounds the events, and no white attacker was ever charged or prosecuted. Researcher Gary Moore, however, discusses and unpacks many of these mysteries while thoroughly documenting the massacre in his book *Rosewood*.[86] As many as 150 died, maybe a third of the town. The origin of the Rosewood Massacre shares much in common with the general pattern of the New Orleans, Atlanta, and Tulsa events described. Whites spread false stories in newspapers of an escaped African American convict raping a white woman. This had been preceded by an era of growing racism and a recent triple lynching eighty-five miles north of Rosewood, in Perry, Florida, that included whites burning African American homes.[87] Whites in nearby Sumner resented Rosewood's prosperity and independence, so an armed white group went to the town, ostensibly to search for the supposed convict-rapist. No evidence supported his being in Rosewood, and, as usual, this story was a flimsy pretext for a long-sought white supremacist goal of eliminating Rosewood.[88] Rosewood armed for self-defense, and perhaps half a dozen whites were killed assaulting the town—all the white dead were near the house of Sylvester Carrier, who fought in the manner of Robert Charles.[89]

Whites spread rumors of an African American uprising, and armed whites and KKK units spread intimidation and slaughter all over rural Levy County and the city of Gainesville. The violence spilled into neighboring counties in western Florida, where local white supremacists assaulted and burned African American communities. In a few locales armed whites actually came out to protect their towns and local African American populations from marauding mobs.

These were not isolated incidents in the early twentieth century. Many towns and even entire counties expelled African Americans. "Sundown" towns and counties allowed no African Americans inside them after sunset and kept them out, often after driving them out as in Rosewood, via continuous violent intimidation. Aftershocks reached into the civil rights movement era. Forysth County, Georgia, and Van Zandt County, Texas, which were known as sundown locales, had racist incidents when African Americans entered them in the 1980s and 1990s. Forsyth had driven out all African Americans in 1912 after rape accusations, white mob violence, and a wave of lynching. Such communities existed throughout the nation, including in the North, where white supremacists often violently excluded African Americans from suburbs.[90] The North's racism and complicity in the triumph of white supremacy in the Southern Civil War made this racial violence possible.

Wilmington, Atlanta, Tulsa, Rosewood, and New Orleans are relatively well-documented clashes that are included in some current history textbooks. Two other violent eruptions of the era are less well known but even better reflect the legacy of the Southern Civil War. Elaine, Arkansas, in 1919 and Slocum, Texas, in 1910 saw massacres and African American resistance that likely had far higher death tolls. Like the great bloodletting of the terror phase of the war from 1865 to 1867, Slocum and Elaine were rural events and so poorly documented that they have no known casualty counts, just as in 1865–1867. Also, they probably represent countless smaller massacres in the twentieth century that have yet to be (and may never be) uncovered, again as was the case in 1865–1867. Just as importantly, Slocum and Elaine were at the heart of the areas of the most warlike states in the guerilla phase of the Southern Civil War. Slocum's East Texas and Elaine's East Central Arkansas were the KKK-style guerilla havens into which Edmund Davis and Clayton Powell sent state militias and police to battle ex-Confederate extremists in 1868.

As with so many massacres and clashes of the Southern Civil War, the 1910 Slocum Massacre began for no real reason at all except white fear and hatred of African Americans, which led to rumors of an African American uprising. As many as three hundred unarmed African Americans were shot by white supremacists, mostly in the back as they ran away. No whites were injured in Slocum. In 2014 E. R. Bills helped uncover the story of Slocum in the searing *1910 Slocum Massacre: An Act of Genocide in East Texas*. Bills writes, "Sheriff Black issued a disturbing statement. 'Men were going about and killing negroes as fast as they could find them,' he said, 'and, so far as I have been able to ascertain, without any real cause at all. These negroes have never done anything that I could discover. There was just a hot-headed gang hunting them down and killing them.'"[91] The Texas state militia went into the Slocum area after the killings, which had all taken place over July 29 and July 30, 1910. Surprisingly, seven white men were indicted for twenty-two of the murders, but, as happened countless times in the Southern Civil War, courts released all of them without trial. Supporters of the killers voted all the local politicians who started the indictments out of office. In 2016 the State of Texas placed a historical marker in Slocum in memory of the slain African Americans. This should just be the start of making the connection of these incidents to the Southern Civil War more central to public histories across the nation. The Southern Civil War built up institutions and traditions of violence that remained in place in the twentieth century. The white supremacist memory of fighting biracial armies in 1865–1877 drove many in the next generations to stay armed and pathologically vigilant against any signs of African American independence or interracial cooperation, let alone any resistance to the victory of ex-Confederate extremists.

In Slocum, white supremacists' fears and traditions of violence ran wild after imaginary rebels, but in Elaine, Arkansas, in 1919, African Americans stood up for themselves, as they did all across the country in that bloody year, and fired back before being slaughtered in the hundreds. Elaine was the most direct echo of the Southern Civil War and resembled both Arkansas's Chicot County War in its origins and the Battle of Colfax in its bloodshed. Phillips County, where Elaine is located, was nearly ninety percent African American. The area had a history of combat in the Southern Civil War. Phillips was three counties north up the Mississippi from Chicot County, where in 1871 African Americans had organized attacks on the KKK and fought the Chicot County War. Elaine in 1919, like Chicot in 1871, witnessed dramatic African American political organization and self-defense. Whites owned the land, but African American sharecroppers began to organize via the Progressive Farmers and Household Union of America in 1918. Added to the systematic terrorism of lynching and other white mob violence, convict leasing in this period was a cruel form of neo-slavery, and so was sharecropping with its debt slavery. Elaine proved how closely terrorism was tied to agricultural enslavement, as it was an attempt by African American sharecroppers to organize that brought a violent white backlash. Racist whites and their newspapers claimed Blacks were planning to rise up and kill whites when they were only seeking simple economic justice. Armed white law enforcement officers came to break up an organizational meeting of about one hundred at an African American church on September 30, 1919. No one knows who fired first, but a white police man died, and another was wounded. Alarms went out throughout outlying white communities, and quickly about a thousand armed whites gathered near Elaine, with scattered other groups rampaging throughout the area. In a mobilization reminiscent of the Southern Civil War paramilitary bands, they systematically scoured the area, killing African American men, women, and children. African Americans fought back and killed five whites but at the cost of hundreds of African American deaths. No solid numbers are available, but at the time whites boasted that they had killed at least two hundred. For days local white newspapers, like the Little Rock–based *Arkansas Gazette*, fabricated stories of an African American "uprising" that stoked continued slaughter.[92] The governor of Arkansas called for federal troops, and more than five hundred restored order—mostly by arresting hundreds of African Americans and by joining the killing of African Americans (one federal soldier died too). Despite the mass arrest of African Americans and charges of capital murder against many, the U.S. Supreme Court and the Arkansas Supreme Court threw out the cases, and all accused African Americans were released by 1925. The legal outcome constituted a turning point in this case, as in some others, but the scale of the Elaine bloodletting dwarfs any other legacy of the event. Historian Grif Stockley, in his 2001 account of Elaine, *Blood in their Eyes: The Elaine Race Massacres of 1919*, sums up: "It is documented that five whites including a soldier died at Elaine, but estimates of African American deaths, made by individuals writing about the Elaine affair [in] 1919–25, range from 20 to 856; if accurate, these numbers would make it by far the most deadly conflict in the history of the United States."[93] Events such as Elaine and Slocum deserve a more prominent place in the narrative of U.S. history. The examples of such white supremacist paramilitary attacks could be greatly expanded. For example, the Thibodaux Massacre in Louisiana in 1887 and the Ocoee Massacre in Florida on Election Day 1920 saw similar African American casualties.[94] They grew out of the culture and institutions of white supremacist violence developed in the South during the Southern Civil War of 1865–1877. Placing the post–Southern Civil War urban and rural racial massacres and clashes in the context of Reconstruction warfare gives them a national and indeed international legacy of lasting import.

CHAPTER FIVE

What Makes a War a War

Assessing Reconstruction

The American Civil War era was messier and more futile than most Americans know.[1] The long-term, unconventional, and brutal war of 1865–1877 and its aftershocks reaching into the twentieth century look like the horrific and complex engagements in modern civil wars in other nations. The Southern Civil War fits the international pattern: a start-and-stop war of political, guerilla, and paramilitary violence and cruel personal reprisals. The war had three distinct phases and a very clear military history, but this does not fit with Americans' images of themselves and their history.[2] No progressive national story can be extracted from the Southern Civil War. Its story instead illuminates lies in the victorious narrative of the American Civil War.

The American Civil War is often called the first modern war since both sides were industrializing, mass democracies. Looking forward at twentieth-century patterns helps clarify the nature of the 1861–1865 war, but the comparative view provides an even better insight into the Southern Civil War and how it expands the entire era of war from 1861 to 1877 and indeed from 1854 to 1965. Twentieth- and twenty-first-century civil wars have been characterized by protracted, irregular fighting (forces engaged in sporadic combat). Civil wars have often followed or grown out of wars of decolonization and independence, as the Southern Civil War did.

Today's U.S. political divisions have their roots in the arguments of Reconstruction but with the roles of the parties flipped: in the twenty-first century we have seen a multiethnic Democratic coalition and white nationalist Republicans. Civil wars often define modern political party divisions within nations, so the Southern Civil War should be at the center of the national historical memory, not forgotten or grossly lied about. It is a great, tragic story filled with heroes Americans can now appreciate and real villains who no longer need to be seen as romantic, redeeming heroes. The nation has built a new racial understanding of its past since the civil rights movement that began in 1954. It has rewritten its curriculum on slavery. National awareness of the horrors of lynching, massacres, and convict leasing has also grown in the last twenty years. Reconstruction is ironically the last unreconstructed part of America's racial memory, but a wave of new history is changing the popular view of the era.

There is a precedent for a forgotten and covered-up war to achieve a new status in American history. The Spanish-American War (1898) once dominated textbooks as a "splendid little war" that defined its era. But, especially since the Vietnam War, the much longer and bloodier consequence of the Spanish-American War, the Philippine-American War (1899–1902) is no longer ignored and gets as much space as the Spanish-American War in good textbooks. Like the Southern Civil War, the Philippine-American War was a vicious guerilla war with massive, uncounted civilian casualties: more than 4,200 U.S. and more than 20,000 Filipino combatants died, as did as many as 200,000 Philippine civilians, compared to 385 combat deaths for the United States in the Spanish-American War (although 2,000 more U.S. soldiers died of disease, and Spanish and Cuban deaths from all causes ran into the tens of thousands).[3] A similar revision is taking place currently with the American Civil War and its consequence, the Southern Civil War, a longer and less conventional war.

Like the Philippine-American War, warfare in Ireland indicates how the Southern Civil War fits patterns of modern war. The Irish War of Independence from 1919 to 1921 was followed by a civil war over the peace settlement, from 1922 to 1923. No one questions the massive and long-term impact of both wars on modern Ireland. The Irish Civil War and its political divisions determined the political parties in Ireland for the rest of the twentieth century. The yearlong Irish Civil War is central to the national history and memory of the Republic. How a peace treaty led to a new war and how families define themselves by their pro- or anti-treaty stance is a matter of powerful popular memory and pride in Ireland. How strange, then, that the American Civil War from 1861 to 1865 looms so large in popular memory, with little acknowledgment of the subsequent twelve-year war that killed ten times the number that died in the Irish Civil War and lasted twelve times longer.

Not only did the Southern Civil War and the Irish Civil War both originate from a previous war of independence, in each case there was also an indirectly involved great power. Britain lurked in the background of the Irish fighting, threatening to intervene but never doing so, just as the federal government largely refused to do in the Southern Civil War. The Irish Civil War began when the treaty that ended the Irish War of Independence divided Ireland and gave limited sovereignty to the Irish rather than a fully independent republic. Anti-treaty hardliners refused to accept the terms of the treaty and continued guerilla tactics, not against the British but against their pro-treaty former compatriots. The pro-treaty side fought with British material support, formed a government, and became the Irish Free State on December 6, 1922. Partisan hatred, assassinations, guerilla raids, battles on a very small scale (incidents, really), and reprisal killings characterized the Irish Civil War. About seven hundred died in combat, and maybe three thousand fighters died in other forms of violence (including summary executions, massacres, and assassinations), and an unknown number of civilians died.[4] No accurate numbers exist, especially for anti-treaty deaths.

No one would think of not calling the Irish Civil War a war, but this is exactly what is done for the much longer, bloodier, and often more conventional combat in the American South from 1865 to 1877. As in Ireland, the Southern Civil War was fought against a peace settlement, with ex-Confederate extremists taking the "anti-treaty" stance (though there was no formal treaty) and resorting to unconventional warfare. Like the Irish Civil War, the exact death toll in the South is unknown and perhaps unknowable, but it was definitely far higher than the Irish Civil War. Unlike the anti-treaty diehards, the ex-Confederate extremists overthrew the settlement of the earlier war and defeated the Republican southern state governments and their biracial forces. This outcome in many ways makes the southern example even more dramatic than the Irish since it reversed some of the results of the previous war. By 1877, ex-Confederate extremists took total control of every southern state government and moved effectively to eliminate Republican politics, African American freedom, and many of their political enemies in reprisal killings and spectacles of public torture by lynching. Like the Irish Civil War, the Southern Civil War has left a legacy of division. In the United States this has never been confined to the South but extends throughout the country today and can be seen in its two-party division. This political divide is rarely connected to its roots in the Southern Civil War of 1865–1877.

The example of the Irish Civil War provides a dramatic contrast to the Southern Civil War's outcome that helps explain the victory of the ex-Confederate extremists. The newly launched Irish Free State won elections, built an army, and defeated anti-treaty guerilla and terrorist tactics. The biracial coalition won democratic elections and set up "free state" governments in Tennessee, Louisiana, Mississippi, Arkansas, Texas, Alabama, Georgia, Florida, Virginia, North Carolina, and South Carolina. These governments also built militias and state police forces but not ones strong enough to defeat guerillas and paramilitaries. The federal government's division and indecisiveness helped lead to the collapse of the new southern biracial governments. England's role in the Irish Civil War illuminates the limitations and mistakes of the federal government and northern politicians. England provided uniforms, artillery, armored cars, rifles, and machine guns that guaranteed that the new Free State army massively outgunned and out supplied the anti-treaty guerillas. The federal government gave no such military support to the biracial governments of southern states that were consistently outgunned by guerillas and paramilitaries drawing on Confederate training and arms.[5] Governor Clayton of Arkansas at the height of his war against the KKK had to draw on his own resources to get rifles. Likewise, Florida's biracial coalition governor Harrison Reed had to go to New York to procure arms for the state militia. Like Clayton too, Reed had his first supply intercepted by KKK guerillas and destroyed.[6] The North's massive resources never reached the biracial governments of the southern states.[7]

The Irish Free State also prosecuted a far different war than the biracial southern governments. Governors Davis and Clayton used martial law, mass arrests, and, especially in Arkansas, judicial and pseudojudicial executions of ex-Confederate extremist guerillas. These executions, however, only numbered a handful. The Irish Free State summarily executed anti-treaty captives in response to guerilla assassinations and terror against Free State targets. The Irish Free State executed eighty-three anti-treaty prisoners by firing squad in the last months of the war.[8] As importantly, the Free State matched anti-treaty killings with equally and often more cruel massacres of suspected anti-treaty guerillas in the field. Historians have never been able to count all the dead from extrajudicial retaliation killings as happen in such small-scale, intimate warfare, but the Free State massacres and assassinations of anti-treaty fighters while in state custody certainly outnumbered the formal executions, as the best current count reaches 125 killed.[9] The anti-treaty forces also killed some prisoners. In comparison, the ex-Confederate extremist guerillas and paramilitaries assassinated and massacred countless thousands more than the Irish anti-treaty forces did over a war that lasted eleven years longer than the Irish Civil War, but ex-Confederate extremists faced virtually no executions or retaliation massacres. The bloodshed of the Southern Civil War was shockingly one-sided. Governors like Davis and Clayton who took up the counterinsurgency tactics needed to combat guerilla terror faced political backlash against the tactics. The English and the Irish Free State in the early 1920s had ample experience of modern warfare and insurgency and did not have the tradition of liberties so dear to nineteenth-century white Americans. Americans, especially white southerners, had a much higher tolerance for nongovernment violence than for governmental violence. America's tradition of limited government meant that the North largely ignored or downplayed "riots" by ex-Confederate extremists that killed thousands but was horrified by southern state governments turning to martial law. The Irish Civil War also points out a limitation in that arena. The Irish Free State detained twelve thousand suspected anti-treaty guerillas without trial in internment camps for the length of the Irish Civil War and long after the end of the war.[10] These were truly mass and long-term detentions. The Free State had a population of less than three million, and America's population in 1870 was 38,558,371. So if the United States had made as serious an attempt to combat the Southern Civil War as the Irish did, 150,000 ex-Confederate extremists would have been detained (that number might have been far higher since the Southern Civil War lasted twelve times longer than the Irish Civil War). When contrasted with the Irish example, the stunning inadequacy of the U.S. reaction to an extremist insurgency is clear. The biracial coalition state governments and the federal government took a small number of ex-Confederate extremists prisoner, but they were not summarily executed or detained for long periods. Instead, they were turned over to the civilian court system, which quickly released even the most brutal of them. Even without mass executions and counterterrorism, the use of long-term, mass detentions and robust prosecution of ex-

Confederate extremists might have kept democratically elected governments in power in the South. These steps were never attempted by state governments or the federal government. At the end of 1871, Grant made use of the federal military only to arrest, not militarily detain, Klansmen in South Carolina. Even that federal foray only emboldened the KKK. Of the 533 arrests in late 1871 and early 1872, only 54 Klansmen were indicted, and all but five of those pled guilty but were released.[11] Of the total of 1,355 indictments under the federal Enforcement Acts, only 102 were not dropped, with 75 pleading out and only 27 convicted. More than 1,250 were simply turned loose.[12] Historian Richard Zuczek has highlighted the failure of federal efforts in South Carolina and pointed out that "civil authorities directed the operations, and neither martial law nor military commissions were utilized."[13] Governors Clayton, Davis, and Holden at least used martial law at the state level but made few arrests prior to public attacks against their tactics. The ex-Confederate extremists exploited traditions of civil liberties. Like the federal troops and unlike the Irish, the biracial governments venerated these traditions and had trouble contemplating, let alone pursuing, such "un-American" tactics as mass detention.

Racism, however, was the main difference between the Southern and Irish Civil Wars, and it was the key to the biracial coalition's defeat. Race was not an issue in the Irish Civil War (religion was), but racism dominated the psychology of nineteenth-century American whites. The North and eventually the white allies of African Americans in the South would not sacrifice much to support African American civil rights. Race-baiting drove southern whites from the biracial coalitions and drove northern politicians from supporting a war or legal action to support African Americans. The mass death of African Americans in the era did not produce the horror in white minds that armed African Americans did or that mass arrests of white people did. Most importantly, ex-Confederate extremist violence forced African Americans out of the voting booths and forced white southerners out of political alliance with them. On paper, the biracial coalition was the majority in most southern states, but fraud and violence based on race made the biracial voting coalition irrelevant.[14] Few whites could contemplate the steps necessary to defeat a white supremacist insurrection, let alone do what the Irish Free State and British did so effectively and so brutally against an insurgent movement in Ireland.

The comparison of the Southern Civil War to the Irish example also shows how remarkably little interest historians and policy experts have about the haunting questions and vital example of the Southern Civil War. How many died? No one has even tried to answer this question systematically. How does the conflict fit into patterns of world history? Clearly, it was a preview of twentieth- and twenty-first-century civil wars and wars over policy, occupation, and nation building (the modern term for "reconstruction"). Modern examples of unconventional warfare, like Ireland, illuminate the southern example, but the southern example also illuminates twentieth- and twenty-first-century examples. The sixteen years of combat during the American Civil War and Southern Civil War and the fifty-plus more years of civil strife that followed are hauntingly familiar looking back at them from the twenty-first century.

The view back now includes the more-than-decade-long conflicts of the United States in Iraq and Afghanistan, where conventional wars and their "settlements" and "reconstruction" have deteriorated in the face of guerilla insurgency and local terror, just as the northern efforts did during Reconstruction. And both of these conflicts were tied into longer wars stretching back to at least 1979 in Afghanistan and the 1990 Gulf War in Iraq. Like the two American wars from 1861 to 1877, these conflicts in Iraq and Afghanistan had phases, starts and stops, and complex reversals of fortune. Saying that civil war stopped in America in 1865 is like stating that the war in Iraq stopped with the President George W. Bush's announcement of the end of "major combat operations" in May 2003. A history that did that for the Iraq War would never be printed. Yet histories of the American Civil War and Reconstruction have done exactly this, stopping the story of warfare in 1865. The look back from the twenty-first century to 1877 also passes over similar long-term, sporadic, and complex civil wars in Russia (1917–1922), China (1927–1950), Algeria (1954–1962 and 1991–2002), Vietnam (1955–1975—or should that be 1941–1979?), Guatemala (1960–1996), Ethiopia (1974–1991), El Salvador (1979–1991), Sri Lanka (1983–2009), Kosovo-Yugoslavia (1990–1999), Chechnya (1994–2014), and the Congo (1998–2008), just to name some of the most significant examples. The separate but related American and Southern Civil Wars should be studied in the context of these protracted, complex, and messy political wars.[15]

Earlier examples teach the same lessons. Civil and political wars have starts and stops and various phases, which often result in odd reversals of victors and protracted time frames stretching across generations. The Taiping War in China from 1851 to 1864 had a North-South element, is increasingly understood as a civil war, overlapped chronologically with the American Civil War, and maybe even went into the years of the Southern Civil War, as Taiping armies were not fully eliminated until 1871. The scale of this nearly generation-long event dwarfed the American Civil War: twenty million or more died.[16] Similarly, the Wars of the Roses (1455–1485) are known as wars despite the fact that little combat was ever going on in most of those thirty years. No historian ends discussion of the Wars of the Roses when one side temporarily appeared to be on top, as the North did in 1865. Likewise, the English Civil War (1642–1651) had three distinct phases, with pauses in between, and the Roundhead victors in the war failed to hold on to power in the end. Southerners' term for their ex-Confederate governments that seized power in the 1870s was "redemption," which equates to "restoration," the term used for the return of the English Stuart monarchs after the English Civil War. "Restoration" was also the term for similar returns, such as that of the Bourbon monarchy in France after the long conflicts of the French Revolution (1789–1815). The patterns of world civil wars before the American and Southern Civil Wars and especially in the 150 years since are clear, showing protracted, unconventional, and sporadic combat just as in the two civil wars in America.

But how could Reconstruction be a war if history textbooks and the public do not call it one? There is a better question. Why is Reconstruction *not* called a war when it so obviously constituted one? The American Civil War did not even technically end until the autumn of 1866, so a state of war demonstrably lasted longer than textbooks say. By 1866 the KKK had been founded, and by 1868 KKK-style guerillas units were in open rebellion against Republican governments across the South. The biracial coalition governments countered the KKK insurgents by raising state militias and going into the field under declarations of martial law—certainly a state of insurrectionary war within those states. After 1871 the state militias faced open paramilitary armies composed of ex-Confederate extremists with thousands in their ranks. So each period of the Southern Civil War easily fit the definition of "war," certainly of "civil war": two armed and organized factions were contesting militarily for political control in a large region with significant bloodshed and pitched battles. True, these forces were trying to capture state governments, not the national one, but the conflict also had a regional character. Ex-Confederate extremists in the Southern Civil War no longer sought a separate nation as Confederates had but instead a return to power inside the South, which would portend a negating power over the federal government in the region and in the halls of power in Washington. This they achieved. The United States was decentralized politically going into the American Civil War, and the ex-Confederate extremist victory after twelve years of the Southern Civil War checked the move toward national consolidation and centralization that began to grow in the aftermath of the American Civil War. The Southern Civil War further had a national character in that federal troops, though little used and limited in number, were nonetheless in the South for the duration of the twelve-year period. The ex-Confederate extremist war was thus partially aimed at forestalling effective occupation and federal military presence in the South. This the ex-Confederate extremists also achieved completely. Federal troops withdrew steadily from the South and the fight, completely vacating the region as part of the Compromise of 1877 that signaled ex-Confederate extremist victory. Not until eighty years later in 1957 with the entry of the 101st Airborne Division into Little Rock, Arkansas, would the national government haltingly reverse this hands-off policy. Ironically, federal military interventions in states during the civil rights movement era and after could be legally justified under Reconstruction Era laws like the Enforcement Acts. The fact that federal forces were largely not ordered to fight in the Southern Civil War does not indicate that no war occurred. This inaction merely insured victory for ex-Confederate extremists. When only one side totally engages in a war, it has an advantage, but that is easy victory, not peace. The national aspect of the Southern Civil War was the least bloody and easiest part of the ex-Confederate extremist victory. Indeed, federal action, via federal court rulings, meant a continuous drawdown of forces and enforcement of federal law, which was coupled with federal refusal to deploy troops even when begged to do so by the biracial coalition. Federal action directly bolstered the ex-Confederate cause.

Stanford political scientist James Fearon has summarized the "128 cases occurring between 1945 and 1999 that satisfy the following criteria" that are present in a civil war:

1. They involved fighting between agents of (or claimants to) a state and organized, non-state groups who sought either to take control of a government, take power in a region, or use violence to change government policies.

2. The conflict killed at least 1,000 people over its course, with a yearly average of at least 100.
3. At least 100 were killed on both sides (including civilians attacked by rebels).[17]

Thus, the Southern Civil War was indeed a war several times over on the state, regional, and national levels.[18] Ex-Confederate extremists battled to take over state governments, to control the South, and to check or deny federal power in the region and advance southern power within the national government. Ex-Confederate extremists weakened and decentralized the national government with the help of the North during the era. Through violence, the extremists took back control from the legitimate state governments, exercised power in the region, and changed federal policies. In many ways the ex-Confederate extremist victors in the Southern Civil War also won powerful national political influence, especially over racial issues, though civil rights continued to be contested after 1877.[19] And, of course, until recently these white supremacist victors of Reconstruction wrote its history, as victors so often do.[20] The victor's history was never convincing, but the lessons of twentieth- and twenty-first-century warfare and the new story of the Southern Civil War render the white supremacist version of the history of Reconstruction untenable. New objective and internationally oriented histories will help displace it as the dominant popular memory of Reconstruction.

Reconstruction is the most misremembered and forgotten period in American history. Civil wars usually have a central place in a nation's memory. Reconstruction constituted a well-defined civil war. The American Civil War of 1861–1865 was fought largely as a conventional battlefield war between uniformed combatants representing nations. Most civil wars are more unconventional and longer term. The longer-term, unconventional, ruthless, and intimate war of 1865–1877 looks more like the horrific and complex engagements in subsequent civil wars around the world. The twelve-year Southern Civil War fit the international pattern in being a start-and-stop war of political, guerilla, and paramilitary violence and brutal personal reprisals. If the United States descends into civil war in the future, it will resemble the Southern Civil War, not the American Civil War.

The military history of Southern Civil War contradicts Americans' images of themselves and their past. American nationalists cannot extract a progressive or triumphant story from this war along the lines of

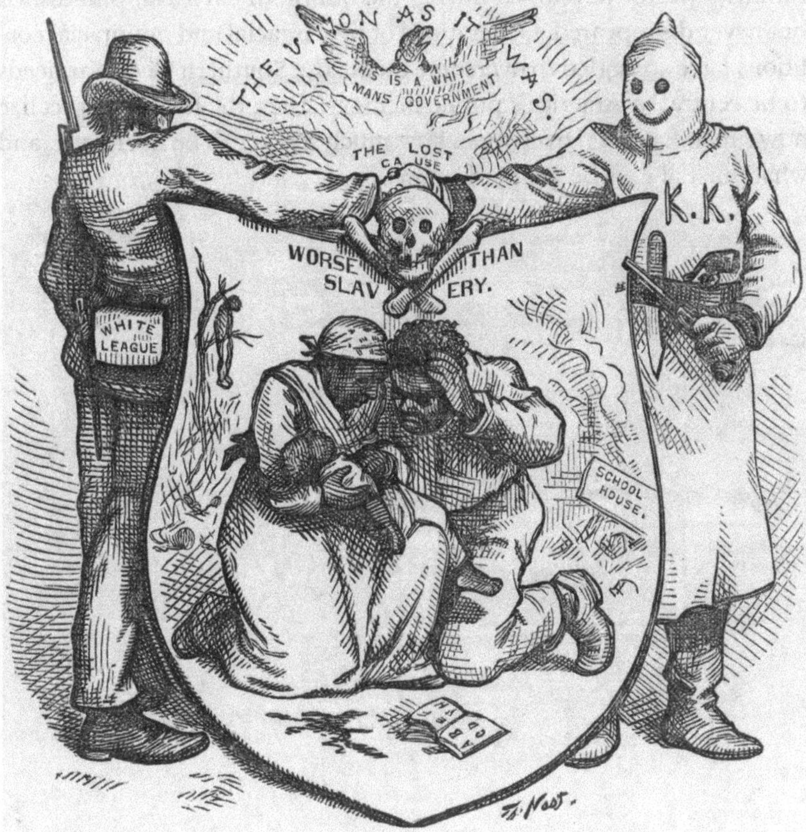

Thomas Nast cartoon, published in *Harper's Weekly* in 1874, showing the triumph of the ex-Confederate KKK guerillas in league with open paramilitary forces. (Library of Congress)

the narrative of the American Civil War. The Southern Civil War underscores the lie in the triumphalist narrative that holds that the American Civil War heroically won lasting moral and institutional progress for the nation. When white supremacist ex-Confederate extremists triumphed in the Southern Civil War, they reinstated a new form of slavery. In effect, they controlled a separate political, economic, and cultural region inside the nation for one hundred years, from 1865 to 1965. There was no Confederate States of America, but, after defeat brought diminished dreams, the Southern Civil War won much of what white supremacist southerners wanted. The war also developed the institutions of violence and deceit that allowed them to hold on to power for so long. The institutions of terror developed during the Southern Civil War diminished but never disappeared. Generations of new biracial and multiracial coalitions have struggled to overcome them. The Southern Civil War needs to be central to America's public memory. Then the nation can realize how much has been overcome, how much has yet to be overcome, and what must always be guarded against.

APPENDIX

Major Incidents of the Southern Civil War

*Battle, massacre, war**	*Date*	*State*	*White supremacists killed*	*Biracial killed*
Early terror massacres	Winter 1865–1866	Across the South	0	Unknown thousands
Norfolk Massacre	April 16, 1866	Virginia	2	8
Memphis Massacre	May 1–3, 1866	Tennessee	2	46 (75 wounded)
New Orleans Street Battle and Massacre	July 30, 1866	Louisiana	1	37 (130 wounded)
Lee-Peacock War	Feb. 1867–June 14, 1871	Texas	25+	25+
Mobile Street Battle	May 14, 1867	Alabama	3+	0
Pulaski attack	Jan. 7, 1868	Tennessee	0	2 (5 wounded)
Camilla Massacre	Sept. 19, 1868	Georgia	0	12 (30+ wounded)
Opelousas Massacre	September 28–29, 1868	Louisiana	0	27
Opelousas battles	Sep. 28–Nov. 3 1868	Louisiana	Unknown (30–50)	Unknown (150–250)
Clayton Militia Wars	Oct. 1868–March 1869	Arkansas	Unknown (6+)	(Unknown dozens)

*A "battle" involved armed struggle between two combatants, whereas a "massacre" (or "attack") involved one armed group killing another unarmed group. The lines between these two events are not always sharp. The Memphis Massacre saw African Americans fighting back in ad hoc street battles but degenerated into a massacre and mostly involved victims fleeing or cornered rather than fighting. The same was true of other street fighting in cities like New Orleans and Norfolk. Other examples, like Colfax and Hamburg and to a lesser extent Coushatta, saw conventional battles between armed sides, and then captured biracial forces were executed later. Other incidents, where ex-Confederate extremists attacked unarmed biracial coalition group at places like marches and courthouses, such as Camilla and Meridian, are rightly designated just massacres though there was fighting around Meridian in the weeks prior to the massacre at the courthouse, and some Black marchers returned fire at Camilla. Opelousas is listed as a separate massacre and following battles, as a massacre initiated a sustained period of chaotic violence and fighting in the region.

"Wars" listed here are so-called because they have long been in the historical record with such names and were sustained struggles within states, with multiple clashes and various violent incidents that included battles and massacres.

Battle, massacre, war	*Date*	*State*	*White supremacists killed*	*Biracial killed*
Municipal War	March 16–April 29, 1870	Virginia	2+	3+
Kirk-Holden War	July–Sept. 1870	North Carolina	Unknown (16+)	12+
Eutaw battle	October 25, 1870	Alabama	0	2–4 (54 wounded)
Meridian Massacre	March 1871	Mississippi	Unknown	Unknown 31+
Grant's attack on the KKK	Oct. 12–Dec. 4, 1871	South Carolina	(500+ arrested)	0
Chicot County War	April 1871–March 1872	Arkansas	Unknown (3+)	Unknown
Pope County Militia War	1872	Arkansas	Unknown	Unknown (5+)
Colfax Massacre	April 13, 1873	Louisiana	3	62–150
Brooks-Baxter War	April 15–May 15, 1874	Arkansas	100+ (100+ wounded)	100+ (100+ wounded)
Coushatta Massacre	Aug. 23–28, 1874	Louisiana	Unknown	11–31
Battle of Liberty Place	Sept. 14, 1874	Louisiana	16–22 (19+ wounded)	13 (60+ wounded)
Eufaula battle	Nov. 3, 1874	Alabama	(12 wounded)	7 (70 wounded)
Vicksburg Massacre	Dec. 7–9, 1874	Mississippi	2 (unknown wounded)	29+ (unknown wounded)
Clinton battle or massacre	Sept. 4–9, 1875	Mississippi	4	34+
Hamburg Battle	July 8, 1876	South Carolina	1	6 (as many as 25 executed)
Ellenton battles and massacres	Sept. 16–21, 1876	South Carolina	6	100+
Cainhoy battle	Oct. 16, 1876	South Carolina	5 (50 wounded)	1
Charleston battle	Nov. 8, 1876	South Carolina	1 (12 wounded)	1 (10 wounded)

NOTES

INTRODUCTION. The Southern Civil War

1. George Rable, *But There Was No Peace: The Role of Violence in the Politics of Reconstruction* (Athens: University of Georgia Press, 2007), 86, 96, 98, 142; Philip Dray, *At the Hands of Persons Unknown: The Lynching of Black America* (New York: Modern Library, 2002), 49.

2. One of the best short, accessible books about the era is Allen C. Guelzo's *Reconstruction: A Concise History* (New York: Oxford University Press, 2018).

3. Key recent works describing a southern civil war after the American Civil War include Douglas Egerton, *The Wars of Reconstruction: The Brief, Violent History of America's Most Progressive Era* (New York: Bloomsbury Press, 2015); Richard Zuczek, *State of Rebellion: Reconstruction in South Carolina* (Columbia: University of South Carolina Press, 1996); Steven Hahn, *A Nation under Our Feet: Black Political Struggles in the Rural South from Slavery to the Great Migration* (Cambridge, Mass.: Belknap Press of Harvard University Press, 2003); James Smallwood, *Murder and Mayhem: The War of Reconstruction in Texas* (College Station: Texas A&M University Press, 2003); James K. Hogue, *Uncivil War: Five New Orleans Street Battles and the Rise and Fall of Radical Reconstruction* (Baton Rouge: Louisiana State University Press, 2006); Nicholas Lemann, *Redemption: The Last Battle of the Civil War* (New York: Farrar, Strauss, and Giroux, 2006); Stephen Budiansky, *The Bloody Shirt: Terror after Appomattox* (New York: Viking, 2008); and LeeAnna Keith, *The Colfax Massacre: The Untold Story of Black Power, White Terror, and the Death of Reconstruction* (London: Oxford University Press, 2008).

4. Frank Wetta and Martin Novelli, *The Long Reconstruction: The Post–Civil War South in History, Film, and Memory* (New York: Routledge, 2013), 10–11. See also Bruce E. Baker, *What Reconstruction Meant: Historical Memory in the American South* (Charlottesville: University of Virginia Press, 2009).

5. David Silkenat, *Raising the White Flag: How Surrender Defined the American Civil War* (University of North Carolina Press, 2019). See also David Silkenat, "Surrender in the American Civil War," *History Today*, May 29, 2019, https://www.historytoday.com/miscellanies/surrender-american-civil-war.

6. Smallwood, *Murder and Mayhem*; Hogue, *Uncivil War*. On Louisiana, see also Frank J. Wetta, *The Louisiana Scalawags: Politics, Race, and Terrorism during the Civil War and Reconstruction* (Baton Rouge: Louisiana State University Press, 2013).

7. Budiansky, *Bloody Shirt*; Lemann, *Redemption* (2006).

8. Mark L. Bradley, *Bluecoats and Tar Heels: Soldiers and Civilians in Reconstruction North Carolina* (Lexington: University Press of Kentucky, 2009); Ben Severance, *Tennessee's Radical Army: The State Guard and Its Role in Reconstruction, 1867–1869* (Knoxville: University of Tennessee Press, 2005). For Georgia, see Mark V. Wetherington, *Plain Folk's Fight: The Civil War and Reconstruction in Piney Woods Georgia* (Chapel Hill: University of North Carolina Press, 2005). For an argument on violence in Alabama, see Michael W. Fitzgerald, *Reconstruction in Alabama: From Civil War to Redemption in the Cotton South* (Baton Rouge: Louisiana State University Press, 2017). On the struggles of Reconstruction in Appalachia, see Andrew L. Slap, ed., *Reconstructing Appalachia: The Civil War's Aftermath* (Lexington: University Press of Kentucky, 2010).

9. Charles Lane, *The Day Freedom Died: The Colfax Massacre, the Supreme Court, and the Betrayal of Reconstruction* (New York: Henry Holt, 2008); Keith, *Colfax Massacre*; Stephen Ash, *A Massacre in Memphis: The Race Riot That Shook the Nation One Year after the Civil War* (New York: Hill & Wang, 2013).

10. Carole Emberton, *Beyond Redemption: Race, Violence, and the American South after the Civil War* (Chicago: University of Chicago Press, 2013); Elaine Frantz Parsons, *Ku-Klux: The Birth of the Klan during Reconstruction* (Chapel Hill: University of North Carolina Press, 2016). On race and gender ideology underlying the violence, see Sharon D. Kennedy-Nolle, *Writing Reconstruction: Race, Gender and Citizenship in the Postwar South* (Chapel Hill: University of North Carolina Press, 2015).

11. Egerton, *Wars of Reconstruction*; Mark Wahlgren Summers, *The Ordeal of the Reunion: A New History of Reconstruction* (Chapel Hill: University of North Carolina Press, 2014); Guelzo, *Reconstruction*. See also Mark Wahlgren Summers, *A Dangerous Stir: Fear, Paranoia, and the Making of Reconstruction* (Chapel Hill: University of North Carolina Press, 2009). Other valuable general studies: Michael W. Fitzgerald, *Splendid Failure: Postwar Reconstruction in the American South* (New York: Ivan R. Dee, 2007); Heather Cox Richardson, *West from Appomattox: The Reconstruction of America after the Civil War* (New Haven: Yale University Press, 2007); Thomas J. Brown, ed., *Reconstructions: New Perspectives on Postbellum America* (London: Oxford University Press, 2006); Richard White, *The Republic for Which It Stands: The United States during Reconstruction and the Gilded Age, 1865–1896* (London: Oxford University Press, 2017); Paul A. Cimbala and Randall M. Miller, *The Great Task Remaining before Us: Reconstruction as America's Continuing Civil War* (New York: Fordham University Press, 2010); Carole Emberton and Bruce E. Baker, eds., *Remembering Reconstruction: Struggles over the Meaning of America's Most Turbulent Era* (Baton Rouge: Louisiana State University Press, 2017).

12. Keith D. Dickson, *No Surrender: Asymmetric Warfare in the Reconstruction South, 1868–1877* (Santa Barbara, Calif.: Praeger, 2017), 1.

13. Gregory P. Downs, *After Appomattox: Military Occupation and the Ends of War* (Boston: Harvard University Press, 2015); Andrew Lang, *In the Wake of War: Military Occupation, Emancipation, and Civil War America* (Baton Rouge: Louisiana State University Press, 2017). Other strong recent military studies are William Blair, "The Use of Military Force to Protect the Gains of Reconstruction," *Civil War History* 51, no. 4 (December 2005), 388–402; John J. McDermott, "Reconstruction and Post-Civil War Reconciliation," *Military Review* 89, no. 1 (January–February 2009), 67–76.

14. Eric Foner, *Reconstruction: America's Unfinished Revolution* (New York: Harper & Row, 1988), 204–205.

15. Emberton, *Beyond Redemption*, 6.

16. James Longstreet, *From Manassas to Appomattox: Memoirs of the Civil War in America* (Philadelphia: J. B. Lippincott, 1896), 234; Jean Edward Smith, *Grant* (New York: Simon & Shuster, 2001), 73.

17. Jay Winik, *April 1865: The Month That Saved America* (New York: HarperCollins, 2001), 78.

18. James L. Alcorn, the Republican governor of Mississippi in 1870–1871, had been a Confederate general of Mississippi state forces at the start of the Civil War but saw no action and left the service.

19. Egerton, *Wars of Reconstruction*, 261, uses the term "white extremists."

20. For an excellent discussion of the meaning of "extremism" and its terror tactics, see J. M. Berger, *Extremism* (Boston: MIT Press, 2018), 23–33.

21. The term "multiracial" would also be valid for the coalition, since Native American groups, like the Lumbees in the Carolinas under the leadership of Henry Berry Lowry in the "Lowry War," fought against ex-Confederate extremists during the Southern Civil War. Many Cajuns in Louisiana and Mexican Americans in Texas also joined the fight against white supremacists. The dominant political coalition and almost all of the military cooperation, however, was between whites and African Americans.

22. Powell Clayton, *The Aftermath of the Civil War in Arkansas* (New York: Neale, 1915), 121–151.

23. *Austin Daily Sentinel*, August 11, 1870; Smallwood, *Murder and Mayhem*, 130; Ann Baenziger, "Texas State Police during Reconstruction: A Re-examination," *Southwestern Historical Quarterly* 72 (April 1969), 470–491.

24. Michael James Martinez, *Carpetbaggers, Cavalry, and the Ku Klux Klan: Exposing the Invisible Empire during Reconstruction* (New York: Rowman & Littlefield, 2007), 113.

25. Emberton, *Beyond Redemption*, 146–152.

26. Smallwood, *Murder and Mayhem*; Zuczek, *State of Rebellion*, 145–166.

27. Other historians are rejecting the term "Reconstruction." See Gregory P. Downs and Kate Masur, eds., *The World the War Made* (Chapel Hill: University of North Carolina Press, 2015), 2–5.

28. For the importance of guerillas in the American Civil War, see Daniel Sutherland, *A Savage Conflict: The Decisive Role of Guerrillas in the American Civil War* (Chapel Hill: University of North Carolina Press, 2009).

29. Hahn, *Nation under Our Feet*, 367–369. Virginia alone among former Confederate states never produced a biracial coalition, Republican-controlled state government.

30. *Charleston News and Courier*, September 25, October 11, 12, 1876.

31. Rable, *But There Was No Peace*, 1. See also Winik, *April 1865*.

CHAPTER 1. The Terror Phase, 1865–1867

1. Kenneth Howell, "The Prolonged War: Texans Struggle to Win the Civil War during Reconstruction," in *Texans and War: New Interpretations of the State's Military History*, ed. Alexander Mendoza and Charles David Grear (College Station: Texas A&M University Press, 2012), 200–204. See also Kenneth Howell, ed., *Still the Arena of Civil War: Violence and Turmoil in Reconstruction Texas, 1865–1874* (Denton: University of North Texas Press, 2012).

2. *Presidential Proclamation 157 of August 20, 1866 by President Andrew Johnson Declaring the Insurrection at an End in Texas, as well as, in the Whole of the United States*, File Unit: Presidential Proclamations 129–179, 1865–1868, Series: Presidential Proclamations, 1791–2011, Record Group 11: General Records of the United States Government, 1778–2006, National Archives, Washington, D.C.

3. Carole Emberton, *Beyond Redemption: Race, Violence, and the American South after the Civil War* (Chicago: University of Chicago Press, 2013), 9. Emberton points out that southern men connected violence and the martial acts with their masculinity.

4. Dan Carter, *When the War Was Over: The Failure of Self-Reconstruction in the South, 1865–1867* (Baton Rouge: Louisiana State University Press, 1985), especially the introduction and chapter 3.

5. Mark L. Bradley, *Bluecoats and Tar Heels: Soldiers and Civilians in Reconstruction North Carolina* (Lexington: University Press of Kentucky, 2009), 3.

6. Richard Zuczek, *State of Rebellion: Reconstruction in South Carolina* (Columbia: University of South Carolina Press, 1996), 145–166.

7. Bruce Hoffman, *Inside Terrorism*, Columbia Studies in Terrorism and Irregular Warfare (New York: Columbia University Press, 2006), 1–4, 33–35.

8. Arie W. Kruglanski and Shira Fishman, "Terrorism between 'Syndrome' and 'Tool,'" *Current Directions in Psychological Science* 15, no. 1 (February 2006), 45–48. The authors highlight how terrorism is a tool and goal oriented.

9. For an excellent description of the Southern Civil War as a war *of* terror met by a war on terror, see Charles Lane, *Freedom's Detective: The Secret Service, the Ku Klux Klan, and the Man Who Masterminded America's First War on Terror* (New York: Hanover Square Press, 2019).

10. Ivan Arreguin-Toft, *How the Weak Win Wars: A Theory of Asymmetric Conflict* (London: Cambridge University Press, 2005); Stathis Kalyvas, *The Logic of Vio-*

lence in Civil War (London: Cambridge University Press, 2006); Jeremy Weinstein, *Inside Rebellion: The Politics of Insurgent Violence* (London: Cambridge University Press, 2006).

11. Andrew Mack, "Why Big Nations Lose Small Wars: The Politics of Asymmetric Conflict," *World Politics* 27, no. 2 (1975): 175–200.

12. Ivan Arreguin-Toft, "How the Weak Win Wars: A Theory of Asymmetric Conflict," *International Security* 26, no. 1 (2001): 93–128; Uri Resnick, *Dynamics of Asymmetric Territorial Conflict: The Evolution of Patience*, (Basingstoke, UK: Palgrave-Macmillan, 2013); Thazha Varkey Paul, *Asymmetric Conflicts: War Initiation by Weaker Powers* (New York: Cambridge University Press, 1994); Michael Allen and Benjamin O. Fordham, "From Melos to Baghdad: Explaining Resistance to Militarized Challenges from More Powerful States," *International Studies Quarterly* 55, no. 4 (2011): 1025–1045.

13. See, for example, David Williams, *Bitterly Divided: The South's Inner Civil War* (New York: New Press, 2008).

14. Lane, *Freedom's Detective*, 25. Historian Elaine Parsons gives a later date for the founding of the Klan, May–June 1866. Elaine Frantz Parsons, *Ku-Klux: The Birth of the Klan during Reconstruction* (Chapel Hill: University of North Carolina Press, 2016), 27. See also Luke Potter Poland, "Affairs in the Late Insurrectionary States," United States House of Representatives, February 19, 1872, 1, 7.

15. Parsons, *Ku-Klux*, 32.

16. Lane, *Freedom's Detective*, 26–27, 178.

17. Stephen Budiansky, *The Bloody Shirt: Terror after Appomattox* (New York: Viking, 2008), 133–135, 140, 221–222; Peter Camejo, *Racism, Revolution, Reaction, 1861–1877* (New York: Monad Press, 1976), 58, 77–78, 83, 144–145; Eric Foner, *Forever Free: The Story of Emancipation and Reconstruction*, 125–127, 134–135, 147–149; Foner, *Reconstruction*, 60–61, 178, 271–291, 342–343; John Hope Franklin, *Reconstruction after the Civil War* (Chicago: University of Chicago Press, 1961), 17–18, 60, 154–156; William Marvel, *Tarnished Victory: Finishing Lincoln's War*, (Boston: Houghton Mifflin Harcourt, 2011) 312–313, 362–369; Howard Means, *The Avenger Takes His Place: Andrew Johnson and the 45 Days That Changed the Nation* (Orlando: Harcourt, 2006), 162–166; George Rable, *But There Was No Peace: The Role of Violence in the Politics of Reconstruction* (Athens: University of Georgia Press, 2007), 82–83, 85–86, 95, 137, 162.

18. Elaine Parsons, *Ku-Klux*, 215–216, 264–266. Parsons notes that the term "Klan" was imposed on local cells. See also Allen Trelease, *White Terror: Ku Klux Klan Conspiracy and Southern Reconstruction* (New York: Greenwood Press, 1979), 7, 113.

19. James Loewen, *Lies across America: What American Historic Sites Get Wrong* (New York: Touchstone, 1999), 237–241.

20. Ben Severance, *Tennessee's Radical Army: The State Guard and Its Role in Reconstruction, 1867–1869* (Knoxville: University of Tennessee Press, 2005), 123, 125, 129. The State Guard deployed and protected ballot boxes in Pulaski, the town where the Klan was founded.

21. Michael W. Fitzgerald, *Splendid Failure: Postwar Reconstruction in the American South* (New York: Ivan R. Dee, 2007), 93.

22. Edward Steers Jr., *Blood on the Moon: The Assassination of Abraham Lincoln* (Lexington: University of Kentucky Press, 2001), 3.

23. Steers, *Blood on the Moon*, 7; Charles Lane, *The Day Freedom Died: The Colfax Massacre, the Supreme Court, and the Betrayal of Reconstruction* (New York: Henry Holt, 2008), 17.

24. Louis P. Masur, *Lincoln's Last Speech: Wartime Reconstruction and the Crisis of Reunion* (New York: Oxford University Press, 2015), xii–xiv.

25. Richard McCaslin, *Tainted Breeze: The Great Hanging at Gainesville, Texas 1862* (Baton Rouge: Louisiana State University Press, 1994), 3–7.

26. Georgia Lee Tatum, *Disloyalty in the Confederacy* (Chapel Hill: University of North Carolina Press, 1934), 31; Daniel Sutherland, *A Savage Conflict: The Decisive Role of Guerrillas in the American Civil War* (Chapel Hill: University of North Carolina Press, 2009), 100–103.

27. Mark Weitz, *A Higher Duty: Desertion among Georgia Troops during the Civil War* (Lincoln: University of Nebraska Press, 2000), 21.

28. Williams, *Bitterly Divided*, 164.

29. Powell Clayton, *The Aftermath of the Civil War in Arkansas* (New York: Neale, 1915), 109.

30. Allen C. Guelzo, *Reconstruction: A Concise History* (New York: Oxford University Press, 2018), 128.

31. Philip Dray, *At the Hands of Persons Unknown: The Lynching of Black America* (New York: Modern Library, 2002), 36–37.

32. "A Great Outrage," Assistant Commissioner's Reports, Bureau of Refugees, Freedmen, and Abandoned Lands (1865–1869), Record Group 105, National Archives, Washington, D.C.

33. *Reconstruction in America: Racial Violence after the Civil War, 1865–1876* (Montgomery, Ala.: Equal Justice Initiative, 2020), 7, https://eji.org/report/reconstruction-in-america.

34. *Reconstruction in America*, 45.

35. Eric Foner, *Reconstruction America's Unfinished Revolution* (New York: Harper & Row, 1988), 119.

36. James K. Hogue, *Uncivil War: Five New Orleans Street Battles and the Rise and Fall of Radical Reconstruction* (Baton Rouge: Louisiana State University Press, 2006), 2; "Grant Reconstruction and the KKK," PBS, https://www.pbs.org/wgbh/americanexperience/features/grant-kkk.

37. Dray, *At the Hands of Persons Unknown*, 49; Dorothy Sterling, ed., *The Trouble They Seen: Black People Tell the Story of Reconstruction* (New York: Doubleday, 1976). The Secret Service estimated twenty-five thousand victims of KKK violence alone. Lane, *Freedom's Detective*, 273.

38. Steven Hahn, *A Nation under Our Feet: Black Political Struggles in the Rural South from Slavery to the Great Migration* (Cambridge, Mass.: Belknap Press of Harvard University Press, 2003), 154–155.

39. Leon Litwack, *Been in the Storm So Long: The Aftermath of Slavery* (New York: Vintage Books, 1980), 276.

40. Earl Schenck Miers, *When the World Ended: The Diary of Emma LeConte* (New York: Oxford University Press, 1957), 105, 119.

41. Margaret M. Storey, *Loyalty and Loss: Alabama's Unionists in the Civil War and Reconstruction* (Baton Rouge, Louisiana State University Press, 2004), 219.

42. Rable, *But There Was No Peace*, 64.

43. *Boston Daily Advertiser*, January 5, 1867.

44. Litwack, *Been in the Storm So Long*, 276; Thomas Jefferson, *Notes on the State of Virginia* (Boston: Lilly and Wait, 1832), 144.

45. Emberton, *Beyond Redemption*, 8.

46. Foner, *Reconstruction*, 119.

47. "Records of the Assistant Commissioner for the State of Texas Bureau of Refugees, Freedmen and Abandoned Lands, 1865–1869," National Archives Microfilm Publication M821, Roll 32, "Registered Reports of Murders and Outrages Sept. 1866–July 1867: Freedmen's Bureau Records—Report of Union Men and Freedmen Murdered in Grason [Grayson] and Fannin Counties, Texas on the Close of the War," http://freedmensbureau.com/texas/shermanoutrages.htm.

48. "Records of the Assistant Commissioner for the State of Texas Bureau of Refugees, Freedmen and Abandoned Lands, 1865–1869," National Archives Microfilm Publication M821, Roll 32, "Registered Reports of Murders and Outrages Sept. 1866–July 1867: Reports of Murders, Outrages &c., Committed on White Men and Freedmen in Washington County, Texas," http://freedmensbureau.com/texas/brenhamoutrages.htm.

49. Foner, *Reconstruction*, 120.

50. "Records of the Assistant Commissioner for the State of Texas Bureau of Refugees, Freedmen and Abandoned Lands, 1865–1869," National Archives Microfilm Publication M821, Roll 32, "Registered Reports of Murders and Outrages Sept. 1866–July 1867: Reports of Murders, Outrages &c., Committed on White Men and Freedmen in Washington County, Texas," http://freedmensbureau.com/texas/brenhamoutrages.htm.

51. Judy Bussell LeForge, "Alabama's Colored Conventions and the Exodus Movement, 1871–1879," *Alabama Review* 63, no. 1 (January 2010): 9.

52. "Records of the Assistant Commissioner for the District of Columbia Bureau of Refugees, Freedmen and Abandoned Lands, 1865–1869," National Archives Microfilm Publication M1055, Roll 21, "Miscellaneous Reports and Lists," http://freedmensbureau.com/washingtondc/outrages.htm.

53. "Records of the Assistant Commissioner for the State of Louisiana Bureau of Refugees, Freedmen and Abandoned Lands, 1865–1869: Miscellaneous Reports and Lists Relating to Murders and Outrages Mar. 1867–Nov. 1868," National Archives Microfilm M1027, Roll 34, "Records Relating to Murders and Outrages," http://freedmensbureau.com/louisiana/outrages/outrages4.htm.

54. Foner, *Reconstruction*, 120.

55. Kim Murphy, *I Had Rather Die: Rape in the Civil War* (Afton, Va.: Coachlight Press, 2014).

56. Dara Kay Cohen, *Rape during Civil War* (Ithaca: Cornell University Press, 2016), 1–11.

57. Hannah Rosen, *Terror in the Heart of Freedom: Citizenship, Sexual Violence, and the Meaning of Race in the Postemancipation South* (Chapel Hill: University of North Carolina Press, 2009), 202, 227.

58. Philip Dray, *Capitol Men: The Epic Story of Reconstruction through the Lives of the First Black Congressmen* (Boston: Houghton Mifflin, 2010), 85.

59. Gilbert James Ryan, "The Memphis Riots of 1866: Terror in a Black Community during Reconstruction," *Journal of Negro History* 62, no. 3 (July 1977): 77–83. See also Hannah Rosen, "Words of Resistance: African American Women's Testimony about Sexual Violence during the Memphis Massacre," in *Remembering the Memphis Massacre: An American Story*, ed. Beverly G. Bond and Susan E. O'Donovan (Athens: University of Georgia Press, 2020).

60. LeForge, "Alabama's Colored Conventions and the Exodus Movement," 12.

61. "Records of the Assistant Commissioner for the State of Louisiana Bureau of Refugees, Freedmen and Abandoned Lands, 1865–1869: Miscellaneous Reports and Lists Relating to Murders and Outrages Mar. 1867–Nov. 1868," National Archives Microfilm M1027, Roll 34, "Records Relating to Murders and Outrages," http://freedmensbureau.com/louisiana/outrages/outrages4.htm.

62. "Affidavit of Rhoda Ann Childs, 25 Sept. 1866," Records of the Subassistant Commissioner for Griffin, Georgia, Bureau of Refugees, Freedmen, and Abandoned Lands, volume 270, 41–42, Record Group 105, National Archives, Washington, D.C.; *Reconstruction in America* (Equal Justice Initiative), 71.

63. "Records of the Assistant Commissioner for the State of Louisiana Bureau of Refugees, Freedmen and Abandoned Lands, 1865–1869: Miscellaneous Reports and Lists Relating to Murders and Outrages Mar. 1867–Nov. 1868," National Archives Microfilm M1027, Roll 34, http://freedmensbureau.com/louisiana/outrages/outrages4.htm.

64. *Reconstruction in America* (Equal Justice Initiative), 71.

65. Hahn, *Nation under Our Feet*, 227–228, 309.

66. Douglas Egerton, *The Wars of Reconstruction: The Brief, Violent History of America's Most Progressive Era* (New York: Bloomsbury Press, 2015), 121.

67. House of Representatives, Doc. No. 57, 40th Congress, 2nd session, 26.

68. Otto Olsen, *Carpetbagger's Crusade: The Life of Albion Winegar Tourgee* (Baltimore: Johns Hopkins University Press, 1965), 54–55.

69. Rable, *But There Was No Peace*, 14, 25.

70. Clayton, *Aftermath of the Civil War in Arkansas*, 117.

71. Hahn, *Nation under Our Feet*, 276–277.

72. *Records of the Assistant Commissioner for the District of Columbia, Bureau of Refugees, Freedmen and Abandoned Lands, 1865–1869*, National Archives Microfilm Publication M1055, Roll 21, "Miscellaneous Reports and Lists."

73. Quoted in Foner, *Reconstruction*, 119; Egerton, *Wars of Reconstruction*, 144; William Mallet to Thaddeus Stevens, May 28, 1866, in Thaddeus Stevens, *The Selected Papers of Thaddeus Stevens*, vol. 2 (Pittsburgh: University of Pittsburgh Press, 1998), 15.

74. Rable, *But There Was No Peace*, 97; Egerton, *Wars of Reconstruction*, 144.

75. Egerton, *Wars of Reconstruction*, 156–164, 205, 293, quote on 156.

76. "Records of the Assistant Commissioner for the State of Alabama Bureau of Refugees, Freedmen and Abandoned Lands, 1865–1870: Freedmen's Bureau List of Murders in the Dist. of Alabama 1866," National Archives Publication M809, Roll 23, https://freedmensbureau.com/alabama/alaoutrages.htm.

77. Litwack, *Been in the Storm So Long*, 329–333.

78. Private Calvin Holly to Major General O. O. Howard, 16 Dec. 1865, H-72 1865, Registered Letters Received, ser. 2052, Mississippi Assistant Commissioner, Bureau of Refugees, Freedmen, & Abandoned Lands, Record Group 105, National Archives, Washington, D.C. .

79. LeForge, "Alabama's Colored Conventions and the Exodus Movement," 13.

80. Litwack, *Been in the Storm So Long*, 319.

81. Litwack, *Been in the Storm So Long*, 368.

82. Michelle Alexander, *The New Jim Crow: Mass Incarceration in the Age of Colorblindness* (New York: New Press, 2020), ix–x. See also David M. Oshinsky, *Worse than Slavery: Parchman Farm and the Ordeal of Jim Crow Justice* (New York: Free Press, 1997); and Douglas A. Blackmon, *Slavery by Another Name: The Re-enslavement of Black Americans from the Civil War to World War II* (New York: Doubleday, 2008).

83. Litwack, *Been in the Storm So Long*, 319.

84. "Riot at Norfolk," House of Representatives, Doc. No. 72, 39th Congress, 2nd session, 3–64; *Richmond Daily Dispatch*, April 21, 22, 1866.

85. Stephen Ash, *A Massacre in Memphis: The Race Riot That Shook the Nation One Year after the Civil War* (New York: Hill & Wang, 2013), 180; *Memphis Daily Post*, May 3, 1866; House of Representatives No. 101, 39th Congress, 1st. session, at 88–116, 315–318.

86. Ash, *Massacre in Memphis*, 82.

87. Ash, *Massacre in Memphis*, 98.

88. Ash, *Massacre in Memphis*, 150; *The Reports of the Committees of the House of Representatives Made during the First Session, Thirty-Ninth Congress, 1865–1866*, vol. 1 (Washington, D.C.: Government Printing Office, 1866), 87. See also Beverly G Bond and Susan E O'Donovan, eds., *Remembering the Memphis Massacre: An American Story*, (Athens: University of Georgia Press, 2020).

89. Ash, *Massacre in Memphis*, 109; *Report of the Select Committee on the Memphis Riots and Massacres* (Washington D.C.: Government Printing Office, 1866); House Reports of the 39th Congress, National Archives and Records Administration, Washington, D.C.

90. Ash, *Massacre in Memphis*, 15.

91. *Reports of the Committees of the House of Representatives Made During the First Session, Thirty-Ninth Congress*, vol. 1, 50–51.

92. James G. Hollandsworth, *An Absolute Massacre: The New Orleans Race Riot of July 30, 1866* (Baton Rouge: Louisiana State University Press, 2001), 3.

93. Rable, *But There Was No Peace*, 54.

94. Justin A. Nystrom, *New Orleans after the Civil War: Race, Politics, and a New Birth of Freedom* (Baltimore: Johns Hopkins University Press, 2010), 68–69.

95. House of Representatives, Doc. 68, 39th Congress, 2nd session, 4–9, 161.

96. Egerton, *Wars of Reconstruction*, 112–114, 227.

97. Rable, *But There Was no Peace*, 71, 76, 78, 94.

98. *Horrible Disclosures: A Full and Authentic Expose of the Ku-Klux Klan*, (Cincinnati: Padrick, 1868), 31.

99. "Letter to Col. H. H. Sibley," *Army Official Records*, Series I, vol. 13, September 28, 1862, 685–686.

100. Michael Les Benedict, *The Impeachment and Trial of Andrew Johnson* (New York: W. W. Norton, 1999), 90.

101. "Alarming," *Harper's Weekly*, June 1, 1867; "Riot in Mobile: Attack by Secessionists upon Judge Kelley—Several Men Shot," May 15, 1867, *New York Times*.

102. Ron Chernow, *Grant* (New York: Penguin Random House, 2017), 601.

103. Strategic goals made a difference in how the federal government fought Native wars as opposed to the Southern Civil War. The government wanted to exterminate or force Natives into detention on reservations, whereas they wanted to rebuild the South and integrate white southern enemies into the nation. Of course, this difference in goals was closely tied to racist attitudes.

104. Foner, *Reconstruction*, 352–364.

CHAPTER 2. The Guerilla Phase, 1868–1872: The KKK Resisted

1. Charles Lane, *Freedom's Detective: The Secret Service, the Ku Klux Klan, and the Man Who Masterminded America's First War on Terror* (New York: Hanover Square Press, 2019), 144–207.

2. Keith D. Dickson, *No Surrender: Asymmetric Warfare in the Reconstruction South, 1868–1877* (Santa Barbara, Calif.: ABC CLIO, 2017), 77–78.

3. Lane, *Freedom's Detective*, 191, 258–259.

4. Lane, *Freedom's Detective*, 192. Many accounts attribute the fading of the KKK to federal action and the Enforcement Acts. The final chapter of this book discusses the ineffectiveness of the Enforcement Acts and federal interventions in South Carolina.

5. Whether historians call this phase of the war from 1868 to 1872 "asymmetrical war" matters little, but I think "guerilla warfare" is a better term since the imbalance of forces was in favor of the KKK guerillas, who triumphed easily in most states. Of course guerilla warfare is often a tactic of asymmetrical warfare but not always. Ex-Confederate extremists were not contesting the "dominant actor," the North, but southern state governments. For an alternative interpreta-

tion and fuller definition of Reconstruction as a period of asymmetrical warfare and the KKK as an asymmetrical actor, see Dickson, *No Surrender*, 1–4, 81–86.

6. Richard Parker and Emily Boyd, "The Great Hanging at Gainesville," *New York Times*, October 16, 2012; Sam Acheson, "George Washington Diamond's Account of the Great Hanging at Gainesville, 1862," *Southwestern Quarterly*, January 1963, 331–414; Richard McCaslin, *Tainted Breeze: The Great Hanging at Gainesville, Texas, 1862* (Baton Rouge: Louisiana State University Press, 1994).

7. James Smallwood, *Murder and Mayhem: The War of Reconstruction in Texas* (College Station: Texas A&M University Press, 2003), 32–41.

8. Smallwood, *Murder and Mayhem*, 45–61.

9. Smallwood, *Murder and Mayhem*, 51.

10. *Washington Post*, December 19, 1883, 2; *Wisconsin State Register*, April 14, 1866, 2, col. 3; Donald R. McClarey, "Sheridan, Hell and Texas," *American Catholic: Politics and Culture from a Catholic Perspective*, April 30, 2010, https://the-american-catholic.com/2010/04/30/sheridan-hell-and-texas.

11. "Militias," in *Encyclopedia of the Reconstruction Era*, ed. Richard Zuczek (New York: Greenwood, 2006), 410–413.

12. Douglas Hales, *A Southern Family in White and Black: The Cuneys of Texas* (College Station: Texas A&M University Press, 2003), 14–16, 58.

13. Adjutant General Records (401–1011), June 30, 1870, Texas State Library and Archives Commission, Austin.

14. Special Orders (401–1012), August 21, 1870, Texas State Library and Archives Commission, Austin, 1.

15. *Flake's Daily Bulletin* (Galveston), November 18, 1870.

16. Letter from J. O. Shelby, Liberty, Texas, September 15, 1871, Edmund Davis Correspondence, Texas State Library and Archives Commission, Austin.

17. For an outstanding account of Davis's war and declarations of martial law, see Carl H. Moneyhon, "The Fight against Lawlessness and Violence," chap. 9 in *Edmund J. Davis of Texas: Civil War General, Republican Leader, Reconstruction Governor* (Fort Worth: Texas Christian University Press, 2010).

18. *Daily State Journal* (Austin, Tex.), April 9, 1872.

19. "Governor's Proclamation," January 31, 1871, Edmund Davis Correspondence, Texas State Library and Archives Commission, Austin.

20. "Copies to House and Senate of Texas October 9th Proclamation," October 10, 1871, Edmund Davis Correspondence, Texas State Library and Archives Commission, Austin.

21. Adjutant General Records, General Orders, Special Order #71 (401–1012), October 10, 1871, Texas State Library and Archives Commission, Austin, 56.

22. General Orders, Adjutant General (401–984), April 1, 1873, Texas State Library and Archive Commission, Austin, 36.

23. "Militias," in *Encyclopedia of the Reconstruction Era*.

24. *New York Herald*, January 18, 1874.

25. Otis A. Singletary "The Texas Militia during Reconstruction," *Southwestern Historical Quarterly* 60, no. 1 (July 1956): 33.

26. Timothy P. Donovan and Willard B. Gatewood Jr., eds., *The Governors of Arkansas: Essays in Political Biography* (Fayetteville: University of Arkansas Press, 1981), 39–43; William H. Burnside, *The Honorable Powell Clayton* (Conway: University of Central Arkansas Press, 1991), 3–5.

27. Rhonda M. Kohl, "Raising Thunder with the Secesh: Powell Clayton's Federal Cavalry at Taylor's Creek and Mount Vernon, Arkansas, May 11, 1863," *Arkansas Historical Quarterly* 64, no. 2 (Summer 2005): 148.

28. Powell Clayton, *The Aftermath of the Civil War in Arkansas* (New York, Neale, 1915), 61.

29. "Large and Enthusiastic Democratic Meeting," *Weekly Arkansas Gazette* (Little Rock), January 7, 1868.

30. Clayton, *Aftermath of the Civil War in Arkansas*, 87.

31. Clayton, *Aftermath of the Civil War in Arkansas*, 65

32. "An Old Tune," *Weekly Arkansas Gazette* (Little Rock), January 14, 1868, 2; "Meddlesome," *Daily Republican* (Little Rock), January 28, 1869.

33. Clayton, *Aftermath of the Civil War in Arkansas*, 62, 91–97.

34. Clayton, *Aftermath of the Civil War in Arkansas*, 91–92.

35. General C. H. Smith to Powell Clayton, October 30, 1868, in Howard C. Westwood, "The Federals' Cold Shoulder to Arkansas' Powell Clayton," *Civil War History* 26 (September 1980), 248.

36. "The Governor's Proclamation," *Weekly Arkansas Gazette* (Little Rock), November 10, 1868, 1; C. H. Smith to Powell Clayton, October 30, 1868.

37. Clayton, *Aftermath of the Civil War in Arkansas*, 60, 64.

38. "The Destruction of the Arms," *Weekly Arkansas Gazette* (Little Rock) October 27, 1868, 1; Allen Trelease, *White Terror: Ku Klux Klan Conspiracy and Southern Reconstruction* (New York: Greenwood Press, 1979), 156.

39. Clayton, *Aftermath of the Civil War in Arkansas*, 106–107.

40. Clayton, *Aftermath of the Civil War in Arkansas*, 11–112, 120.

41. Clayton, *Aftermath of the Civil War in Arkansas*, 151.

42. Clayton, *Aftermath of the Civil War in Arkansas*, 128, 153.

43. Thomas A. DeBlack, *With Fire and Sword: Arkansas, 1861–1874* (Little Rock: University of Arkansas Press, 2003), 188.

44. Burnside, *Honorable Powell Clayton*, 32.

45. Clayton, *Aftermath of the Civil War in Arkansas*, 147. See also Grif Stockley, *Ruled by Race: Black/White Relations in Arkansas from Slavery to the Present* (Little Rock: University of Arkansas Press, 2008), 80.

46. Clayton, *Aftermath of the Civil War in Arkansas*, 65.

47. Clayton, *Aftermath of the Civil War in Arkansas*, 111–112.

48. *Contested Election Case of John M. Clayton vs. C. R. Breckinridge, from the Second Congressional District of Arkansas: Ordered to be Printed by the Committee on Elections* (Washington, D.C.: U.S. Government Printing Office, 1890), 29.

49. Clayton, *Aftermath of the Civil War in Arkansas*, 128.

50. Nancy Williams, *Arkansas Biography: A Collection of Notable Lives* (Fayetteville: University of Arkansas Press. 2000), 297–299.

51. Clayton, *Aftermath of the Civil War in Arkansas*, 68.

52. Paul A. Cimbala, *Veterans North and South: The Transition from Soldier to Civilian after the American Civil War*, Reflections on the Civil War Era (Santa Barbara: Praeger, 2015), 100.

53. Trelease, *White Terror*, 168.

54. Nancy Snell Griffith, "Chicot County Race War of 1871," *Encyclopedia of Arkansas*, https://encyclopediaofarkansas.net/entries/chicot-county-race-war-of-1871-7615.

55. "A Little Negro Rebellion and How Clayton Brought It About," *Atlanta Constitution*, May 5, 1871, 2.

56. "Negro Militia in Arkansas," House of Representatives Doc. no. 209, 42nd Congress, 2nd session, 23; "Report of T. W. Morrison, 2nd Lieutenant, 16th Infantry, U.S. Army [January 29, 1872]," in *Documentary History of Reconstruction: Political, Military, Social*, vol. 2, ed. Walter L. Fleming (Cleveland, Ohio: Arthur H. Clark, 1907), 99–101.

57. "What the Mob of Chicot County Did," *Arkansas Gazette*, January 3, 1872, 1.

58. "Murder and Pillage by Armed Negroes," *Edgefield (S.C.) Advertiser*, December 28, 1871, 2; "Chicot: The Bloody Riot—Effect of the News in Little Rock," *Memphis Daily Appeal*, December 25, 1871, 17; "Chicot," *Memphis Daily Appeal*, March 2, 1872, 2; "Our Great Calamity," *Memphis Daily Appeal*, January 31, 1872, 1; "Effect of Radical Teachings," *Galveston Daily News*, January 4, 1872, 2.

59. "Chicot County," *Arkansas Gazette*, February 4, 1872, 1; "Bloody Chicot," *Arkansas Gazette*, February 10, 1874, 1.

60. "The Arkansas Troubles," *New York Times*, December 27, 1871, 1; "The Arkansas Troubles: Emphatic Denial by the Governor—a Singular Narrative of Events as Given by an Eye-Witness," *New York Times*, December 29, 1871, 2; "Arkansas," *Bangor (Me.) Daily Whig and Courier*, January 3, 1872, 3.

CHAPTER 3. The Guerilla Phase, 1868–1872: The KKK Triumphant

1. *St. Landry Progress* (Opelousas, La.), September 9, 1868.

2. Carolyn E. DeLatte, "The St. Landry Riot: A Forgotten Incident of Reconstruction Violence," *Louisiana History* 17, no. 1 (Winter 1976), 47.

3. Lorraine Boissoneault, "The Deadliest Massacre in Reconstruction-Era Louisiana Happened 150 Years Ago," *Smithsonian*, September 28, 2018, https://www.smithsonianmag.com/history/story-deadliest-massacre-reconstruction-era-louisiana-180970420.

4. *Supplemental Report of Joint Committee of the General Assembly of Louisiana on the Conduct of the Late Elections and the Condition of Peace and Order in the State* (New Orleans: A. L. Lee, State Printer, 1869), 38–40.

5. Matthew Christensen, "The 1868 St. Landry Massacre: Reconstruction's Deadliest Episode of Violence," master's thesis, University of Wisconsin-Milwaukee, 2012, 60–62, 64–67.

6. DeLatte, "St. Landry Riot," 48.

7. "Madness of the South," *New York Times*, October 20, 1868, 4.

8. "The Southern Outrages—How to End them," *New York Times*, October 6, 1868, 6.

9. Eric Foner, *Reconstruction: America's Unfinished Revolution* (New York: Harper & Row, 1988), 425.

10. Foner, *Reconstruction*, 426.

11. Foner, *Reconstruction*, 427.

12. Steven Hahn, *A Nation under Our Feet: Black Political Struggles in the Rural South from Slavery to the Great Migration* (Cambridge, Mass.: Belknap Press of Harvard University Press, 2003), 287.

13. Ted Tunnell, *Crucible of Reconstruction: War, Radicalism, and Race in Louisiana, 1862–1877* (Baton Rouge: Louisiana State University Press, 1984), 117–119.

14. DeLatte, "St. Landry Riot," 41–49.

15. *New Orleans Republican*, October 5, 1868.

16. Ray Granade, "Violence: An Instrument of Policy in Reconstruction Alabama," *Alabama Historical Quarterly*, Fall/Winter 1968, 181–202.

17. *Index to the Reports of the Committees, The Senate of the United States, for the 2nd Session of the Forty-Second Congress 1871–1872*, vol. 2, part 2, 221–223.

18. Margaret M. Storey, *Loyalty and Loss: Alabama's Unionists in the Civil War and Reconstruction* (Baton Rouge, Louisiana State University Press, 2004), 225.

19. Storey, *Loyalty and Loss*, 227.

20. Charles Lane, *Freedom's Detective: The Secret Service, the Ku Klux Klan, and the Man Who Masterminded America's First War on Terror* (New York: Hanover Square Press, 2019), 145.

21. "Editorial," *Richmond Daily Enquirer and Examiner*, March 26, 1868.

22. "Racial Terror and Reconstruction: A State Snapshot," Equal Justice Initiative, n.d., https://eji.org/report/reconstruction-in-america/documenting-reconstruction-violence/#racial-terror-and-reconstruction-a-state-snapshot.

23. "Richmond was blessed or cursed, as the case may he, with two mayors and two sets of police." "The Richmond Mayoralty," *Richmond Daily Dispatch*, April 8, 1870.

24. "The Municipal War," *Richmond Daily Dispatch*, March 29, 1870.

25. "The Municipal War," *Richmond Daily Dispatch*, March 31, 1870.

26. Michael B. Chesson, *Richmond after the War, 1865–1890* (Richmond: Virginia State Library, 1981), 112–14; Richard Lowe, "Another Look at Reconstruction in Virginia," *Civil War History* 32, no. 1 (March 1986), 56–76; Richard Lowe, *Republicans and Reconstruction in Virginia, 1856–70* (Charlottesville: University of Virginia Press, 1991).

27. "The Terrible Calamity," *Richmond Daily Dispatch*, April 28, 1870; "The Calamity," *Richmond Daily Dispatch*, May 2, 1870; Harry Kollatz Jr., "1870: The Worst. Year. Ever," *RichmondMag*, August 21, 2020. See also W. L. Sheppard, "The Richmond Calamity—Interior of Hall of Delegates—Getting Out the Dead and Wounded," *Harper's Weekly*, May 14, 1870, 312.

28. "Riot at the Third Precinct, Jefferson Ward," *Richmond Daily Dispatch*, May 18, 1870; "Row at Precinct No. 3 in Jefferson Ward," *Richmond Daily Dispatch*, May 13, 1870.

29. For a complete account of all these events in Richmond, see Chesson, *Richmond after the War*, 111–120.

30. Charles Lane, *The Day Freedom Died: The Colfax Massacre, the Supreme Court, and the Betrayal of Reconstruction* (New York: Henry Holt, 2008), 4.

31. Lane, *Freedom's Detective*, 21–22.

32. *Records of the Assistant Commissioner for the State of Georgia Bureau of Refugees, Freedmen and Abandoned Lands, 1865–1869, Outrages*; Jonathan M. Bryant, "The KKK in the Reconstruction Era," *New Georgia Encyclopedia*, https://www.georgiaencyclopedia.org/articles/history-archaeology/ku-klux-klan-reconstruction-era.

33. Lane, *Freedom's Detective*, 144.

34. Hahn, *Nation under Our Feet*, 289–292.

35. Carole Emberton, *Beyond Redemption: Race, Violence, and the American South after the Civil War* (Chicago: University of Chicago Press, 2013), 138–140.

36. Lee W. Formwalt, "The Camilla Massacre of 1868: Racial Violence as Political Propaganda," *Georgia Historical Quarterly* 71, no. 3 (Fall 1987): 399–426.

37. "The Camilla Massacre," *Today in Georgia History*, September 19, 1868.

38. Joseph Grégoire de Roulhac Hamilton, *Reconstruction in North Carolina* (New York: Columbia University Press, 1914), 497.

39. "Life in North Carolina: The Murder of Senator John W. Stephens—a Terrible Scene—Shall His Assassins Be Amnestied?" *New York Times*, February 26, 1873.

40. Mark L. Bradley, *Bluecoats and Tar Heels: Soldiers and Civilians in Reconstruction North Carolina* (Lexington: University Press of Kentucky, 2009), 4. Bradley emphasizes that the terror "employed any means necessary."

41. Richard Zuczek, ed., *Encyclopedia of the Reconstruction Era* (New York: Greenwood, 2006), 410–413. Zuczek lists them as all white for June–August 1870.

42. Letter from Holden to Chief Justice R. M. Pearson, Raleigh, July 26, 1870, in *The Memoirs of W. W. Holden* (Durham, NC: Seeman Printery, 1911), 153–157.

43. For the best modern account of the Kirk-Holden War, see Bradley, *Bluecoats and Tar Heels*, 217–234.

44. Bradley, *Bluecoats and Tar Heels*, 259.

45. Bradley, *Bluecoats and Tar Heels*, 262.

46. Philip Dray, *Capitol Men: The Epic Story of Reconstruction through the Lives of the First Black Congressmen* (Boston: Houghton Mifflin, 2010), 180–181.

47. "Southern Outrages, Another Rebel Version of the Meridian (Miss.) Massacre," *New York Tribune*, March 8, 1871.

48. Dunbar Rowland, *Encyclopedia of Mississippi History: Comprising Sketches of*

Counties, Towns, Events, Institutions and Persons, vol. 2 (Madison, Wis.: Selwyn A. Brant, 1907), 221–223.

49. "Riot in Mississippi," *New York Times*, March 8, 1871 The *Charleston Daily News*, South Carolina, March 8, 1871, reported Moore dead.

50. "Fatal Affray in Mississippi," *New York Tribune*, March 7, 1871. This earlier account has African Americans starting the courtroom firing.

51. Lane, *Freedom's Detective*, 145; George Rable, *But There Was No Peace: The Role of Violence in the Politics of Reconstruction* (Athens: University of Georgia Press, 2007), 97.

52. William Sturgis, *New York Daily Tribune*, March 16, 1871.

53. Lane, *Day Freedom Died*, 18–19.

54. Michael James Martinez, *Carpetbaggers, Cavalry, and the Ku Klux Klan: Exposing the Invisible Empire during Reconstruction* (New York: Rowman & Littlefield, 2007), 120–121.

55. Richard Zuczek, "The Federal Government's Attack on the Ku Klux Klan: A Reassessment," *South Carolina Historical Magazine*, January 1996, 48–49; Zuczek, *Encyclopedia of the Reconstruction Era*, 410–413; Martinez, *Carpetbaggers, Cavalry, and the Ku Klux Klan*, 124.

CHAPTER 4. The Paramilitary Phase, 1872–1877

1. Alabama had fewer than six hundred federal troops in the whole state by that date, basically the same number as had been in the state in 1868. Margaret M. Storey, *Loyalty and Loss: Alabama's Unionists in the Civil War and Reconstruction* (Baton Rouge: Louisiana State University Press, 2004), 225.

2. Earl F. Woodward, "The Brooks and Baxter War in Arkansas, 1872–1874," *Arkansas Historical Quarterly* 30, no. 4 (Winter 1971): 321–322.

3. Richard Zuczek, ed., *Encyclopedia of the Reconstruction Era* (New York: Greenwood, 2006), 103–104.

4. Sources vary widely on the dead and wounded at this battle, but the *New York Times*, May 30, 1874, listed twenty-one dead and over seventy wounded.

5. Jimmy Hefley, "The Brooks-Baxter War," *Arkansas Historical Quarterly* 14, no. 2 (Summer 1955): 188.

6. James Loewen, *Lies across America: What American Historic Sites Get Wrong* (New York: Touchstone, 1999), 237–241.

7. Cory M. Pfarr, *Longstreet at Gettysburg: A Critical Reassessment* (Jefferson, N.C.: McFarland, 2019), 3–28.

8. James L. Alcorn, the Republican governor of Mississippi in 1870–1871, had been a Confederate general of Mississippi state forces at the start of the Civil War but saw no action and left the service. Confederate general James Fleming Fagan of Arkansas saw action in the American Civil War and later commanded African American militias in the Brooks-Baxter War, but unlike Longstreet he was not a major commander in the Confederacy.

9. Fox Butterfield, *All God's Children: The Boskett Family and the American Tradition of Violence* (New York: Vintage Books, 2008), 1–26.

10. William Garrett Piston, *Lee's Tarnished Lieutenant James Longstreet and His Place in Southern History* (Athens: University of Georgia Press, 1987), 3.

11. Piston, *Lee's Tarnished Lieutenant*, 5; James Longstreet, *From Manassas to Appomattox: Memoirs of the Civil War in America* (Philadelphia: J. B. Lippincott, 1896), 234; Jean Edward Smith, *Grant* (New York: Simon & Schuster, 2001), 73.

12. Jay Winik, *April 1865: The Month That Saved America* (New York: HarperCollins, 2001), 78.

13. Eric Foner, *Reconstruction: America's Unfinished Revolution* (New York: Harper & Row, 1988), 119; James K. Hogue, *Uncivil War: Five New Orleans Street Battles and the Rise and Fall of Radical Reconstruction* (Baton Rouge: Louisiana State University Press, 2006), 1–15.

14. Steven Hahn, *A Nation under Our Feet: Black Political Struggles in the Rural South from Slavery to the Great Migration* (Cambridge, Mass.: Belknap Press of Harvard University Press, 2003), 297; Zuczek, *Encyclopedia of the Reconstruction Era*, 410–413.

15. Justin A. Nystrom, *New Orleans after the Civil War: Race, Politics, and a New Birth of Freedom* (Baltimore: Johns Hopkins University Press, 2010), 162–185; Justin A. Nystrom, "Battle of Liberty Place," *64 Parishes* (Louisiana Endowment for the Humanities), January 3, 2021, https://64parishes.org/entry/the-battle-of-liberty-place.

16. *New Orleans Daily Picayune*, September 15, 1874; *New Orleans Bulletin*, September 16, 1874.

17. Foner, *Reconstruction*, 119; Hogue, *Uncivil War*, 1–15.

18. Nicholas Lemann, *Redemption: The Last Battle of the Civil War* (New York: Farrar, Strauss, and Giroux, 2006), 160–202.

19. LeeAnna Keith, *The Colfax Massacre: The Untold Story of Black Power, White Terror, and the Death of Reconstruction* (London: Oxford University Press, 2008), 1–21.

20. Charles Lane, *The Day Freedom Died: The Colfax Massacre, the Supreme Court, and the Betrayal of Reconstruction* (New York: Henry Holt, 2008), 224, 257; Keith, *Colfax Massacre*, 77, 79, 162.

21. Keith, *Colfax Massacre*, 73–74.

22. Lane, *Day Freedom Died*, 57.

23. Lane, *Day Freedom Died*, 265–266. U.S. marshals counted 62 African American dead, which is the source of the lower number. Later army and congressional reports have a higher, more accurate count, which Lane puts at a minimum of 105, though local traditions have a higher number of 150. See also George Rable, *But There Was No Peace: The Role of Violence in the Politics of Reconstruction* (Athens: University of Georgia Press, 2007), 128.

24. House of Representatives Rep. No. 21, part 3, 43rd Congress, 2nd session, 857–859.

25. *U.S. v. Cruikshank, et al.*, 25 Federal Case 707, 1874.

26. Rable, *But There Was No Peace*, 130.

27. *New York Herald*, September 4, 1874, 7; "Southern Outrages," *New York Tribune*, September 4, 1874, 1.

28. "Testimony of Mathilda Floyd and Other Negroes about Murder of Her Husband by a Group of White Men, Warrants of Arrest, Statements about Violence in Parish, Coushatta, August 1874," Marshall Harvey Twitchell Papers, box 1, folder 2, University Archives and Special Collections, Prescott Memorial Library, Louisiana Tech University, Ruston, Louisiana.

29. Marshall Henry Twitchell Papers, box 1, folder 2.

30. House of Representatives Rep. No. 261, part 3, 43rd Congress, 2nd session, 489–505.

31. Loewen, *Lies across America*, 113.

32. Nystrom, "Battle of Liberty Place."

33. Yasmeen Serhan, "The Dismantling of New Orleans's Confederate Monuments," *Atlantic*, May 11, 2017, https://www.theatlantic.com/news/archive/2017/05/jefferson-davis-monument-removal/526314; "Confederate Monuments Are Coming Down," *New York Times*, August 28, 2017; "Cities Want to Remove Toxic Monuments," *New York Times*, June 18, 2020; Bonnie Berkowitz and Adrian Blanco, "Confederate Monuments Are Falling, but Hundreds Still Stand," *Washington Post*, June 17, 2020.

34. Lane, *Day Freedom Died*, 224, 257; Keith, *Colfax Massacre*, 162.

35. Foner, *Reconstruction*, 458–459.

36. James Sefton, *The United States Army and Reconstruction* (Baton Rouge: Louisiana State University Press, 1967), 223.

37. Stephen Budiansky, *The Bloody Shirt: Terror after Appomattox* (New York: Viking, 2008), 227–237.

38. Hahn, *Nation under Our Feet*, 307–308.

39. Hahn, *Nation under Our Feet*, 307

40. Rable, *But There Was No Peace*, 173.

41. *Charleston News and Courier*, September 25, October 11, 12, 1876.

42. Rable, *But There Was no Peace*, 156–158.

43. *Daily Clarion* (Jackson, Miss.), February 9, 1876.

44. U.S. Congress, *Mississippi in 1875: Report of the Selected Committee to Inquire into the Mississippi Election of 1875* (Washington, D.C.: Government Printing Office, 1875).

45. Lemann, *Redemption*, 128–130; Zuzanna Wisniewska, "Charles Caldwell (ca. 1831–1875)," BlackPast.org, December 2, 2018, https://www.blackpast.org/african-american-history/caldwell-charles-c-1831-1875.

46. Blanche Ames, *Adelbert Ames, 1835–1933, General, Senator, Governor: The Story of His Life and Times and His Integrity as a Soldier and Statesman in the Service of the United States of America throughout the Civil War and in Mississippi in the Years of Reconstruction* (New York: Argosy Antiquarian, 1964); Lemann, *Redemption*, 128–130. Kennedy wrote: "No state suffered more from carpetbag rule than Mississippi. Adelbert Ames, first Senator and then Governor, was a native of Maine, a

son-in-law of the notorious 'butcher of New Orleans,' Ben Butler. He admitted before a Congressional committee that only his election to the Senate prompted him to take up his residence in Mississippi. He was chosen Governor by a majority composed of freed slaves and Radical Republicans, sustained and nourished by Federal bayonets. One Cardoza, under indictment for larceny in New York, was placed at the head of the public schools and two former slaves held the offices of Lieutenant Governor and Secretary of State. Vast areas of northern Mississippi lay in ruins. Taxes increased to a level fourteen times as high as normal in order to support the extravagances of the reconstruction government and heavy state and national war debts." John F. Kennedy, *Profiles in Courage*, memorial ed. (London: Hamish Hamilton, 1964), 181.

47. For the best scholarly treatment of Ames's career, see Benson Harry King, "The Public Career of Adelbert Ames, 1861–1876," PhD diss., University of Virginia, 1975.

48. Stuart B. Lord, "Adelbert Ames, Soldier and Politician: A Reevaluation," *Maine Historical Society Quarterly* 13, no. 2 (1973), 81–97.

49. Rable, *But There Was No Peace*, 156.

50. *Appleton's Annual Cyclopaedia and Register of Important Facts of the Year* (New York: D. Appleton, 1875), 516.

51. Lemann, *Redemption*, 71.

52. Hahn, *Nation under Our Feet*, 297–298.

53. Lemann, *Redemption*, 91.

54. Budiansky, *Bloody Shirt*, 192–194; Lemann, *Redemption*, 92.

55. *Chicago Tribune*, August 5, 1879, 6.

56. A. T. Morgan, *Yazoo; Or, On the Picket Line of Freedom in the South* (1884; repr., New York: Russell and Russell, 1968), 439–455, 481–485; Senate Report No. 527, 44th Congress, 1st session, 1647–1663.

57. Budiansky, *Bloody Shirt*, 145.

58. Rable, *But There Was No Peace*, 160.

59. "The Election Murder Trial; Close of the Testimony on Both Sides," *New York Times*, May 14, 1884.

60. Loewen, *Lies across America*, 156.

61. Richard Zuczek, *State of Rebellion: Reconstruction in South Carolina* (Columbia: University of South Carolina Press, 1996), 145–166.

62. Lord, "Adelbert Ames, Soldier and Politician," 81–89, 96–97.

63. See the discussion of the Compromise and end of Reconstruction in Mark Wahlgren Summers, *The Ordeal of the Reunion: A New History of Reconstruction* (Chapel Hill: University of North Carolina Press, 2014), 360–397.

64. Warren A. Ellen, "The Overthrow of Reconstruction in Mississippi," *Journal of Mississippi History* 54, no. 2 (1992): 175–201.

65. James Loewen, "Democracy Betrayed: The Wilmington Race Riot of 1898 and Its Legacy," *Southern Cultures* 6, no. 3 (Fall 2000): 90.

66. John DeSantis, "Wilmington, N.C., Revisits a Bloody 1898 Day," *New York Times*, June 4, 2006.

67. William Ivy Hair, *Carnival of Fury: Robert Charles and the New Orleans Race Riot of 1900* (Baton Rouge: Louisiana State University Press, 1976), 1–36.

68. Philip Dray, *At the Hands of Persons Unknown: The Lynching of Black America* (New York: Modern Library, 2002), 127–130.

69. Hair, *Carnival of Fury*, 185.

70. Hair, *Carnival of Fury*, 169–173.

71. Rebecca Burns, *Rage in the Gate City: The Story of the 1906 Atlanta Race Riot* (Athens: University of Georgia Press, 2009), 173.

72. Rebecca Burns, *Rage in the Gate City*, 22.

73. *Atlanta Journal*, June 4, 1905, January 10, 1906; *Atlanta Constitution*, January 11, 1906. See also Dewey W. Grantham Jr., "Georgia Politics and the Disfranchisement of the Negro," *Georgia Historical Quarterly* 32, no. 1 (March 1948): 5–9.

74. Charles Crowe, "Racial Massacre in Atlanta, September 22, 1906," *Journal of Negro History* 54 (April 1969), 150–160.

75. Sarah Case, "1906 Race Riot Tour," *Journal of American History* 101 (December 2014): 880.

76. David F. Godshalk, *Veiled Visions: The 1906 Atlanta Race Riot and the Reshaping of American Race Relations* (Chapel Hill: University of North Carolina Press, 2005); Gregory Mixon, *The Atlanta Riot: Race, Class, and Violence in a New South City* (Gainesville: University Press of Florida, 2005); Mark Bauerlein, *Negrophobia: A Race Riot in Atlanta, 1906* (San Francisco: Encounter Books, 2001).

77. James Hirsch, *Riot and Remembrance: The Tulsa Race War and Its Legacy* (New York: Houghton Mifflin, 2002). For journalistic retelling of the massacre, see Tim Madigan, *The Burning: Massacre, Destruction, and the Tulsa Race Riot of 1921* (New York: St. Martin's Press, 2001).

78. *Tulsa Race Riot: A Report by the Oklahoma Commission to Study the Tulsa Race Riot of 1921* (Tulsa: The Commission, 2001), https://www.okhistory.org/research/forms/freport.pdf.

79. Rowland and Page may have known each other, but any description of the incident is in part speculation and no source supports a sexual assault. See *Tulsa Race Riot*, 57.

80. *Tulsa Race Riot*, 57.

81. A. G. Sulzberger, "As Survivors Dwindle, Tulsa Confronts Past," *New York Times*, June 19, 2011.

82. Alfred Brophy, "Tulsa (Oklahoma) Riot of 1921," in *Encyclopedia of American Race Riots*, ed. Walter Rucker and James Upton (New York: Greenwood, 2007), 645–656.

83. Robert L. Brooks and Alan H. Witten, "The Investigation of Potential Mass Grave Locations for the Tulsa Race Riot," in *Tulsa Race Riot*, 123–130.

84. *Tulsa Race Riot*, 21–22.

85. Edward González-Tennant, *The Rosewood Massacre: An Archaeology and History of Intersectional Violence* (Gainesville: University Press of Florida, 2018). 1, 29–30.

86. Gary Moore, *Rosewood: The Full Story* (Memphis: Manantial Press, 2015), 525; González-Tennant, *Rosewood Massacre*, 2.

87. González-Tennant, *Rosewood Massacre*, 26–28.

88. Moore, *Rosewood*, 526; R. Thomas Dye, "Rosewood, Florida: The Destruction of an African American Community," *Historian* 58, no. 3 (Spring 1996), 605–622.

89. "Rosewood Massacre: A Harrowing Tale of Racism and the Road toward Reparations," *Guardian*, January 4, 2016.

90. James Loewen, *Sundown Towns: A Hidden Dimension of American Racism* (New York: Touchstone, 2005).

91. E. R. Bills, *The 1910 Slocum Massacre: An Act of Genocide in East Texas*, (Charleston, S.C.: History Press, 2014), 25.

92. *Arkansas Gazette* (Little Rock), October 3, 1919.

93. Grif Stockley, *Blood in Their Eyes: The Elaine Race Massacres of 1919* (Fayetteville: University of Arkansas Press, 2001), xiv.

94. González-Tennant, *Rosewood Massacre*, 26.

CHAPTER 5. What Makes a War a War

1. Michael C. C. Adams, *Living Hell: The Dark Side of the Civil War* (Baltimore: Johns Hopkins University Press, 2016), 7, 210.

2. Bruce E. Baker, *What Reconstruction Meant: Historical Memory in the American South* (Charlottesville: University of Virginia Press, 2009), 84. Baker says that the Reconstruction Era war of terror against African Americans has been described by historians since the 1950s but "could not be incorporated into public discourse."

3. "The Philippine-American War, 1899–1902," U.S. Department of State, Office of the Historian, https://history.state.gov/milestones/1899-1913/war; "America's Wars," Department of Veterans Affairs, Office of Public Affairs Washington, https://www.va.gov/opa/publications/factsheets/fs_americas_wars.pdf. For the best discussion of the "War of 1898" in global context, see Thomas David Schoonover, *Uncle Sam's War of 1898 and the Origins of Globalization* (Lexington: University Press of Kentucky, 2005).

4. Senia Paseta, *Modern Ireland: A Very Short Introduction* (London: Oxford University Press, 2003), 87; Michael Hopkinson, *Green against Green: The Irish Civil War* (New York: St. Martin's Press, 1988), 69–73.

5. Gideon Welles, *The Diary of Gideon Welles: Secretary of the Navy under Lincoln and Johnson*, vol. 3, *January 1, 1867–June 6, 1869* (Boston: Houghton Mifflin, 1911), 460.

6. Steven Hahn, *A Nation under Our Feet: Black Political Struggles in the Rural South from Slavery to the Great Migration* (Cambridge, Mass.: Belknap Press of Harvard University Press, 2003), 286.

7. Welles, *Diary of Gideon Welles*, vol. 3, 461–462. An exception to this lack

of provision of military supplies to southern governments was Grant's making weapons available to Governors Scott and Holden of the Carolinas. Hahn, *Nation under Our Feet*, 286.

8. Sean Enright, *The Irish Civil War: Law, Execution and Atrocity* (Newbridge, Ireland: Merrion Press, 2019), 6.

9. Enright, *Irish Civil War*, 6.

10. Enright, *The Irish Civil War*, 112, 61, 131.

11. Richard Zuczek, "The Federal Government's Attack on the Ku Klux Klan: A Reassessment," *South Carolina Historical Magazine*, January 1996, 55–56.

12. Zuczek, "Federal Government's Attack on the Ku Klux Klan," 63 (and see also 56).

13. Zuczek, "Federal Government's Attack on the Ku Klux Klan," 63–64.

14. If the African American population of a state at the time is added to the white unionist population in the state, 50 percent of the population would be reached in most former Confederate states. States like Arkansas and Tennessee, with only about 25 percent of their populations African American (1870 census), had many white unionists. However, white unionists did not necessarily vote Republican during Reconstruction, and so it is hard to determine the strength of the political base of the biracial coalition. In states with an African American majority or at least 40 percent of the population, it is safe to conclude that there was a majority for the biracial coalition.

15. David Armitage, *Civil Wars: A History in Ideas* (New York: Alfred A. Knopf, 2017).

16. Stephen R. Platt, *Autumn in the Heavenly Kingdom: China, the West, and the Epic Story of the Taiping Civil War* (New York: Knopf, 2012), xxiii–xxv.

17. James D. Fearon, "Why Do Some Civil Wars Last So Much Longer than Others?," *Journal of Peace Research* 41, no. 3 (2004): 278.

18. Well over a hundred ex-Confederate extremists were killed in the course of the war, but most of their losses were in forces captured. Ex-Confederate extremists killed thousands and probably tens of thousands of unionists. That the biracial coalition usually captured rather than killed its ex-Confederate extremist enemies is more a demonstration of a one-sided war than the lack of a war. See also the discussion of the definition of a civil war in David Armitage, *Civil Wars: A History in Ideas*, especially 201–205.

19. For how the issue of civil rights played out in national politics after the Southern Civil War in a "long Reconstruction," see Charles W. Calhoun, *From Bloody Shirt to Full Dinner Pail: The Transformation of Politics and Governance in the Gilded Age* (New York: Hill and Wang, 2010); and especially Calhoun, *Conceiving a New Republic: The Republican Party and the Southern Question, 1869–1900* (Lawrence: University Press of Kansas, 2006).

20. Baker, *What Reconstruction Meant*, 69. Baker says this white supremacist story of Reconstruction was "as close to hegemonic as any part of American historical memory had ever been."

INDEX

Page numbers in *italic* refer to illustrations.

Adams, D. L. ("Doc"), 118
Afghanistan, 147
African Americans: army regiments of, 50, 83; as congressmen, 95, 104; migration of, 18, 48, 95–96, 132; school and church arsons, 35, 43–44, 49, 85, 133; as state legislators, 90, 111, 115, 116, 119
—militias, 100; Arkansas, 106; Georgia, 134; Louisiana, 111; Mississippi, 120, 123; South Carolina, 117, 118
—self-defense, 12, *13*, 14, 51; Arkansas, 79–80, 138–139; Atlanta, 133, 134; Florida, 136; Louisiana, 99, 111, 114, 132–133; Mississippi, 95, 96, 97, 124, 125
—voting, 5, 16, 31, 32, 51, 55–59 passim, 85; Georgia, 89, 134; Mississippi, 97, 119. *See also* voter intimidation
Akerman, Amos T., 89
Alabama, 40–48 passim, 62, 85, 86, 104–105; emigration, 95–96; Eufaula Battle, 154; Eutaw Battle, 86, 154; Mobile Street Battle, 55, 153; Secret Service, 61
Alcorn, James L., 10, 157n18, 170n8
Alexandria, Va., 52
Ames, Adelbert, 72, 107, 119–127 passim, *123*, 172–173n46
Appomattox surrender, 21, 53
Arkansas, 43, 44, 60, 61, 71–80, 102, 105–106, 176n14; Elaine Massacre, 137, 138–140; Little Rock, 105, 149; Pope County Militia War, 154
arson, 35, 43–44, 85; Greenville, Ala., 46; Memphis Massacre, 49; Meridian Massacre, 97; New Orleans, 133; Rosewood Massacre, 136, 137; Tulsa Massacre, 136; Wilmington, N.C., 132
Ashburn, George W., 89
assassinations, 32, 34, 83–84; Alabama, 86; Arkansas, 72, 77–78, 79, 80; Florida, 61; Georgia, 89, 90; Ireland, 145; Lincoln, 31–32; Louisiana, 114; Mississippi, 120, 126; North Carolina, 91; Texas, 68
asymmetrical warfare, 28
Atlanta massacres (1906), 133–135

Badger, A. S., 110
Baker, Cullen, 76
ballot destruction. *See* election fraud and ballot destruction
Battle of Gettysburg, 107
Battle of Liberty Place (1874), 1–2, *3*, 10, 109–110, 154
Battle of Palarm, 106
Baxter, Elisha, 105, 106
Bentley, Emerson, 82, 83
Bills, E. R., 138
Birth of a Nation, The (Griffith), 4–5, *5*, 6
Black Codes, 25, 26, 40, 88
Bloody Sunday (Selma, Ala., Mar. 7, 1965), 85
Booth, John Wilkes, 31–32, *33*
Bradley, Mark, 25
Bramlette, E. L., 98
Breckinridge, Clifton, 78
Breckinridge, John C., 78
Brogdon, Curtis, 94
Brooks, Joseph, 105, 106
Brooks-Baxter War (1874), 10, 79, 102, 105–106, 154
Brownlow, William G., 31

Burns, Ken, 22
Butler, Benjamin, 121, 126, 172–173n46
Butler, Matthew, 118

Cainhoy (S.C.) Battle (Oct. 16, 1876), 118, 154
Caldwell, Charles, 12, 14, 116, 119–120
Caldwell, Tod, 94
Calhoun, William Smith, 111
Camilla (Ga.) Massacre (Sept. 19, 1868), 90, 153
capital punishment. *See* executions
Catterson, Robert F., 75, 76
Chahoon, George, 87, 88
Charles, Robert, 132–133
Chicot County War, 79–80, 138, 154
Childs, Rhoda Ann, 42
church and school arson. *See* African Americans: school and church arsons
Civil Rights Act of 1866, 26, 95, 96
civil rights movement, 85, 149
Civil War, The (Burns), 22
civil wars: comparative cases, 141–150; defining criteria, 149–150; rape in, 41
Clayton, John, 77–78
Clayton, Powell, 12, 61, 71–79, *73*, 91, 106, 107, 126–127; Ames compared, 121
Clayton Militia Wars, 71–80, 154
Clinton, James, 85
Clinton (Miss.) battle or massacre (Sept. 1875), 119–120, 154
Clopton, William, 95, 97, 98
Coleman, Gillford, 86
Colfax Massacre (Apr. 13, 1873), 8, 109, 110–114, 154
Collier, Clarence, 79
Compromise of 1877, 103, 127, 128, 130–131
Confederate Home Guard, 31, 32, 34, 37, 53
Confederate monuments. *See* monuments and markers
Confederate re-enfranchisement, 31, 105
congressmen, African American, 95, 104
constitutional amendments. *See* Fifteenth Amendment; Fourteenth Amendment; Thirteenth Amendment
convict-leasing system, 48, 96, 139, 142
court cases: *Cruikshank*, 113; Hamburg, S.C., 117; Louisiana, 113; Meridian, Miss., 97–98; perjury and jury tampering, 69, 93; *Plessy*, 32, 129; Richmond, Va., 88; Texas, 69, 70; *Williams v. Mississippi*, 129
Coushatta (La.) Massacre (1874), 114, 154
Crosby, Peter, 124
Cruikshank case, 113
Cuney, Norris Wright, 67

Dakota War of 1862, 53–54
Danforth, Keyes, 76
Davidson, John, 69, 70
Davis, Edmund, 12, 61, 65–71, *67*, 107, 126–127; Ames compared, 121
Davis, Jefferson, 66, 107, 109
Day, Damascas D., 42
Demby, Josiah H., 76
Dent, Julia, 108
Dotsie, A. P., 52
Durand, C. E., 83

Elaine (Ark.) Massacre (1919), 137, 138–140
election fraud and ballot destruction, 78, 85, 88, 90, 104–105, 125, 146; defense against, 100–101
Ellenton (S.C.) battles and massacres (1876), 118, 154
Ellyson, Henry, 87, 88
Enforcement Acts of 1870–1871, 61, 84, 95, 118, 146, 149
English Civil War, 148
Eufaula (Ala.) Battle (Nov. 3, 1874), 104, 154
Eutaw (Ala.) Battle (Oct. 25, 1870), 86, 104, 154
executions, 54, 145; mass, 54, 63; summary, 74, 76, 77, 80, 83, 91–92, 118, 144

Fagan, James Fleming, 10, 170n8
Fearon, James, 149–150
Fifteenth Amendment, 4, 23, 56, 57, 58, 129
Florida, 61, 84, 144; Rosewood Massacre, 136–137
Foner, Eric, 39
Forrest, Nathan Bedford, 29–31, *30*, 59, 88–89, 106
Fort Davis, 66
Fort Pickering, 50
Fort Pillow Massacre, 29
Fortune, Emanuel, 84
Fourteenth Amendment, 4, 23, 25, 32, 56, 57, 58, 129; *Cruikshank* case, 113

Freedmen's Bureau incident reports, 35–36, 37–38, 39, 42, 44–46
Frost, A. B., 125
Fusion movement, 131–132

Gainesville, Tex., mass hanging (Oct. 1862), 54, 63
Georgia, 42, 85, 88–90; Andersonville prison, 24; Atlanta massacres (1906), 133–135; Camilla Massacre, 90, 153; Longstreet, 108, 114; sundown towns, 137
Gettysburg, Battle of, 107
Gone with the Wind (film), 5, *6*, 6–7
Gordon, John B., 89–90
Grant, Ulysses S., 26, 61, 62, 146, 176n14; Ames relations, 121, 123, 125; Arkansas and, 106; election of 1868, 85; Longstreet relations, 108–109; Pope letter to, 56; South Carolina and, 17, 61; Texas and, 71
Griffith, D. W., 4–5, *5*
Guelzo, Allen C., 35

Hahn, Steven, 84
Hamburg (S.C.) Battle (July 8, 1876), 100, 116–119, 154
Hamilton, Andrew Jackson, 43
Harris, Essic, 41–42
Hart, Hardin, 64
Hayes, Rutherford B., 103, 120
Haynes, A. J., 79
Hindman, Thomas, 72
Hinds, James M., 72
historical markers. *See* monuments and markers
historiography, 7–9, 19, 22, 84, 126, 128
Holden, William, 12, 61, 90–91, 93–94, 176n14
Holly, Calvin, 46–47
Home Guard, Confederate. *See* Confederate Home Guard
Houston, Sam, 66

Iraq, 147
Irish Americans, 49–50
Irish War of Independence and Civil War, 142–144, 146–147

James, Jesse, 121
Jenkins, Sam, 69
Jim Crow laws, 25, 132, 133, 134
Johnson, Andrew, 21–22, 25, 31–32, 37, 55, 65, 107
Johnston, Joe, 23–24
Joiner, Phillip, 90

Keiley, Anthony M., 88
Kelley, William, 55
Kellogg, William Pitt, 110
Kennard, Adam, 96, 97
Kennedy, John F., 121, 172–173n46
King, Horace, 40
Kirk, George W., 93–94
Kirk-Holden War, 92–94, 154
Knights of the White Camellia, 81–82, 99, 109
Ku Klux Klan (KKK), 16–17, 29–31, 36, 53, 62, 84–101 passim, 131; Alabama, 102, 104; Arkansas, 71–80 passim; Confederate Home Guard and, 37; Enforcement Acts, 61, 95; federal government action against, 61, 62, 118, 146; in films, 5, *5*; Florida, 144; founding, 29; Georgia, 84, 88–90; historiography, 8; Knights of the White Camellia and, 82; Louisiana, 85, 114; Mississippi, 95–96, 98; North Carolina, 91–94, 100; regalia, *60*; South Carolina, 61, 100–101, 118, 146; Tennessee, 29, 59; Texas, 64; Virginia, 86–88; White League and, *151*

Lane, Charles, 99
Laurensville, S.C., 100
LeConte, Emma, 37
Lee, Bob (guerilla leader), 64
Lee, Robert E., 1, 10, 53, 66, 107, 109; Appomattox surrender, 21, 53
Lee-Peacock War, 64–65, 153
Lewis, David P., 104
Liberty Place, Battle of. *See* Battle of Liberty Place
Lincoln, Abraham, 53, 130; assassination, 31–32; assassination plots, 24; offer to Robert E. Lee, 66; presidential election, 22–23, 103; second inauguration, *33*; Sioux Uprising, 54; "ten percent plan," 25
Lindsay, Robert Burns, 104
Little Rock, Arkansas, 105, 149

Litwack, Leon, 46, 48, 49
Longstreet, Augustus Baldwin, 108
Longstreet, James, 1, 2, 10, 107–109, *108*, 110, 126–127; Ames compared, 121
Louisiana, 40–44 passim, 98–99, 102–103, 109–115; Jim Crow laws, 133–134; Mississippi compared, 122; Opelousas Massacre and battles, 81–83, 84–85, 153. *See also* New Orleans
lynching, 36, 131; Alabama, 45, 86; Florida, 136; Georgia, 137; Louisiana, 114; Mississippi, 124; North Carolina, 92; Oklahoma, 135; threats, 129

Mahone, William, 10
Mallory, Samuel, 75–76
Mason, James W., 79–80
massacres of African Americans, 18, 29, 34–40 passim, 49–52, 153–154; Arkansas, 137, 138–140; Florida, 136–137, 140; Louisiana, 8, 83, 99, 109–114 passim, 140, 153, 154; Memphis, 8, 42, 49–51, 153; Mississippi, 98, 124; Tulsa, 135–136; Wilmington, N.C., 132
mass executions, 54, 63
Matthews, John, 126
Matthews, Print, 12, 126
McClure, F. A., 77
McNelly, Leander H., 69
Meade, George, 55
memorial markers. *See* monuments and markers
Memphis, Tenn., 74, 78
Memphis Massacre (1866), 8, 42, 49–51, 153
Meridian (Miss.) Massacre (Mar. 1871), 95, 96–98, 154
militias. *See* African Americans: militias; state militias
Militia Wars (Ark.), 71–79, 154
Mississippi, 47, 72, 96–98, 102, 119–126, 154; Copiah County, 126; Louisiana compared, 122; Yazoo County, 124–125
Mobile (Ala.) Street Battle (1867), 55, 153
monuments and markers, 106–107, *113*, 114–115, *115*, 126, 138
Moore, J. Aaron, 95, 97, 98
Morgan, Albert T., 124
Morgan, John, 85
Mosby, John Singleton, 10
Municipal War (Richmond, Va., 1870), 87–88, 154

Nash, Christopher Columbus, 111, 112
Nast, Thomas, *130*, *151*
National Guard: Texas, 67; Tulsa Massacre, 135
Native Americans, 53–54, 56, 93, 157n21, 164n103
New Orleans: Butler and Civil War occupation, 121; "Robert Charles Riots" (1900), 132–133; street battle and massacre (1866), 51–52, 153. *See also* Battle of Liberty Place
newspapers, rumor-mongering and false reports by, 133, 134, 135, 136, 139
Norfolk Massacre (1866), 49, 153
North Carolina, 43, 61, 62, 81, 84, 85, 90–95; KKK, 91–94, 100; Wilmington clash and massacre, 131–132
Nueces Massacre (Aug. 10, 1862), 64

Ocoee (Fla.) Massacre (1920), 140
Oklahoma, 135–136
Opelousas (La.) Massacre and battles (1868), 81–83, 84–85, 153
Outlaw, Wyatt, 92, 93

Palarm, Battle of, 106
Panic of 1873, 104, 127
Peacock, Lewis, 64, 65
Pettus, Edmund, 85
Philippine-American War, 142
Pickett, A. C., 77
Plessy v. Ferguson, 32, 129
Poe, John, Jr., 87
Pope, John, 53–56, 108
Pope County (Ark.) Militia War (1872), 154
presidential elections: (1860), 22–23, 103; (1868), 74, 85, 99; (1876), 103, 127, 128
Presidential Reconstruction, 25
Price, Daniel, 96–97
Profiles in Courage (Kennedy), 121, 172–173n46
Pulaski, Tenn.: KKK attack (Jan. 7, 1868), 59, 153; KKK founding, 29

Rable, George, 18
"Radical Republican" (term), 9, 11
rape, 35, 41–42, 43

Reconstruction Acts of 1867, 26, 56, 58
Red Shirt paramilitaries, 116, 117, 119, 124
Reed, Harrison, 144
"restoration" of European monarchies, 148
Richmond, Va., Municipal War (1870), 87–88, 154
Rivers, Prince, 12, 14, 116–119, *117*
Rosewood (Fla.) Massacre (1923), 136–137
runaway slaves, 20, 34, 96, 116

Schofield, John, 73, 87
school and church arson. *See* African Americans: school and church arsons
Scott, Ben, 87
Scott, Robert, 100–101, 176n14
Secret Service, 61
Sefton, James, 118
Selma, Ala., 85
Senter, Dewitt Clinton, 31
sharecroppers and sharecropping, 35, 96, 139
Sheridan, Phil, 21, 28, 54, 66–67, 121, 124
Sherman, William Tecumseh, 23–24, 28, 54, 121
Sioux Uprising, 53–54
slave patrols, 31, 34, 38, 96
slavery, 38, 39, 130; Indian Territory, 135; Texas, 63, 64, 65. *See also* runaway slaves
Slocum (Tex.) Massacre (July 1910), 137–138
Smith, Hoke, 134
Smith, William Hugh, 85
South Carolina, 61, 62, 81, 99–101, 146, 154; Edgefield District, 107–108, 116; Emancipation Day, *117*; Hamburg Battle, 100, 116–119, 154
Spanish-American War, 142
state militias, 41, 57, 144, 148; Arkansas, 71–79 passim; Georgia, 134; Louisiana, 109, 111; North Carolina, 90–91, 93, 94; Tennessee, 31; Texas, 67, 70, 71, 138; Third Enforcement Act, 61
state terror, 27–28
Stephens, John W., 91–92, 93
Stockley, Grif, 139
Stoneman, George, 50
Sturgis, William, 95, 96, 97, 98
sundown towns, 137
Supreme Court, U.S. *See* U.S. Supreme Court

Taiping Civil War, 148
Tennessee, 29–31, 34, 62, 153, 176n14; East-West division, 63; Forrest markers and monuments, 106; Fort Pillow Massacre, 29; Memphis, 74, 78; Memphis Massacre, 8, 42, 49–51, 153; State Guard, 31. *See also* Pulaski, Tenn.
Texas, 21, 39, 43, 61, 63–71; Great Hanging at Gainesville, 54, 63; Slocum Massacre, 137–138; State Police, 67, 68, 69; sundown towns, 137
Thibodaux (La.) Massacre (Nov. 1887), 140
Third Colored Heavy Artillery Regiment, 50
Thirteenth Amendment, 3–4, 21, 48, 129
Throckmorton, James Webb, 21
Tilden, Samuel J., 128
Tourgee, Albion W., 84
Travis Rifles, 71
Tulsa Massacre (1921), 135–136
Turner, Henry McNeal, 89, 132
Twenty-Fifth Colored Infantry Regiment, 83
Tyler, Warren, 95, 97, 98

United States v. Cruikshank, 113
Upham, D. P., 75, 77
U.S. Constitution. *See* Fifteenth Amendment; Fourteenth Amendment; Thirteenth Amendment
U.S. Supreme Court, 32, 113, 129, 139

Vance, Zebulon, 94
Vicksburg, Miss., 123–125, 132, 154
Virginia, 85, 86–88, 154, 158n29; Norfolk Massacre, 49, 153; State Capitol disaster of 1870, 88
voter intimidation, 85–90 passim, 127–128, 129, 146; Alabama, 85, 86, 104; Florida, 140; Mississippi, 126; North Carolina, 94; South Carolina, 118, 119; Virginia, 88
voting fraud. *See* election fraud and ballot destruction

Walker, Gilbert, 87
Ward, William, 12, 14, 111, 115–116
Wars of the Roses, 148
Washington, D.C., 43–44, 94
Wheeler, Ras, 126
White, George H., 95

White League, 104, 109, 111, 113–114, 120, 123, *151*
Whitley, Hiram C., 61
Wilkes, James, 100
Williams, Joseph, 95
Williams v. Mississippi, 129
Wilmington, N.C., 131–132
Woods, Jim, 100
Wynn, Wathal, 80

Zuczek, Richard, 146

UnCivil Wars

Weirding the War: Stories from the Civil War's Ragged Edges
EDITED BY STEPHEN BERRY

Ruin Nation: Destruction and the American Civil War
BY MEGAN KATE NELSON

America's Corporal: James Tanner in War and Peace
BY JAMES MARTEN

The Blue, the Gray, and the Green: Toward an Environmental History of the Civil War
EDITED BY BRIAN ALLEN DRAKE

Empty Sleeves: Amputation in the Civil War South
BY BRIAN CRAIG MILLER

Lens of War: Exploring Iconic Photographs of the Civil War
EDITED BY J. MATTHEW GALLMAN AND GARY W. GALLAGHER

The Slave-Trader's Letter-Book: Charles Lamar, the Wanderer, and Other Tales of the African Slave Trade
BY JIM JORDAN

Driven from Home: North Carolina's Civil War Refugee Crisis
BY DAVID SILKENAT

The Ghosts of Guerrilla Memory: How Civil War Bushwhackers Became Gunslingers in the American West
BY MATTHEW CHRISTOPHER HULBERT

Beyond Freedom: Disrupting the History of Emancipation
EDITED BY DAVID W. BLIGHT AND JIM DOWNS

The Lost President: A. D. Smith and the Hidden History of Radical Democracy in Civil War America
BY RUTH DUNLEY

Bodies in Blue: Disability in the Civil War North
BY SARAH HANDLEY-COUSINS

Visions of Glory: The Civil War in Word and Image
EDITED BY KATHLEEN DIFFLEY AND BENJAMIN FAGAN

Household War: How Americans Lived and Fought the Civil War
EDITED BY LISA TENDRICH FRANK AND LEEANN WHITES

Buying and Selling Civil War Memory in Gilded Age America
EDITED BY JAMES MARTEN AND CAROLINE E. JANNEY

The War after the War: A New History of Reconstruction
BY JOHN PATRICK DALY

Printed in the USA
CPSIA information can be obtained
at www.ICGtesting.com
CBHW010326130724
11541CB00016B/566

9 780820 361901